The Celestial Tradition

A Study of Ezra Pound's *The Cantos*

Demetres P. Tryphonopoulos

Wilfrid Laurier University Press

This book has been published with the help of a grant from the Humanities and Social Sciences Federation of Canada, using funds provided by the Social Sciences and Humanities Research Council of Canada.

We acknowledge the support of the Canada Council for the Arts for our publishing program.

We acknowledge the financial support of the Government of Canada through the Book Publishing Industry Development Program for our publishing activities.

Library and Archives Canada Cataloguing in Publication

Tryphonopoulos, Demetres P., 1956–
    The celestial tradition : a study of Ezra Pound's *The Cantos*

Includes bibliographical references and index.
ISBN 978-0-88920-202-3 (cloth).—ISBN 978-1-55458-250-1 (paper).—
ISBN 978-0-88920-578-9 (PDF).—ISBN 978-1-55458-805-3 (epub).

1. Pound, Ezra, 1885–1972. Cantos. I. Title

PS3531.082C289 1992   811'.52   C92-093361-0

© 1992 Wilfrid Laurier University Press
    Waterloo, Ontario N2L 3C5, Canada
    www.wlupress.wlu.ca

Cover design by Connolly Design Inc.

Every reasonable effort has been made to acquire permission for copyright material used in this text, and to acknowledge all such indebtedness accurately. Any errors and omissions called to the publisher's attention will be corrected in future printings.

No part of this publication may be reproduced, stored in a retrieval system or transmitted, in any form or by any means, without the prior written consent of the publisher or a licence from The Canadian Copyright Licensing Agency (Access Copyright). For an Access Copyright licence, visit www.accesscopyright.ca or call toll free to 1-800-893-5777.

THE CELESTIAL TRADITION

A STUDY OF EZRA POUND'S *THE CANTOS*

Demetres P. Tryphonopoulos

Despite the painstaking work of Pound scholars, the *mythos* of *The Cantos* has yet to be properly understood — primarily because until now its occult sources have not been examined sufficiently. Drawing upon archival as well as recently published material, this study traces Pound's intimate engagement with specific occultists (W.B. Yeats, Allen Upward, Alfred Orage, and G.R.S. Mead) and their ideas. The author argues that speculative occultism was a major factor in the evolution of Pound's extraordinary aesthetic and religious sensibility, much noticed in Pound criticism.

The discussion falls into two sections. The first section details Pound's interest in particular occult movements. It describes the tradition of Hellenistic occultism from Eleusis to the present, and establishes that Pound's contact with the occult began at least as early as his undergraduate years and that he came to London already primed on the occult. Many of his London acquaintances were unquestionably occultists.

The second section outlines a tripartite schema for *The Cantos* (*katabasis/dromena/epopteia*) which, in turn, is applied to the poem. It is argued here that *The Cantos* is structured on the model of an initiation rather than a journey, and that the poem does not so much describe an initiation rite as enact one for the reader.

In exploring and attempting to understand Pound's "occultism" and its implications to his [Pound's] oeuvre, Tryphonopoulos sheds new light upon one of the great works of modern Western literature.

Demetres P. Tryphonopoulos *teaches American Literature at the University of New Brunswick. His current projects include an edition of Ezra Pound's letters to Olivia Rossetti Agresti as well as a collection of essays on modernism and the occult.*

for
Leon Surette

CONTENTS

ABBREVIATIONS ix

PREFACE xi

I. THE *CANTOS* AS PALINGENESIS 1
    1. The *Cantos* as Palingenesis 1
    2. Poetry as Revelation 9
    3. "The Celestial Tradition" 11
       Notes 18

II. THE OCCULT TRADITION 23
    1. "The Rising Psychic Tide" 23
    2. A History of the "Occult Tradition" 28
       Notes 54

III. POUND'S OCCULT EDUCATION 59
    1. American Beginnings: Katherine Ruth
       Heyman and H.D. 59
    2. Pound's Catechesis in London (1):
       Yeats and the Shakespears 69
    3. Pound's Catechesis in London (2):
       Upward and Orage 74
    4. "Echoes from the Gnosis": G.R.S. Mead
       and Pound 82
       Notes 92

IV. PALINGENESIS: *KATABASIS / DROMENA / EPOPTEIA* 101
    1. Palingenesis: *Katabasis / Dromena / Epopteia* 101
    2. "The Cave of Nerea": Canto 17 108

3. "Never with this Religion / Will You Make
   Men of the Greeks": Canto 23 127
4. "Yet Must Thou Sail after Knowledge":
   The *Katabasis* after Gnosis in Canto 47 142
   Notes 152

V. "THE SUBTLE BODY": CANTOS 90 AND 91 159
   1. "Out of Erebus": Canto 90 159
   2. "The Subtle Body": Canto 91 169
   Notes 184

APPENDIX I 189
APPENDIX II 192
WORKS CITED AND CONSULTED 193
INDEX 207

ABBREVIATIONS

The following abbreviations are used in the text and in endnotes to designate reference works. (For full bibliographical information see "Works Cited and Consulted.")

ABCR	*ABC of Reading*
Companion	Terrell, *A Companion to the Cantos of Ezra Pound*
EP/JT	*Ezra Pound and John Theobald Letters*
EP/DS	*Ezra Pound and Dorothy Shakespear, Their Letters: 1909-1914*
GK	*Guide to Kulchur*
L	*Selected Letters of Ezra Pound, 1907-1941*
LE	*Literary Essays*
Light	Surette, *A Light from Eleusis: A Study of Ezra Pound's "Cantos"*
SP	*Selected Prose, 1909-1965*
SR	*The Spirit of Romance*
T	*The Translation of Ezra Pound*

PREFACE

Most of Ezra Pound's sympathetic readers have begun with the assumption that "the significance and form [of *The Cantos*] are hidden in an iterative and kaleidoscopic pattern for the assiduous and intelligent to discover" (*Light* 1). Daniel S. Pearlman's *The Barb of Time: On the Unity of Ezra Pound's Cantos* is representative of this kind of criticism which usually attempts to prove that *The Cantos* display "perfect coherence." Since there is no narrative line, Pearlman defines the major form of the poem in terms of temporal modalities: ephemeral/recurrent/eternal. Pearlman's study, like several other studies of *The Cantos*, is well researched and knowledgeable; it fails, nonetheless, to give due attention to the visionary or occult component of the poem.

Despite all the painstaking work which has been done on *The Cantos*, the poem's *mythos* has yet to be fully explored. In *A Light from Eleusis*, Leon Surette brings us close to a proper understanding of the poem's *mythos* by chronicling Pound's revisionist rendering of the Odyssean myth in terms of the Eleusinian mysteries (40-66). According to Surette, the *mythos* of *The Cantos* is based on a fantasy history which can be traced in part to Joséphin Péladan, a French Rosicrucian of the late nineteenth and early twentieth centuries (34-39, 57-60). This finding raises one aspect of Pound which has been largely neglected: his involvement with the occult.[1] It is the aim of this study to consider the relationship between Pound's ideas about poetry and his occult studies which began as early as 1904 or 1905. It is suggested that an understanding of Pound's "occultism" sheds new light upon the *mythos* of *The Cantos*. The present study builds upon Surette's pioneering work which still underestimates the extent of Pound's involvement with the occult.

The note to the Preface is found on p. xviii.

The term "occult" commonly designates the study of supernatural or unusual phenomena: from psychic experiences in séances to Black Magic and such pseudo-sciences as numerology and astrology. However, in this study the emphasis is placed on "metaphysical occultism" — which is different from the practice of theurgy or occult arts. I take "occult" to mean the whole body of speculative, heterodox religious thought which lies outside all religious orthodoxies and includes such movements as Gnosticism, Hermeticism, Neoplatonism, Cabalism, and Theosophy. Occultism always involves mysticism, a belief in the possibility of *gnosis*, or direct awareness of the Divine attained through *myesis*, or ritual initiation. This distinction between the popular notions of occultism and "metaphysical occultism" should be kept in mind because Pound, unlike W.B. Yeats, was not susceptible to the attractions of theurgy.

During his London years (1908-21) many of Pound's close associates — Yeats, G.R.S. Mead, Allen Upward, A.R. Orage, and Olivia and Dorothy Shakespear — had strong connections with occult groups. That Yeats was interested in all sorts of occult doctrines and practices is well known, and there is evidence that Pound observed some of Yeats's occult experiments without, however, participating in or being attracted by them (Harper, *Yeats and the Occult* 165; Longenbach, *Stone Cottage* passim). Pound's association with Mead, Upward, and Orage has not been much explored. Recently published correspondence between Pound and his future wife, Dorothy Shakespear, and Pound's letters to John Theobald and Margaret Cravens clearly demonstrate Pound's interest in the occult during the years preceding the genesis of *The Cantos*. Additional evidence for Pound's interest in the occult is found in unpublished Pound letters at the Lilly Library (Ezra Pound Collection, Indiana University at Bloomington), the Beinecke Rare Book and Manuscript Library (Collection of American Literature, Yale University), and the British Museum (Patricia Hutchins Collection). Drawing primarily upon Pound's published letters and unpublished letters to his parents, to Olivia Rossetti Agresti, and to Patricia Hutchins, this study traces Pound's intimate engagement with specific occultists (Yeats, Upward, Orage, and Mead) and their ideas, and argues for the importance of speculative or "metaphysical" occultism in the shaping of his aesthetic theories and poetry. In other words, it is argued here, first, that it is implausible to suppose Pound could have been ignorant of those occultists who at the turn of the century were the constant subject of gossip in the press of the day, and second, that Pound is often drawing on a body of opinion, belief, and experience that he encountered first hand among friends and acquaintances.

For a study of this nature, the state of Yeats scholarship is instructive.

With regard to the significance of the occult for Yeats, scholars can be divided into two camps: those who have sought to evade the fact of Yeats's intense, lifelong interest in occult doctrines and activities of every sort because they have regarded them as "embarrassing"; and those who are sympathetic to occult ideas. Examples on each side of this critical dichotomy may be found in the work of Richard Ellmann and of Kathleen Raine.

Recent criticism no longer avoids discussion of Yeats's occultism. In his introduction to *Yeats and the Occult* (1975), George Mills Harper writes that "the time has passed when it was necessary, in order to preserve intellectual respectability, to express either astonishment or dismay at the nature of Yeats's intellectual pursuits" (xv). As a result, a number of critics have written books devoted to Yeats's long search in hermetic studies. The same cannot be said of Pound. With the notable exception of Elliott and Surette, the little that has been done on Pound and the occult usually does not go far enough—the extent and nature of Pound's connection with occultism remain largely unexplored.

With regard to the question of Pound's occultism, scholars may be divided into three camps. Mainstream Pound scholarship—with Hugh Kenner representing the most authoritative and orthodox position—has entirely bypassed this dimension of Pound. Even when the subject is broached, Pound's occult connections are either denied or loosely described as Neoplatonism or "visionary." For example, in her discussion of Pound's understanding of myth, Wendy Flory states that the poet "is not committed to occult study as Yeats is" (14); and James J. Wilhelm, who notes that Pound's "philosophical training was very heavily influenced by Neoplatonics" (*Dante and Pound* 137), returns time and again to the poet's Neoplatonism without suspecting that this movement's roots are to be found in Hellenistic occultism.

Other critics are less categorical than Flory in their estimations. Thus, the second camp is made up of critics who recognize Pound's involvement with the occult but are not willing to concede that it has any importance other than its role in shaping his aesthetic theories. For example, James Longenbach identifies Pound's intense interest in the occult during his London years, and more specifically during his time with Yeats at Stone Cottage (1913-16), but concludes that "It is finally not so much the subject matter as the allusive, aristocratic attitude of the occult that was most important for modernism [and for Pound]" ("The Order of the Brothers Minor" 398). In this second camp we may include Clark Emery, Sharon Meyer Libera, Herbert N. Schneidau, Ian F.A. Bell, A. Walton Litz, and Longenbach. The best assessment of the impact of the occult on Pound's aesthetics is still Schneidau's early study, *Ezra Pound: The Image and the Real* (1969), which includes a brief discussion of Pound's early poetics "at the time when he was entertaining esoteric ideas from people like Mead and Upward" (125).

The third camp is made up of critics who recognize the importance of occult speculation to Pound's work: Noel Stock, Akiko Miyake, Carroll F. Terrell, Angela Elliott, Leon Surette, William French, Colin McDowell, Timothy Materer, and Kevin Oderman are the most published of these. With the exception of Elliott, the earlier of these critics treat the occult dimension of Pound's poetry and prose with excessive respect, labelling it his "arcanum," "secretum," or "mysterium." Of these critics Surette, in *A Light from Eleusis*, goes further than anyone else in his discussion of Joséphin Péladan and the supposition of the existence of an underground mystery cult and "the idea of formulating history in terms of such a secret cult" (37). Pound's belief in this secret cult, which he calls "Eleusis," was encouraged, Surette stresses, by his contact "with the unusual interests in religious backwaters of G.R.S. Mead, Allen Upward, A.R. Orage and Yeats" (37). But Surette failed to appreciate fully the occult provenance of Pound's "secret religion."

As new evidence accumulates, Pound's enduring interest in the occult is becoming increasingly clear. Colin McDowell and Timothy Materer conclude in their discussion of Pound and Yeats's early acquaintance that "both poets were in fact deeply committed to occult studies" (345). They go so far as to state that Pound initially sought out Yeats as much for his mystical themes as for his technical masterfulness.

Even with accumulating evidence and commentary, persuading Poundians that Pound was seriously interested in the occult is a formidable task. Pound never attempted to construct a system, like Yeats did, but remained to the end an Odysseus fishing "by obstinate isles." Nonetheless, *The Cantos* are enriched and shaped by Pound's esoteric studies. The question of whether or not Pound was, strictly speaking, an occultist is not addressed here; there is no evidence I have found that he ever joined any occult group. And his denial of any interest in Yeats's ghosts seems genuine. Pound seems not to have been interested in "phenomena" — in ghosts, poltergeists, "masters," metempsychosis, divination and the rest of the paraphernalia of the credulous.

My discussion falls into three large sections. Part 1 (Chapter I) deals with *The Cantos* as palingenesis. It is argued here that *The Cantos* are intended to be read as are the Hermetic writings on rebirth. Also noted here is the occult component of Pound's cultural and aesthetic theories. There is, of course, a good deal of "history" in *Guide to Kulchur*. This book is examined as an essentially occult document. Part 1 also documents the early onset and persistence of Pound's occult studies by (a) establishing the importance of "religious" thought to *The Cantos*; (b) establishing the Hellenistic provenance of the poem's "religious" thought; (c) introducing the *topos* of palingenesis; and (d) establishing the pertinence of a double-reading or exoteric/esoteric technique for the poem.

Part 2 (Chapters II and III) begins with a discussion of what I call "the rising psychic tide," a phrase I borrow from Mead, that is, the extraordinary ubiquity of occult speculation in Europe between 1880 and 1920. Chapter II also discusses Pound's contact with particular occult movements and formulates a coherent account of modern philosophical occultism. It is emphasized here that the intellectual content of the occult is almost wholly derived from the Hellenistic period; that the historical continuity claimed by the modern occult is a constantly rediscovered fiction; and that the late nineteenth and early twentieth centuries were periods of unusual vitality in the history of occultism. The ubiquity of occultism in the 1880s and 1890s was part of the reaction against the scientific materialism and positivism of the nineteenth century. Some attention is paid to the character and the ubiquity of occult ideas within literary culture from the pre-Romantics to the moderns.

Integrating information from personal letters and biographical and critical sources, Chapter III relies on hard data to establish the following: (a) that Pound's contact with the occult began as early as his undergraduate years, and (b) that many of his London acquaintances were undisguised occultists. This chapter traces his involvement in the intellectual community to which Yeats, Upward, Orage, Mead, and Olivia and Dorothy Shakespear—Pound's future mother-in-law and wife respectively—belonged. I argue that Pound found Upward's and Mead's varieties of occultism more congenial than Yeats's, and substantially adopted them for *The Cantos*. Special attention is paid here to Mead's work on Gnosticism and its contribution to the formation of Pound's religious views.

The last section (Chapters IV and V) is devoted to an examination of selected cantos (17, 23, 47, and 90-91) in the light of the occult context established in the preceding sections. Close analysis establishes the extent to which Pound's occultism contributed to the content of his "tale of the tribe." Chapter IV begins with a discussion of a tripartite palingenetic schema for *The Cantos*: *Katabasis/dromena/epopteia*. It is argued that the model of an initiation is needed to supplement or replace the Odyssean journey motif relied upon by commentary. The poem does not describe or report on an initiation rite; instead, it enacts an initiation for the reader. Thus it is suggested that Pound read Homer's *Odyssey*, Virgil's *Aeneid*, and Dante's *Divine Comedy* as esoteric texts—in other words, the journeys in

Homer, Virgil, and Dante are the exoteric experiences and palingenesis is the esoteric sense. The balance of Chapter IV offers an explication of cantos 17, 23, and 47.

Chapter V is an analysis of cantos 90 and 91. These cantos are read as a spiritual drama enacted by the illuminated soul undergoing initiation. It is argued that canto 90 illustrates the motif of palingenesis or rebirth to a higher plane of existence, and that canto 91 illustrates the nature of that higher plane as understood through the doctrine of the "subtle body."

It is a pleasure to record my grateful thanks to those who have, in various ways, made this study possible. For his considerable patience, advice, generosity, and encouraging criticism, I wish to thank Professor Leon Surette. Professor Surette's contributions have been so numerous that it would be impossible to acknowledge them as they occur in the text. I am also deeply indebted to Professor Stephen J. Adams, not only for his judicious suggestions and advice, but also for his constant encouragement and patient energy over several years. Along with Professors Timothy Materer, Michael Groden, David M.R. Bentley, and M.J. Moscovich (to all of whom I am also very grateful), Professors Surette and Adams have read this text in its entirety and have made useful suggestions. Michael Ballin and Gerald Noonan, my former colleagues at Wilfrid Laurier University, have also read and helpfully commented on parts of the manuscript.

I am also most grateful to the following persons for various kinds of help, advice, and encouragement: R.M. Stingle, R.J. Shroyer, D.F. Chapin, Carroll F. Terrell, Pat Dibsdale, James Laughlin, Andrzej Sosnowski, Joseph Webster, Shawn Malley, and Shao-Pin Luo. For her Penelopean patience and love, I want to thank my wife, Litsa.

The book could hardly have been written without the support I received from the faculty and staff of the English Department, University of Western Ontario. Wilfrid Laurier University, where I taught while I was completing this manuscript, provided financial support through two research grants, making it possible for me to visit The Beinecke Rare Book and Manuscript Library. Finally, I am grateful to everyone who worked on this book at Wilfrid Laurier University Press: Sandra Woolfrey and the staff at WLUP have been most co-operative and patient in dealing with the manuscript—my special thanks to William Fizet and Maura Brown.

For permission to quote from Ezra Pound's unpublished letters to his parents and his correspondence with Olivia Rossetti Agresti, I am indebted to the Ezra Pound Literary Property Trust which holds the copyright on all such quotations.

Parts of this manuscript have either appeared or are about to appear in print. A longer version of Chapter I has appeared as "*The Cantos* as

Palingenesis" in *Paideuma* 18 (1989): 7-33. A version of Chapter III, section 4 will appear in the *Journal of Modern Literature* as "Ezra Pound's Occult Education." Finally, a revised version of Chapter II, section 1 has appeared in *Ezra Pound and America*, a collection of essays on Pound edited by Jacqueline Kaye; the title of this paper is " 'That Great Forty-Year Epic': Ezra Pound, Katherine Ruth Heyman & H.D."

Grateful acknowledgment is given to New Directions Publishing Corporation for permission to quote from the following copyrighted works of Ezra Pound: *ABC of Reading* (all rights reserved); *The Cantos* (copyright © 1934, 1937, 1940, 1956, 1959, 1962, 1963, 1966, and 1968 by Ezra Pound); *Collected Early Poems* (copyright © 1976 by the Trustees of the Ezra Pound Literary Property Trust); *Ezra Pound and Dorothy Shakespeare* (copyright © 1976, 1984 by the Trustees of the Ezra Pound Literary Property Trust); *Gaudier-Brzeska* (copyright © 1970 by Ezra Pound); *Guide to Kulchur* (copyright © 1970 by Ezra Pound); *Literary Essays* (copyright © 1918, 1920, 1935 by Ezra Pound); *Selected Letters 1907-1941* (copyright © 1950 by Ezra Pound); *Selected Prose 1909-1965* (copyright © 1960, 1962 by Ezra Pound, copyright © 1973 by the Estate of Ezra Pound); *Translations* (copyright © 1954, 1963 by Ezra Pound); H.D.: *End to Torment: A Memoir of Ezra Pound* (copyright © 1979 by New Directions Publishing Corporation). Previously unpublished material by Ezra Pound copyright © (1909-12, 1937-59) by the Trustees of the Ezra Pound Literary Property Trust; used by permission of New Directions Publishing Corporation, agents.

Acknowledgment is hereby also made for kind permission to reprint excerpts from the following copyrighted material: Richard Ellmann, *The Identity of Yeats* (New York: Oxford University Press, 1964); George Mills Harper, *W.B. Yeats and W.T. Horton: The Record of an Occult Friendship* (London: Macmillan, 1980); Clark Emery, *Ideas into Action: A Study of Pound's Cantos* (Coral Gables, FL: University of Miami Press, 1958); Sharon Mayer Libera, "Ezra Pound's Paradise: A Study of Neoplatonism in the *Cantos*," Diss., Harvard University, 1971; Hans Jonas, *The Gnostic Religion* (Boston: Beacon Press, 1967); Frances A. Yates, *The Occult Philosophy in the Elizabethan Age* (London: Routledge, 1979) and *The Rosicrucian Enlightenment* (London: Routledge, 1972); Gershom G. Scholem, *Major Trends in Jewish Mysticism* (London: Thames and Hudson, 1955); Peter Kuch, *Yeats and A.E.: 'The Antagonism that Unites Dear Friends'* (Gerrards Cross, Buckinghamshire: Colin Smythe, 1986); Allen Upward, *Divine Mystery* (Santa Barbara: Ross Erikson, 1976); Thomas Taylor, *Thomas Taylor the Platonist: Selected Writings*, edited by Kathleen Raine and George Mills Harper (Princeton, NJ: Princeton University Press, 1969); Porphyry, *Porphyry: "On the Cave of the Nymphs,"* translated by Robert Lamberton (Barrytown, NY: Station Hill,

1983); Noel Stock, *Reading the Cantos: A Study of Meaning in Ezra Pound* (London: Routledge, 1966); and Leon Surette, *A Light from Eleusis* (Oxford: Clarendon Press, 1979); Kevin Oderman, *Ezra Pound and the Erotic Medium* (Durham: Duke University Press, 1986); James J. Wilhelm, *The American Roots of Ezra Pound* (New York: Garland, 1985); and to *Paideuma* [p. xvii].

Every effort has been made to trace the ownership of all copyright material reprinted in the text. The author and publisher regret any errors, and will be pleased to make necessary corrections in subsequent editions.

This book has been published with the help of a grant from the Canadian Federation for the Humanities, using funds provided by the Social Sciences and Humanities Research Council of Canada.

Note

1. So far as I know, the first one to mention Pound's contact with occult ideas was Noel Stock. In "The Pagan Mystery Religions," one of the chapters in *Poet in Exile* (1964), Stock writes: "During his years in London, from 1908 until 1921, Pound read and talked with a number of authors who were interested in mysticism, the occult and old religions, among them W.B. Yeats, G.R.S. Mead, and Allen Upward. All three of these men were well-read in their fields and Pound learned much from them.... It is well then to keep these authors in mind when discussing Pound's attitude to religion, for they contributed to it and coloured his subsequent thinking" (20-21). Though Stock was the first to make explicit references to Pound's interest in occult ideas, Clark Emery, in *Ideas into Action* (1958), had already dealt with Pound's religion in a way that suggests that he, too, understood "the tradition of the undivided light" as an Hellenist, heteroclite, eclectic, syncretic, occultist movement (11). The fact that the poet read a version of *Ideas into Action* "and often set [him] right when [he] was dead wrong in fact or theory" (viii) adds credence to Emery's account of Pound's religion — it will be evident in the pages that follow that my own understanding of Pound's religious beliefs derives, to a certain extent, from Emery and, even more so, from Surette.

    The most comprehensive treatment of Pound's occultism is to be found in Angela Elliott's "Light as Image in Ezra Pound's *Cantos*." As her title suggests, Elliott builds on Emery's argument concerning the centrality of the Neoplatonic tradition of "the undivided light" and its symbolism for *The Cantos*. She identifies the occult provenance of many of Pound's ideas and gives an excellent account of his debt to a variety of occult concepts (ranging from Gnosticism to Theosophy) which influenced his thought and art. Though she is concerned neither with the chronology of Pound's involvement with the occult nor with the *mythos* of the poem (which are among the principal concerns of the present study), she does examine some of the same issues presented here, and I am in general agreement with her as to the occult provenance of Pound's thought.

    See also Akiko Miyake's treatment of some of these issues in *Ezra Pound and the Mysteries of Love* (Durham: Duke University Press, 1991). Professor Miyake's book appeared so recently that I have been unable to indicate some points of agreement as well as several points of disagreement between us — for instance, I disagree with Miyake's contention that Pound is writing from within the Christian mystical tradition.

I

THE CANTOS AS PALINGENESIS

1. THE CANTOS AS PALINGENESIS

Pound's "religious" ideas form a mosaic out of elements selected from a wide variety of pagan mystery religions and occult movements. The mosaic seems to be pieced together out of randomly chosen bits. Being neither a systematic philosopher nor a methodical student of religions, Pound nowhere takes the step of attempting to organize his religious ideas into a coherent system. Yet there is a governing principle directing the process of selection and presentation. As with many occult writers and thinkers, Pound's predilection for some elements and his rejection of others were determined by a need to serve the purposes of a value system with more or less defined perimeters. Pound formulated a framework on a priori grounds and kept enriching it — sometimes overburdening it — with analogies drawn from diverse systems. Gathered in this way, the analogies are later used to underpin the legitimacy of the original structure. *The Cantos* constitute, I think, such a structure: a collection of fragments gathered according to a predetermined plan for the purpose of validating the author's original value system. This is a perception which the reader of *The Cantos* must bear in mind while examining the poem's evolution, one the poet himself, contemplating his labours, describes in one place in this way:

> From time's wreckage shored,
>   these fragments shored against ruin.[1]

The notes to Chapter I are found on pp. 18-21.

For Pound, the "essential thing in a poet is that he builds us his world" (qtd. in *SP* 7). Pound's cosmos is built out of his sense and understanding of the "mysterium" — that is, Pound's cosmos is imbued with his "religious" understanding, an understanding whose provenance and form are traced in this chapter.

Noel Stock notes in *Poet in Exile* that Pound was never a deep student of the Christian religion. But, as already evident from the preceding discussion, I regard Pound as a "deep" student of religion, including the Christian religion — even though he repeatedly took up Christianity in order to denigrate it. I do agree, however, with the following observation by Stock: "[Pound's] is the work of a man with a theory, . . . deriving after a fashion from the mysteries of Eleusis" (16). Pound's belief in the importance of these mysteries was so strong that he went so far as to claim that the Catholic church's decline is the direct result of its neglect of the mysteries:

> Latin is sacred, grain is sacred. Who destroyed the mystery of fecundity, bringing in the cult of sterility? Who set the Church against the Empire? Who destroyed the unity of the Catholic Church with this mud-wallow that serves the Protestants in the place of contemplation? Who decided to destroy the mysteries within the Church so as to be able to destroy the Church itself by schism? Who has wiped the consciousness of the greatest mystery [Eleusis] out of the mind of Europe — to arrive at an atheism proclaimed by Bolshevism . . . ? (from *A Visiting Card* in *SP* 317).

Pound's rhetorical questions allude to a number of his lifelong concerns (all of which find poetic expression in *The Cantos*), including the connection between mystery rites and fecundity; the "emptying out" of the real meaning in the present-day Church ritual of the Mass; and the suppression of the mysteries and their adherents. Pound believes that the loss of mystery has reduced the collective consciousness of Europe to atheism, making it incapable of experiencing the *theos* that Pound calls "an eternal state of mind" (*SP* 47).[2]

Elsewhere in *A Visiting Card*, Pound describes historical events and conditions as products generated through the interaction of two antithetical forces:

> We find two forces in history: one that divides, shatters, and kills, and one that contemplates the unity of the mystery. . . .
>
> There is the force that falsifies, the force that destroys every clearly delineated symbol, dragging man into a maze of abstract arguments, destroying not one but every religion.
>
> But the images of the gods, or Byzantine mosaics, move the soul to contemplation and preserve the tradition of the undivided light (*SP* 306-307).

The rhetoric of antithesis is used here to build a polarized structure of values contrasting the sterile, labyrinthine, blurring, destructive, dark, hylic force, which Pound usually identifies with usury and personifies as "Usura" or "Geryon" (49/245, 51/251, 88/583, etc.), with the sacred, fecund, clear, dynamic force identified with the "unity of the mystery," and symbolized by the "tradition of the undivided light."

Throughout *The Cantos*, Pound is concerned with delineating these two opposing forces. "Usura," and all that Pound associates with it, is represented in the imaginative world of *The Cantos* as the evil, fatal force which stands in diametrical opposition to the *energeia* or creative, vital force derived from contemplation of the "unity of the mystery." In Pound's cosmos the mythic opposition between the corn goddess, Demeter, and Pluto, the god of the Underworld, is replaced by the poet's own antithesis of the "mysterium" and the abstract, demonic "Usura." Of course, Pound's imagination is firmly rooted in the mythic cosmos. The terms of the "mysterium"/"Usura" antithesis are always being transformed and replaced, so that the single antithesis has a polymorphous, proliferating pattern. The protean character of the antithesis allows Pound to include in his epic examples from many different realms: mythical, cultural, historical, religious, and economic. A paradigmatic rendition of the antithesis is found in canto 51 where the opposition is between the *forma* "That hath the light of the DOER" and the "sour song" arising from the belly of the usurious Geryon.[3]

The importance Pound attaches to the "mysterium" points to one of his primary *topoi* in *The Cantos*, a *topos* which I shall call *palingenetic*. Pound's interest in apotheosis, the ascent into a higher or divine life, is closely linked with the *topos* of palingenesis or rebirth. It has often been noted that scenes of transformation can be found in *The Cantos* and the early poems, and that his source is often Ovid. In response to Eliot's "What Mr. Pound believes?" Pound blames modern ills on the overshadowing of the mysteries "by an over-emphasis on the individual" in our time, and offers the following personal belief:

> I assert that the Gods exist. . . .
> I assert that a great treasure of verity exists for mankind in Ovid and in the subject matter of Ovid's long poem, and that only in this form could it be registered (GK 299).

The subject matter of Ovid's poem is metamorphosis, and in speaking about it Pound is thinking of metamorphosis "not as a poetic fiction, but as a metaphor for the relationship between the human and the divine, the third subject of *The Cantos*, 'the magic moment or moment of metamor-

phosis, bust thru from quotidien into "divine or permanent world"'"
(*Light* 100). Pound often tries to catch the fluid nature of metamorphosis.
But why are Ovid's myths the only "form" in which these moments
could be registered?

In his discussion of the development of initiation mystery rites during
the Hellenistic period, Richard Reitzenstein turns to Apuleius's *Golden Ass*
in order to trace the motif of palingenesis, that is, "rebirth" or "second
birth," death of the old, physical life and rebirth to a new spiritual life of
the *mystes* or initiate into the mysteries. Through god's miraculous power,
the *mystes* is elevated into a better and higher nature. Reitzenstein explains
that in the arts, palingenesis is typically depicted as metamorphosis:

> This rebirth is a transformation of essence, the assumption of a new
> form; *renasci* alternates with *reformari*, and even the transformation from
> the form of an ass into human form means for the community a part of
> that divinely wrought rebirth. The word παλιγγενεσία is in fact also
> used in Hellenistic literature for the "migration of souls," the assump-
> tion of a new form. Underlying it is the view that in that migration
> through the twelve hours of the night which is reenacted in the mystery
> the deceased person, like the deity, assumes twelve different forms, the
> forms of animals, before he attains or regains the divine form. A *transfig-
> uration*, a μεταμορφοῦσθαι or μεταβάλλεσθαι, is for this conception
> indissolubly bound up with the rebirth, the παλιγγενεσία; hence the
> account can form the conclusion of a book of "Metamorphoses"
> (39-40).

The connection between μεταμόρφωσις (metamorphosis) and
παλιγγενεσία (palingenesis) as outlined by Reitzenstein points to the possibility that Pound read Ovid's *Metamorphoses* as an account of initiations,
of palingeneses of the soul. On this reading the transformation of animals
in Ovid would be representations of the soul's apotheosis or *soteria*.
Pound's assertion that the *Metamorphoses* contains a thesaurus of *aletheia* or
wisdom hidden in the poem whose nature, once understood, is revelatory
makes sense in the light of such an esoteric reading.[4] The application of a
similar hermeneutics to Pound's epic could go a long way toward helping
us understand its often obscure, dense, and impenetrable surface.

Edgar Wind emphasizes, in *Pagan Mysteries in the Renaissance*, that the
term "mysteries" has several meanings.[5] He distinguishes among three.
The first and original meaning of "mysteries," exemplified by the festival
of Eleusis, is of a popular, secret ritual of initiation in which the neophytes
were given assurance of a higher status, the sense of a closer relationship
with the divine, and the hope of some sort of blessedness in the hereafter.

They were also bound to keep the mystery secret. The second meaning derives from Plato, who used the imagery and terminology of initiation playfully in the *Euthydemus* and with the most solemn seriousness in the *Symposium*. For Plato any deep understanding of the universe could not be communicated as mere information or technique. Thirdly, Plato and his Neoplatonic disciples grafted onto philosophy a figurative use of the language of the popular rites. But, as Wind remarks, "the adoption of the ritual terminology to assist and incite the exercise of intelligence proved exceedingly useful as a fiction, but ended, as such fictions are likely to do, by betraying the late Platonists into a revival of magic" (15).

The Renaissance Italian humanists, among them Pico della Mirandola and Marsilio Ficino, seeing the mysteries through the eyes of Platonic philosophers, erroneously assumed that the figurative interpretation was part of the fabric of the original mysteries.[6] Pound first became acquainted with the mysteries through his reading of the Italian humanists (ca. 1906), where he would have encountered a mixture of the ritual, the figurative, and the magic. Stock suggests that the influence of Frazer and Frobenius led Pound to devote more attention to the original, ritualistic phase of the mysteries. I will argue that Pound's initial acquaintance with the *mystères littéraires* (Festugière's term for the literary use of mystery as opposed to *mystères culturels*, or ritual initiation[7]) was later reinforced through his contact with Mead and his circle, long before his reading of Frazer or Frobenius.

Stock argues that Pound's response to the mysteries would be similar to the half-skeptical bemusement of Pico della Mirandola, as described by Wind:

> The enjoyment Pico derived from occult authors was vicarious and poetical; they exercised his imagination in the employment of outlandish metaphors. It never occurred to him, as it did to less speculative minds, that the turgid love of the dialectical magi might be put to a more nefarious use than amplifying the Platonic *mystères littéraires*. Black magic, in the sense that it appealed to Agrippa of Nettesheim, he rejected as a vile superstition (Wind 17-18).

Pound did, indeed, maintain a highly skeptical attitude toward theurgy or practical magic.

Having suggested that Pound's response to the mysteries parallels that of Pico della Mirandola, Stock makes no further use of Wind; had Stock explored further, he might have taken up Wind's central argument concerning the double nature of many Renaissance paintings which provides what appears to be a useful hermeneutical paradigm for our reading of *The*

Cantos. Wind discusses a deliberate obliqueness in the use of metaphor in some of the greatest Renaissance paintings, and he speaks of "the presence of unresolved residues of meaning" in many of these (22). He writes that some Renaissance works "were designed for initiates, hence they require an initiation," that is, they possess an esoteric meaning hidden or occluded beneath an exoteric surface; they are "cryptic art" (22). In his discussion of Michelangelo's *Last Judgement*, Wind notes the basic paradox of cryptic art: "[it] addresses itself to the very audience from which it professes to be hidden" (157). Thus the discourse presented by such works as Michelangelo's *Last Judgement* has an esoteric as well as an exoteric sense; it is both private and public. The art and its exoteric meaning can be appreciated by the "vulgar" as well as by those few learned who possess the key to an encrypted esoteric meaning.

Wind illustrates the experience of cryptographic texts with hieroglyphs: "Unless one knows what a hieroglyph means, one cannot *see* what it says. But once one has acquired the relevant knowledge, 'unfolded' by more or less exoteric instruction, one can take pleasure in finding it 'infolded' in an esoteric image or sign" (170). According to this cryptological hermeneutics, the "esoteric" meaning can be deciphered when one comes to the possession of the appropriate key, that is, when one comes to the possession of the rule of "infolding" or encrypting, a possession gathered by instruction or learning.

A cryptological reading of *The Cantos*, where the exegesis is governed by the logic of concealment and where enlightenment and obscurity are tightly linked, has attracted some scholars; but I do not think that *The Cantos* are cryptographic, even though they are often cryptic.[8] The poet and his art would be better served by a pneumatic or gnostic reading — that is, a reading which brings to bear on the poem the writings of the ancient wisdom tradition, a tradition to which Pound devoted considerable study.

I believe *The Cantos* are intended to be read in a fashion similar to Hermetic palingenetic literature. With this model, the author plays the role of the mystagogue and presents a description of a "mystery" in the hope that his presentation will have the same impact upon the reader as a ritual revelation or mystical vision. Only the willing "neophyte" will be able to perceive and experience the mystery; the doubter and skeptic will remain ignorant of the import of the words he is reading.[9] As Richard Reitzenstein explains,

> Anyone who published these mysteries [the literary mysteries of the Hermetic writings] as books expected that the reader, if God chose to favor him, would, upon reading them, feel the same effect as Thoth [the Egyptian god of wisdom, learning and literature] felt upon hearing;

the miraculous power of God's message functions even in the written word: the vision, the experience, occurs. But he also expected that the unbeliever into whose hand the book might fall would not understand it; indeed, for him it must remain dead, just because the vision does not occur (62).

There is an exoteric as well as an esoteric side. The text can be read and understood on a superficial level; but the text is specifically designed to bring about, in those readers who are open, pure of heart and willing to hear, the "full Ειδώς" (81/520) — that is, true and complete seeing and knowing. The text can be the bridge ("a bridge over worlds" [Notes for CXVII et seq./802]) through which the initiate can attain revelation, the unmediated vision of the deity. At the same time, there is no danger that the esoteric dimension of the mystery might be perceived by the profane.[10]

Pound himself seems to have read certain texts in this way. I have already discussed his reading of Ovid's *Metamorphoses*. *Guide to Kulchur* provides additional examples. In the section entitled "The Promised Land," Pound criticizes Luigi Valli's *Il Linguaggio Segreto di Dante e dei "Fideli d'Amore"* because that author's "wanderings in search of a secret language (for Dante, Guido, and the rest of them) are, at mildest estimate, unconvincing" (294). Pound's position is stated even more clearly in his "Cavalcanti" essay. In that essay Valli is criticized because Pound cannot find justification for his "theories *re* secret conspiracies, mystic brotherhoods, widely distributed (and uniform) cipher in 'all' or some poems of the period, etc." (*LE* 173). And yet, despite his objections to Valli's arguments about Dante's employment of a secret language in the *Divine Comedy*, Pound seems to have read Dante's poem as an esoteric document — in a 1956 letter he goes so far as to endorse Dante's [and Swedenborg's] "schema of increasing enlightened consciousness."[11] Pound's laborious quarrel with Valli has been misunderstood, or at best misconstrued, by Pound scholars. What is at issue here is not Valli's assumption that Dante's work contains a secret code but rather the nature of that code. Valli reads Dante's work as secret Ghibelline communications, containing a political message. Pound objects not to the presence of a message but to its nature: for Valli the message is secret and political; for Pound it is esoteric.[12]

Again, much more directly and near the spirit of this discussion this time, in his account of the differences between prose and poetry, Pound shifts into a consideration of the art of poetry in terms of the "mysteries":

> Beyond its [prose's] doors are the mysteries. Eleusis. Things not to be spoken save in secret.
>
> The mysteries self-defended, the mysteries that *can* not be revealed. Fools can only profane them. The dull can neither penetrate the secretum nor divulge it to others (*GK* 144-45).

These "mysteries are *not* revealed, and no guide book to them has or will be written," Pound writes to Henry Swabey in a 1939 letter (*L* 327); and in another 1939 letter, to Douglas McPherson this time, he adds: "The minute you proclaim that the mysteries exist *at all* you've got to recognize that 95% of yr. contemporaries will not and can not understand *one* word of what you are driving at. And you can *not* explain" (*L* 328-29). One could hardly wish for clearer and less uncompromising appeals to the exoteric/esoteric principle.

I suggest that *The Cantos* constitute a text designed to produce initiates as much as it is for initiates; the text's purpose is to occasion a palingenesis achieved through participation in the "mystery" contained in the text. For the initiands or neophytes who are able to participate in this mystery, the text constitutes a *leitourgia*, a service or act performed for the benefit and common interest of the participants. Since the "mystery" Pound has in mind belongs to an esoteric tradition, only the "*catechumens*" (*GK* 145) are expected to participate and understand fully the experience of the poem's *mythos*.

The obscurity of *The Cantos* may be the result not merely of the intractability of their cryptic allusions or their polymorphous, heterogeneous surface. The poem's obscurity is deliberate; meant as an mystery text, the poem has an esoteric as well as an exoteric side. The poem's obscurity also has a rhetorical purpose: the enlightenment of the reader! (Whether or not the committed reader ever achieves the enlightenment Pound sought is another matter.) Finally, the poem's obscurity can be penetrated somewhat by knowledge of the wisdom literature. Presumably Pound himself knows what it is that he wants to reveal in the *telete* or mystic rites of his poem, but he refrains from stating this anywhere in *The Cantos* (or anywhere else for that matter).

Pound's method is perfectly consistent with the idea found in the Hermetic tradition regarding the secrecy of the esoteric side of the sacred text. Mysteries are "things not to be spoken save in secret." *The Cantos*, like the sacred Hermetic texts, have an outer or exoteric form whose "meaning" is for general consumption; but the poem can also be understood by the initiates or illuminated souls who are in possession of *gnosis* as an inner or esoteric revelation.[13] Such popular metaphors of the poem's structure as the Odyssean journey belong to an exoteric reading of the poem. In turn, the poem's recondite surface can be justified by the occult assumption of the impenetrability and incommunicability of its *gnosis*.

2. POETRY AS REVELATION

Pound's interest in esoteric ideas shows up in a number of essays, spanning his early London years to the late 1930s; but most importantly in *Guide to Kulchur* (1938), that rather curious, idiosyncratic effort which resembles *The Cantos* in terms of organization and content.[14] Despite Stock's assertion that Pound's occult interests faded between his early London years and the time of the writing of *Guide to Kulchur*, a number of observations Pound makes in his prose writings suggest his continued interest in things occult.[15]

In defence of the "ideogrammic method" Pound states, early in *Guide to Kulchur*, that his aim as a writer is "revelation" (51). The word "revelation" is used in this early chapter, "ZWECK or the AIM," as a poetic term designating the moment of *gnosis* in the text, the moment when "one gets off the dead and desensitized surface of the reader's mind, onto a part that will register" (*GK* 51). Laszlo Géfin writes that Pound's purpose here is to show

> that the accumulated data will at one point cease to be just a "heap" of detail. As in a flash, the whole subject or phenomenon will appear, in the form of an image, in the reader's consciousness. What Pound avers here is that *revelation is a process*, the final stage of a cumulative agglomeration of detail (38).

Pound is interested in the "rain of factual atoms [particular things]," not so much for their own sake but because they are a necessary part of a process of revelation.

Elsewhere in *Guide to Kulchur*, Pound uses an analogy, borrowed from science, to explain both the method and the aim of his poetry:

> The *forma*, the immortal *concetto*, the concept, the dynamic form which is like the rose pattern driven into the dead iron-filings by the magnet, not by material contact with the magnet itself, but separate from the magnet. Cut off by the layer of glass, the dust and filings rise and spring into order (152).

Herbert N. Schneidau observes that this expresses the Vorticist conception of the ideal artist who projects the force of his "will and consciousness" into his material, aiming at inducing form which is latent in the material itself (*The Image and the Real* 152).

Notwithstanding the display of scientific language, it is important to recognize that during his London years, the major years of Pounds's activity as a theoretician, his statements are equally full of the language and attitude of the visionary experience.[16] Pound's prose is full of descriptions of the poetic moment of revelation, none more important or famous than the third item in his outline of the main scheme of *The Cantos*: "The 'magic moment' or moment of metamorphosis, bust thru from quotidien into 'divine or permanent world.' Gods, etc." (*L* 210). And, finally, the metaphor used by Pound in "A Retrospect" (1918) to define the "Image" is also concerned with the moment of revelation:

> An "Image" is that which presents an intellectual and emotional complex in an instant of time. . . .
>
> It is the presentation of such a "complex" instantaneously which gives that sense of sudden liberation; that sense of freedom from time limits and space limits; that sense of sudden growth, which we experience in the presence of the greatest works of art (*LE* 4).

For Pound the purpose of poetry is to help the reader arrive at the "full Eιδώς"; the aim of the poetics of the ideogram is to give the reader "a sudden insight." The language of the "mysterium" is to be found everywhere in Pound's statements, from the *Spirit of Romance* (1910) to *Gaudier Brzeska* (1916). "Sudden insight," "ecstasy," "great art is made to call forth, or create, an ecstasy," "sudden liberation," "revelation," "delightful psychic experience" and direct knowledge ("An Image . . . is real because we know it directly") are terms or phrases which one finds scattered throughout Pound's prose writings. In general, all of Pound's poetic theories, ranging from his theory of "language beyond metaphor" in *The Spirit of Romance* and his discussion of the "luminous detail" in "I Gather the Limbs of Osiris" (1911-12) to his formulation of the "image" and the "vortex" (1913-16), are concerned with an artistic process that has as its ultimate objective a "revelation" and its registration in art.

Pound displays an aversion for vagueness and, in the case of the Troubadours for example, he finds that "the ecstasy is not a whirl or a madness of the senses, but a glow arising from the exact nature of the perception" (*SR* 91). Thus, even when registering moments of vision, Pound "predicated exactness, precision, [and] definition as the life-giving component" (Schneidau, *The Image and the Real* 124). This explains in part the cohabitation in Pound's aesthetics of the impulse to register moments of revelation together with the insistence on the use of language that is clear and painstakingly precise.

To emphasize the importance of precision, Pound uses scientific terms to define his aesthetic ideals. In "Psychology and Troubadours" he talks about the need for "hyper-scientific precision" and defines poetry as "a sort of inspired mathematics, which gives us equations, not for abstract figures, triangles, spheres, and the like, but equations for the human emotions" (*SR* 14). Elsewhere he speaks of "The arts, literature, [and] poesy, [as] a science, just as chemistry is a science" (*LE* 42). Later, in describing the ideogrammic method, he likens poetry to the science of biology: "That, you see, is very much the kind of thing a biologist does (in a much more complicated way) when he gets together a few hundred or thousand slides, and picks out what is necessary for his general statement" (*ABCR* 22). These examples make clear Pound's preoccupation with couching moments of vision in a language which registers the exact nature of the perception.

Schneidau notes that in Pound's definition of Imagism there is heavy emphasis on its visionary potential and adds that this in no way compromises his quest for precision and exactness.[17] To prove his point that Pound cannot have felt any conflict between experiencing phantasmagoric states and his desire to create a "poetry of reality," Schneidau quotes from Pound's obituary article on Ford Madox Ford: "That Ford was almost an *halluciné* few of his intimates can doubt. He felt until it paralysed his efficient action, he saw quite distinctly the Venus immortal crossing the tram tracks" (*SP* 461). Schneidau, like most other critics, takes these remarks figuratively; I think they should be taken literally. And since Pound sees nothing paradoxical about Ford's visionary experiences and his insistence on exactness and precision, one has to assume that Pound would not view his own mix of activities as paradoxical either.

3. "The Celestial Tradition"

In this section I will trace the presence of a number of Poundian beliefs, already surveyed in the foregoing discussion, in *Guide to Kulchur*. This book remains the most authoritative guide to Pound's religious beliefs. These beliefs are based on Pound's understanding of the "occult" or, using Pound's own phrase, "celestial tradition"—a single tradition reaching back to the remotest antiquity and embracing many of the enlightened souls found in the pages of *The Cantos*. It is within this tradition that Pound discovers the *topos* of palingenesis and the justification for constructing a paradigm that allows for the exoteric/esoteric reading of history which we find in *The Cantos*.

The apparent capriciousness of *Guide to Kulchur*[18] is symptomatic of Pound's obsessive assumption of everything under the sun under a fairly simple set of categories set out in the following discussion.

Pound's views on poetic revelation become much clearer in his chapter on the "NEO-PLATONICKS ETC." in the *Guide to Kulchur*. The major criterion here involves the kind of language employed, and Pound distinguishes between "prose rhapsody" of which he disapproves, and the quest for "real theology" which he applauds. The first, he says, "undoubtedly excites certain temperaments, or perhaps almost anyone if caught at the right state of adolescence or in certain humours" (222). Having criticized the "prose rhapsody" for its vagueness and abstruseness, he nevertheless goes on to assert that there is nothing wrong with describing mystical experiences when the proper, precise, disciplined language is employed:

> Man drunk with god, man inebriated with infinity, on the one hand, and man with a millimetric measure and microscope on the other. I labour and relabour the discipline of real theology or of any verbal combat or athletics that forces or induces him to define his terms clearly.
>
> And this can NOT be limited to mere definition of abstract concepts. There is no doubt whatsoever that human beings are subject to emotion and that they attain to very fine, enjoyable and dynamic emotional states, which cause them to emit what to careful chartered accountants may seem intemperate language . . . (223).

Pound then examines the phenomenon of divine *ekstasis* in terms reminiscent of those employed in discriminating the "mysterium" from "Usura":

> Two mystic states can be dissociated: the ecstatic-beneficent-and-benevolent, contemplation of the divine love, the divine splendour with goodwill toward others.
>
> And the bestial, namely, the fanatical, the man on fire with God and anxious to stick his snotty nose into other men's business or reprove his neighbour for having a set of tropisms different from that of the fanatic's, or for having the courage to live more greatly and openly.
>
> The second set of mystic states is manifest in scarcity economists, in repressors etc.
>
> The first state is a dynamism. It has, time and again, driven men to great living, it has given them courage to go on for decades in the face of public stupidity. It is paradisical and a reward in itself seeking naught further . . . perhaps because a feeling of certitude inheres in the state of feeling itself. The glory of life exists without further proof for this mystic (223-24).

Those who belong to the first group form a sort of brotherhood whose concerns are philanthropic and whose reward is a feeling of equanimity and certitude; those who belong to the second group are fanatical, dogmatic, and concerned with repressing anything and everything they perceive as different from their own set of petrified beliefs.

Pound's speculations about the two mystic states derive from his understanding of Hellenistic religious thought. "NEO-PLATONICKS ETC." opens with another glimpse of this brotherhood: "Alongside or rather a long way from alongside of factual study, for 2000 or more years has run the *celestial tradition* [italics mine]" (222). The first group obviously belongs to the "celestial tradition," which Pound believes to have had a long history stretching back to Hellenistic times and beyond. Sharon Mayer Libera observes that Pound sees Neoplatonism as "part of a 'celestial tradition'" and that the "ETC." of the chapter's title "seems to justify the inclusion of a curious assortment of figures, such as Gemistus Plethon, Swedenborg, and G.R.S. Mead" (40). However, as far as Pound is concerned, this is not at all a "curious assortment of figures."

Pound places a digest of Confucius' *Analects* at the beginning of his *Guide to Kulchur* and the subject of economics is a constant thread; but the real spine of the book is a Gnostic or Hermetic reading of history which Pound calls the *Secretum*. Pound's list of philosophical heroes and villains in the *Guide to Kulchur* reveals his own commitment to this gnostic or hermetic tradition. This list is similar to the list of magi Frances Yates has retraced in *Giordano Bruno and the Hermetic Tradition*. Pound includes Pythagoras, Plato,[19] Plotinus, Iamblichus, Porphyry, Psellus, Plethon, the *Corpus Hermeticum*, Scotus Erigena, Grosseteste, the Masons, Ficino, Pico della Mirandola, Heydon, Blavatsky, Mead, and Yeats. To these names others can be added from the pages of *Guide to Kulchur*: Manes, Albertus Magnus, Dante, Swedenborg, Orage, Upward, H.D., Balzac, Brancusi, Cocteau, and Gurdjieff. The tradition that Pound is tracing is the Hermetic or Gnostic one. He calls it "Eleusis" (294-95). The centrality of this tradition is made clear in the frontispiece to *Guide to Kulchur* where his reverence for Plethon is manifested. It is underlined later on in *Guide to Kulchur* when the tradition is named:

> Gemistus Plethon brought over a species of Platonism to Italy in the 1430s.... and his conversation must have been lively. Hence (at a guess) Ficino's sinecure, at old Cosimo's expense, trained to translate the greek neoplatonists. Porphyry, Psellos, Iamblichus, Hermes Trismegistus....
>
> Whence I suppose what's-his-name and the English mystics with reference to greek originals sometimes (John Heydon etc.) (224-25).[20]

There are others who belong to this tradition (such as Appolonius of Tyana, Ocellus, Mozart, and Péladan); but the list is quite complete as it stands. There can be no mistake in recognizing the Gnostic/Hermetic tradition which Pound wants to reveal and discuss in the *Guide to Kulchur*, even if finally he does not avow his intention clearly. Nonetheless, Pound's hesitation is not translated into silence in the *Guide to Kulchur*. In spite of himself, it would seem, he comes back to the "celestial tradition."[21]

The idea of a secret, hidden, mystery tradition or history is a constant motif in Pound's "paideuma." In the chapter on "ROYALTY AND ALL THAT" in *Guide to Kulchur*, for example, Pound identifies the participants in this tradition in its medieval phase, and baptizes it as a "conspiracy of intelligence" which, he says, "outlasted the hash of the political map. Avicenna, Scotus Erigena in Provence, Grosseteste in Lincoln, the Sorbonne, fat faced Frankie Petrarch, Gemisto, the splendour the xvth century, Valla, the over-boomed Pico, the florentine collectors and conservers..." (263). Pound goes on to explain that the "secret history" appears in two distinct and opposed manifestations, a negative one which he associates with the "marasmus" and usurious conspiracies and a positive one which he associates with the sacredness of grain, fecundity, and the rite of ἱερός γάμος (*hieros gamos*):

> Shallow minds have been in a measure right in their lust for "secret history." I mean they have been dead right to want it, but shallow in their conception of what it was. Secret history is at least twofold. One part consists in secret corruption, the personal lusts, avarices, etc. that scoundrels keep hidden, another part is the "plus," the constructive urges, a *secretum* because it passes unnoticed or because no human effort can force it on public attention (264).

The reader who would look for an explicit and unambiguous description of the *secretum* in the *Guide to Kulchur* must be disappointed. The *secretum* and the *arcanum* exist and Pound is very categorical on this point: "Sober minds have agreed that the arcanum is the arcanum. No man can provide his neighbour with a Cook's ticket thereto" (292).[22] But Pound continuously harps on the blindness and deafness of his contemporaries, who fail to see the revelation he tirelessly holds up before them. He seems to believe that modern man has lost the ability or insight needed to absorb and comprehend the *gnosis* which is "perceptible in our own minds only with proper 'lighting,' fitfully and by instants" (295). The *gnosis* communicated through the mysteries will always be secret, "the mysteries will never be legal" and, Pound warns, the "law should keep from them" (156).

Besides providing some of the names of those who belong to the "celestial tradition" and hinting at the nature and history of the *secretum*, Pound also incorporates in his account some occult concepts, and his language is also imbued with terminology borrowed from this tradition. A notable example is his discussion, along Neoplatonic lines, of *nous* or *pleroma*, the transcendent field which Pound describes beautifully as a "sea crystalline and enduring, of the bright as it were molten glass that envelops us, full of light" (*GK* 44). Another example is Pound's version of the emanationist theory of *ekpyrosis* according to which the end of the world, when all things return to the One, is pictured as a supreme conflagration — dispersal through death conceived as an act of creation:

> God the architectural fire, *pur texnon*. . . .
> . . . The soul a blob of the first fire, apospasma, a torn-off shred, stuck in the human chest whence the voice proceeded, the word a creative force.
> The one individual soul an instrument of the world-soul lasting while the world-soul lasts, and after a new ekpyrosis be again frayed off from the pneuma.
> The body a dwelling-place . . . (124).

The picture which emerges from reading *Guide to Kulchur* is reaffirmed when one turns to Pound's essays, especially those essays which have been conveniently gathered in *Selected Prose of Ezra Pound: 1909-1965*. Such ideas as the tradition of *gnosis*, the belief in the existence of an arcanum available to those with great intelligence, the need for recapturing the "consciousness of the greatest mystery [Eleusis]" (*SP* 317), reconstituting the fragments of the tradition, and achieving a "greek pagan revival" (*GK* 191), and the belief in "the universal religion of all men [that is, theosophy]" (*GK* 141-42) are ideas which are reiterated in some of these essays.[23]

Interesting in this context is Pound's reading of myths as esoteric fictional records of the psychic experiences of the most intelligent individuals of a culture, and the connection he sees between myths and the mysteries. In the well-known paragraph from "Psychology and Troubadours" (1912), Pound commits himself to the following belief:

> I believe in a sort of permanent basis in humanity, that is to say, I believe that Greek myth arose when someone having passed through delightful psychic experience tried to communicate it to others and found it necessary to screen himself from persecution. Speaking aesthetically, the myths are explications of mood: you may stop there, or you may probe deeper. Certain it is that these myths are only intelligi-

ble in a vivid and glittering sense to those people to whom they occur. I know, I mean, one man who understands Persephone and Demeter, and one who understands the Laurel, and another who has, I should say, met Artemis. These things are for them *real* (SR 92).

There are two points which must be emphasized here. First, for Pound the status of the experience is never in doubt; and second, he sees the myth-making process as a masking or transformation of the real experience — that is, he sees it as corresponding to the exoteric side of the mysteries. Myth-making, then, is an imaginative transformation or fictionalization of the real experience, a transformation motivated by a fear of persecution.[24]

The status of the psychic experience is never doubted by Pound in "Psychology and Troubadours" or elsewhere. In *Guide to Kulchur*, written over twenty years later, Pound is equally emphatic:

> What remains, and remains undeniable to and by the most hardened objectivist, is that a great number of men have had certain kinds of emotion and, *magari*, of ecstasy.
>
> They have left indelible records of ideas born of, or conjoined with, this ecstasy (225).

To return to "Psychology and Troubadours," an additional point of interest is Pound's testimony concerning his acquaintance with a number of people who have had psychic experiences. It is difficult to say who these people were, although Ford Madox Ford who "saw the Venus immortal," as Pound wrote in his obituary article on him, was certainly one of them. Regardless of who the other friends were, one begins to see that Pound probably counts himself among those who "understand or have even 'met' Artemis." Here we need to remember that in Pound's "rite [which is] made for the West" "a God is [simply] an eternal state of mind," a state that man can both "perceive" as a "Vision" as well as enter (*SP* 47-48). Pound's belief that "the Gods exist" also explains the veneration he felt for Gemistus Plethon who "had distinct aims, [for the] regeneration of greek people so they wd. keep out the new wave of Barbarism (Turkish) etc." (*GK*, 224) by reinstating the pagan gods. Pound himself echoes Plethon's aim when he says that he "wd. set up the statue of Aphrodite again over Terracina. I doubt, ... whether you can attain a living catholicism save after a greek pagan revival" (*GK* 191).

Besides believing in the reality of extraordinary or mystic experiences Pound also believed in the preservation of mystical insights which have their origins in the mystery cults of antiquity. "Terra Italica," an essay first published in *The New Review* (Winter 1931-32), shows clearly his desire to return to the psychic fountain of religion, here identified with Eleusis.²⁵ After discussing the importance of eros in the religious institutions of paganism, Pound presents the religious experience as something which should not and cannot be institutionalized into dogma. He follows this with an attempt at defining the positive elements of paganism and Hellenistic polytheism which evokes, at the same time, all that is negative in fossilized church doctrine:

> For certain people the *pecten cteis* is the gate of wisdom. The glory of the polytheistic anschauung is that it never asserted a single and obligatory path for everyone. It never caused the assertion that everyone was fit for initiation and it never caused an attempt to force people into a path alien to their sensibilities.
> Paganism never feared knowledge. It feared ignorance and under a flood of ignorance it was driven out of its temples (*SP* 56).²⁶

The motif of the restoration of the temples becomes very important in the later cantos. There the task of resurrecting the ancient places of worship (the statue of Aphrodite at Terracina, the altar in the garden, etc.) becomes closely associated with the idea of recollection and reconstitution of the *gnosis* of the "ancient wisdom" (*SP* 57). Pound calls for a "pagan revival" to be achieved by discovering and following the principles of the "celestial tradition," a tradition which at various points in history emerges as a light that energizes and determines the nature of exceptional human achievement — for example, Pound thought of Dante and Swedenborg as having achieved this *gnosis* or "enlightened consciousness." He sees the *gnosis* of the "celestial tradition" as "a light from Eleusis [which] persisted through the middle ages and set beauty in the song of Provence and of Italy" (*SP* 53).²⁷

The rediscovery of or return to the polytheistic ethos of pagan and Hellenistic esoteric rituals is, as noted earlier, the basis of Pound's admiration for Plethon. At the same time, Pound's conception of *gnosis* is closely linked with the cognizance of the divine ("full Εἰδὼς"), rooted for him in ordinary sensory experience. In addition, ritual sex and the significance of pagan ceremonies and sun festivals are central to his idea of what constitutes *gnosis*. This is the point made in "Religio" (1939), which I quote in its entirety:

> Paganism included a certain attitude toward; a certain understanding of, coitus, which is the mysterium.
> The other rites are the festivals of fecundity of the grain and the sun festivals, without revival of which religion can not return to the hearts of the people (*SP* 70).

This note contains in a nutshell Pound's religious beliefs and provides an apt conclusion for this discussion. It defines the *hieros gamos* or ritual copulation as a "mysterium" central to paganism's conception of the relationship between man and the divine and calls for a "revival," a return, a *nostos* to the religious sense shared by the pagans through their ancient rites and mysteries which had palingenesis as their focal point and motivation.

The palingenetic *topos* found in "Religio" is ubiquitous in *The Cantos*. The foregoing account of the importance of Hellenistic religious thought for Pound looks forward to the relevance of such thought to *The Cantos* which is explored in the final section of this book. But before turning to the poem itself, we must examine first the heteroclite family of opinions and beliefs which have their provenance in the celestial or occult tradition and, second, this set of opinions and beliefs in the form in which Pound encountered them during his early Hamilton College and Pennsylvania years and later during his Kensington years.

Notes

1. Ezra Pound, *The Cantos of Ezra Pound* (New York: New Directions, 1972), 781. Hereafter, *The Cantos* are cited by canto number and page only; therefore, (110/781) refers to canto 110, page 781.
2. Mary de Rachewiltz has pointed out to me that the Catholic Church held a strong appeal for Pound (letter dated 24 September 1989). In a May 1949 letter to Olivia Rossetti Agresti, Pound attributes the church's decline to the "spread" of the New Testament: "The Church of Rome decayed, got steadily stupider pari passu as the jew books were put into circulation, and stupidities engrafted on the clean greek and roman ideas of the early Church. . . . The New Test[ment] is ANTI the old, or omit all but a very few pages of it. A few good ideas, and much and increasing corruption" (Collection of American Literature, Beinecke Rare Book Library, Yale University, Pound Collection; hereafter cited as BRBL). Agresti herself was a staunch Catholic; the exchanges between them make clear Pound's sympathy for the early Church as well as his contempt for the modern-day Catholic Church. Pound believed that the Catholic Church stayed healthy as long as the pagan and Hellenistic elements outweighed the Judaic ones. In another letter to Agresti he notes that "The Hellenic element IN Xtianity never corrupted no one" (n.d. but Agresti responded to it in December 1953). Finally, in still another letter to Agresti, Pound gives a succinct statement that contains in a nutshell many of the ideas outlined in this study and, more specifically, anticipates much of the discussion in this chapter: "Fanaticisms are from abstract statements & a religion hatched in slums & cut off from agriculture is a *curse* whether of 1000 or 3000 years" (n.d. but Agresti responded to it on 14 July 1947). For more on Pound's attitude towards the Catholic Church, see Emery (esp. 3-4 and 15-16).

3. In *Polite Essays* Pound writes: "Forma to the great minds of at least one epoch meant something more than dead pattern or fixed opinion. 'The Light of the DOER, as it were a form cleaving to it' meant an ACTIVE pattern, a pattern that set things in motion" (51).
4. This reading is also supported by Pound's assertion, in a 16 July 1922 letter to Harriet Monroe, that he considers "the *Metamorphoses* a sacred book" (L 183). See also Emery's discussion of Pound's views on Ovid (6-7).
5. I am indebted to Noel Stock's *Pound in Exile* for alerting me to the usefulness of Wind's arguments. However, I find Stock's application of Wind's argument incomplete. Though he considers the relevance of Hellenistic "religious" thought to Pound's *paideuma*, Stock fails to appreciate it fully.
6. Wind writes that "Thus Plato appeared to them not as a critic or transposer of mysteries, but as the heir and oracle of an ancient wisdom for which a ritual disguise had been invented by the founders of the mysteries themselves" (17).
7. These terms are borrowed by Wind from A.-J. Festugière, *L'idéal réligieux des Grecs et l'Evangile* (1932).
8. The example of Forrest Read's *'76: One World and the Cantos of Ezra Pound* must be avoided. In his book Read proposes that there is a cryptic plan behind *The Cantos*. This plan involves a system of correspondences between the sections of *The Cantos* and such documents as the Declaration of Independence, the U.S. Constitution, a mysterious calendar published anonymously in the *Little Review* in 1922, and the symbols of the Great Seal of the United States.
9. The reading proposed here shares much with Wind's cryptological hermeneutics — but there is a sharp distinction to be made: Wind's hermeneutics presupposes that anyone can arrive at an esoteric reading or understanding of the secret meaning of a work of art provided that he or she first masters the appropriate key or learning; the pneumatic or occult hermeneutics proposed here presupposes that unless one is in possession of *gnosis* or wisdom (arrived at by way of a revelation or direct communication with the ineffable) he or she cannot penetrate the exoteric form of the text and attain an esoteric revelation or meaning that cannot be communicated directly.
10. In *Ezra Pound and the Erotic Medium*, Kevin Oderman also argues that Pound's writing has an exoteric as well as an esoteric side: "following the lead of the 'trobar clus' [Pound] hoped to be writing essays and poems that were available on two levels, one for the crowd, one for the elect. So there is always an element of obfuscation in his treatment of 'mystic phenomena'" (135). As can be gathered from my own discussion, I am in general agreement with Oderman. However, he seems to be attributing Pound's perception of the exoteric/esoteric sides of a work of art wholly to his understanding of the "trobar clus." I, on the other hand, argue for Pound's understanding of the Gnostic/Hermeticist/Rosicrucian tradition which also colours his view of troubadour art.
11. In this 7 December 1956 letter to Olivia Rossetti Agresti, Pound writes that "Dan[te] and Swed.[enborg] are both sound in their schema of increasing enlightened consciousness" (BRBL).
12. In both "Cavalcanti" (LE 173-82) and *Guide to Kulchur* Pound devotes a great deal of space to Valli. In *Provence and Pound*, Peter Makin writes that "In 1928 Luigi Valli published a book called *Il Linguaggio Segreto di Dante*, which 'proved' that Dante and his friends were writing into their poems a cipher concerning Manichaeist 'secret conspiracies, mystic brotherhoods,' and so on" (242). Makin's claim that Valli

proved anything is absurd. Valli is, of course, another eccentric who proved nothing. Kevin Oderman makes some sensible suggestions about Pound's disagreement with Valli (65-67). See also Angela Elliott's discussion of Pound's reading of Valli's contention ("Light as Image" 161-62). My own understanding of Pound's attitude to Valli derives from "The Birth of Modernism," Leon Surette's work-in-progress.
13. *Gnosis*, from the Greek γνῶσις, is any teaching according to which *soteria* or salvation depends upon initiatory knowledge—that is, revealed, self-realized, spiritual knowledge; *gnosis* is knowledge that is more profound than that available to intellectual or philosophical inquiry (ἐπιστήμη or *episteme*). For a more comprehensive definition of the term *gnosis*, see Chapter II.
14. For a discussion of the economic and artistic threads found in *Guide to Kulchur*, see Chapter II in Emery's *Ideas into Action*. Emery points out that *Guide to Kulchur* "may be described as the prose complement of the *Cantos*" (27).
15. The argument regarding the fading of Pound's interest in "things occult" after the early London years until the late 1930s or even the early 1950s, at which time it is said to have been rekindled, has been advanced by other critics besides Stock. William French argues for the early 1950s as the time for the reawakening of Pound's interest—this is the time French helped Pound proofread *The Spirit of Romance*. French claims that the rereading of this book helped renew Pound's interest in esoterica. Boris de Rachewiltz is in general agreement with French on this point (177). For details on this position see Timothy Materer, "Ezra Pound and the Alchemy of the Word" (119-20). I suggest that Pound's interest in the occult never really waned. Pound's letters to John Theobald and Patricia Hutchins, in which he reminisces about his London years, suggest that his interest in the occult was unbroken. An essay like "Terra Italica" (1931-32) also shows that this interest was strong in the early 1930s. *Guide to Kulchur* (1938), as I argue in this chapter, constitutes the strongest proof for Pound's continued interest in "things occult."
16. Max Nänny, in *Ezra Pound: Poetics for an Electric Age*, writes that, "As paradoxical as it may sound, it was exactly Pound's 'mystical' desire for immediate experience and perception that was instrumental in his replacing the purely verbal 'approach of logic' by the intuitional and factual approach of science" (63).
17. Schneidau quotes from *Instigations of Ezra Pound* to show Pound's concept of visionary poetry: "poetry wherein the feelings of painting and sculpture are predominant (certain men move in phantasmagoria; the images of their gods, whole countrysides, stretches of hill and forest, travel with them)" (145).
18. Pound himself is aware of the "difficult" nature of his book and in at least two places admits as much. In Chapter 52, "The Promised Land," he describes it as "a book of yatter such as the present is" (292). Further on in the same chapter he makes a comparison between his poetry and *Guide to Kulchur*, admitting that "the foregoing pp. are as obscure as anything in my poetry" (295).
19. Plato is alternately blamed and praised in *Guide to Kulchur* (222, 347).
20. For more on Plethon see Chapters II and IV.
21. As I will explain more fully in a subsequent chapter, this "celestial tradition" involves four more or less distinct strands: Gnosticism, Hermeticism, Neoplatonism, and the Cabala.
22. Following common occultist practice, Pound implies that the secret tradition is too *profound* to be communicated directly.
23. See especially "Part Two: Religio" (*SP* 45-72).

24. Pound critics have much to say about the first point; it is Ian F.A. Bell in *Critic as Scientist* who makes the second point: "Commentators have rightly attended to the notion of 'delightful psychic experience' but have usually ignored its coda, the possibility of 'persecution' as its consequence.... As Pound's 1915 essay on Arnold Dolmetsch testified, he was concerned throughout his early years in London with a 'persecution' that took the form of mockery at all his talk of the 'gods' or consisted in calling him a liar" (138). Bell goes on to say that the status of the experiences is never in doubt in Pound's mind; instead, Pound's problem is the discovery of a discourse fit for modern audiences in the way that myth was a fit discourse for the ancients: "[the problem is to find] an available lexicon for experience that was seemingly arcane and certainly private and communicatively unintelligible; of sustaining a public, and publishable, status for the myths of psychic or mystic phenomena" (138).
25. In *Ez As Wuz*, James Laughlin, who knew Pound quite well, has this to say about Pound's "religion": "He believed in such cults as the Eleusinian Mysteries, not in Christianity or Buddhism. The appeal to him of Confucius was precisely that it was ethics, not religion as most of us conceive it" (28).
26. Elsewhere Pound discusses the "mysterium"/usurious dogma antithesis in these terms: "Tradition *inheres*... in the images of the gods, and gets lost in dogmatic definitions. History is recorded in monuments, and *that* is why they get destroyed" (from *A Visiting Card*, qtd. in *SP* 322).
27. In his discussion of canto 39, Clark Emery also identifies this tradition. Emery writes that Pound alludes to "an unbroken tradition of fertility ritualism extending from pre-historic Egypt, through Eleusis, into Roman Catholicism" (146). In addition, Emery discusses the attainment of *gnosis* (though he does not use this term) in Pound's work. For example, he discusses the Neoplatonic notions of *nous* in this way: "The neo-Platonists have borne witness that men can achieve a state in which clarity of intellect and harmony of soul obtain" (10). Emery also discusses the idea of the "Permanent" of which "we have moments of awareness, moments of... clarity of vision" (17).

II

The Occult Tradition

1. "The Rising Psychic Tide"

Ezra Pound's stay in London coincided with a time of intense public interest in the occult. He arrived in London in September 1908, attracted, he said later, by the prospect of meeting William Butler Yeats, whom he considered to be the most important poet alive. Olivia Shakespear introduced Pound to Yeats in the early months of 1909, and by the middle of of that year he was a regular in the older poet's Monday evening "at homes" in Woburn Buildings.[1] Pound boasts of his intimacy with Yeats in a May 1911 letter to his father: "Yeats I like very much. I've seen him a great deal, almost daily.... He is, as I have said, a very great man, and he improves on acquaintance."[2]

At the time of his first acquaintance with Pound, Yeats was, as indeed he was throughout his adult life, actively involved in the occult movement. His involvement in various occult groups (Dublin Hermetic Society, Blavatsky Lodge of the London Theosophical Society, Hermetic Order of the Golden Dawn) has been well documented in a number of studies published in the last three decades.[3]

The most important and lasting of all the occult influences in Yeats's case was probably that exerted by Theosophy. In 1885 Yeats, together with Charles Johnson and a few others, founded a theosophical association, the Dublin Hermetic Society, to discuss "occult sciences." When Yeats moved to London in 1887 he immediately joined the London Lodge of the Society, falling under the influence of Madame Blavatsky. Though he later severed his formal ties with the Theosophical Society, it was Theosophy that gave him his first systematic introduction to the occult tradition. Graham Hough stresses the importance of Blavatsky and her movement for

---

The notes to Chapter II are found on pp. 54-58.

Yeats: "again and again we find that many obscure, puzzling and apparently original elements in Yeats's esoteric doctrine, even towards the end of his life, turn out to have their roots in the Theosophical teaching he first encountered in his early twenties [ca. 1887]" (35).

Blavatsky's influence was so widespread and far-ranging that, as Warren S. Smith writes in *The London Heretics, 1870-1914*, her impact "on the London intelligentsia during her fleeting visit of 1884 and during her residence there in the last four years of her life [1887-91] makes it impossible to ignore either her or her organization in any consideration of the local heresies of the day" (141-42).

The late nineteenth and early twentieth centuries were periods of unusual vitality in the history of the occult—perhaps prompted by the complete triumph of positivist science over religious faith. In Yeats's case, he was lured to the occult by the promise of liberation from materialism. In *The Identity of Yeats*, Richard Ellmann remarks on the poet's personal need for a belief in a heterodox dogma that would allow him to dispute the claims of modern science:

> Yeats found in occultism, and in mysticism generally, a point of view which had the virtue of warring with accepted belief.... He wanted to secure proof that experimental science was limited in its results, in an age when science made extravagant claims; he wanted evidence that an ideal world existed, in an age which was fairly complacent about the benefits of actuality; he wanted to show that the current faith in reason and in logic ignored a far more important human faculty, the imagination (3).

Yeats's motivation and occult connections being undoubted, it is hardly surprising that he introduced Pound to his occult circle.

I intend to return to the subject of Pound's involvement with Yeats, Olivia and Dorothy Shakespear, Upward, Orage, and Mead in the next chapter. At this point I would like to present a brief definition of the term "occult" before going on to discuss the London scene during the first years of Pound's stay there. The rest of the chapter then is devoted to a general discussion of the "celestial or occult tradition," from its origins to certain of its various manifestations during the late Victorian and early Edwardian periods. I also use the term "wisdom tradition" to mean that branch of occultism which deals with metaphysics and history—as opposed to theurgy or practical magic.

Operating outside established, orthodox religion, occultism comprises theories and practices based on esoteric knowledge. Derived from the Latin root *occulere* (to cover over, hide, conceal), "occult" signifies anything hidden or secret, in the sense of being mysterious to ordinary understanding or scientific reason.[4] It is an axiom of the occult that presently mysterious phenomena may be understood or explained in the future. However, there are other phenomena, said to be intrinsically occult, inherently unknowable by scientific reason, but still accessible to occult modes of cognition latent in everyone. In what has been described as "still the best short statement of the technical meaning of the term" (and from which this discussion is largely derived), Mead writes that occultism points to the limitations of normal senses and advances the belief that "the range of the senses can be enormously extended psychically, and so the imperfections and inaccuracies of the normal senses can be progressively corrected by the natural development of the powers of the human organism itself" ("Occultism" 445).[5] Thus occultism makes a "claim to knowledge of a scientific nature which is inaccessible to the accepted methods of positive objective scientific research" (Mead, "Occultism" 445).

An ancient body of literature, formulating a profound and coherent system, is thought to pass on occult or esoteric knowledge whose source is divine. The title of Mead's study of the philosophies and practices of various Gnostic groups of the early centuries of the Christian era, *Fragments of a Faith Forgotten* (1900), suggests both the preoccupations and the method of occult scholars. Esoteric knowledge is found in venerable texts severally containing the key to all wisdom; occultists believe that these texts were known to the ancients but have since been forgotten or lost. The occult scholar must therefore labour to discover and reassemble the scattered "fragments" in an attempt to trace the contour of the original structure of "ancient wisdom." In fact, despite the claims made by occult groups regarding their ancient origins, the intellectual content of the occult is almost all derived from the Hellenistic period. Characteristically, occult texts from that period attribute their wisdom to Egypt.

Even though human history presents an unbroken line witnessing humanity's incessant fascination with magic, there have been a number of periods when popular interest in the occult has peaked. One of those periods spanned the late nineteenth and early twentieth centuries. The causes of this particular manifestation of interest in the occult are numerous, one of the major stimuli being a reaction against the restrictive world view of posivitism. The dominant role assumed by science in modern culture, and science's exclusion of all knowledge that is not quantifiable sparked the interest in the occult. Many of the occult movements of the period begin with a formulaic denial that science represents the only legitimate access to reality.

However, science is not rejected outright by the occult. On the contrary, the occult often expresses itself in scientific or quasi-scientific terminology and derives much of its appeal from the claim that it bridges the traditional split between religion and science. Rather than repudiating science, occultism claims that it uses the methods of scientific analysis to provide empirical evidence for concepts and beliefs (such as the immortality of the soul) which religion asks that we accept on grounds of faith. The synthesis of occultism and science, aimed primarily at the educated reader, results in what Robert Galbreath calls "intellectualized versions of occultism." Galbreath sees these "versions of occultism" as seeking

> to go beyond science by placing it in a higher synthesis in which metaphysical questions are joined with personal experience and systematic investigation. It is likely that it is the self-proclaimed incompetence of science to handle metaphysical questions which provides the chief justification for the intellectualized syntheses of modern occultism ("Explaining Modern Occultism" 31).

The reaction against science during the late Victorian and Edwardian years, then, was a reaction against its monopoly and an attempt to resist the omnipresent threat of materialism — a threat which Ellmann identified as the single most important cause of Yeats's turning to esotericism. The occult's appeal was as an alternative to the strictly rational, empiricist outlook of the times. In *The Edwardian Turn of Mind*, Samuel Hynes discusses the occult as one of a number of "often apparently unconnected movements [which] shared a common concern for the liberation of men from the restrictions of materialistic thought and materialistic values" (134).[6] In addition to its appealing opposition "to conventional Victorian ideas," the occult also filled the gap left by the failure of Christian Churches to satisfy the need for "sacramental experiences" and personal as well as collective *renovatio* (Eliade, *Occultism* 63-65).

Whatever the reasons for the mushrooming of occult sects during the late Victorian and Edwardian periods, Pound's stay in London (1908-21), as already noted, coincided with a time of intense public interest in occultism. In an article published in *The Quest*, Mead reports on the kinds of occult activities Pound would have encountered during his Kensington years — activities he would not have failed to notice. Writing in early 1912, Mead notes that "the idea of the adept and initiate in secret knowledge, the ideal of the divine man or woman, of the god-inspired, or at any rate of the human with superhuman powers, is in the air" (420). And in this article, aptly entitled "The Rising Psychic Tide," he goes on to say that if we look for them,

> In many directions we may see . . . revivals of divination, seers and soothsayers and prophets, pythonesses, sibyls and prophetesses, tellers of dreams and of omens, mantics of every description and by every sort of contrivance; astrologists and even alchemists; professors of magical arts and ceremonies; cosmologists and revelationists; necromancy and communion with spirits; enthusiasm trance and ecstasy. And with all this, as of old, keeping pace with religious unrest and loss of faith in traditional beliefs and blank denial of anything beyond the range of the physical, there is what looks very much like the bringing in of new gods and new saviours and new creeds, the blending of cults and syncretism of religions; societies and associations open and secret, for propagating or imparting new doctrines, new at any rate to their adherents though mostly old enough (410).

What Mead describes here is a city (London, ca. 1912) experiencing the revival of Rosicrucianism, the Cabala, Hermeticism, and esoteric Buddhism: a city flooded by waves of reincarnationists, palmists, astrologers, and all sorts of groups absorbed in various arcane activities. The list is impressive in breadth as well as length. Mead claims that these occult activities represent a "repetition" of the past; but the claims of direct ancient lineage and historical continuity which permeate all of Mead's works as well as the works of other occultists are a constantly rediscovered fiction.

Furthering his claim for the antiquity of modern occult movements, Mead searches the past to discover any periods when the "psychic tide" paralleled in intensity that of his own time. Noting that there can be no "exact parallel . . . in any epoch in the past," he, nonetheless, finds striking similarities between his London and the Alexandria of the Hellenistic period (409). In *Fragments of a Faith Forgotten*, Mead describes the "rising psychic tide" one would encounter in "the city [Alexandria] where Egypt and Africa, Rome and Greece, Syria and Arabia met together" (120). He sees the Alexandria of Hellenistic times as a "melting pot" into which philosophy, science, religio-philosophy, and theosophy of every kind were poured.

That the late nineteenth and early twentieth centuries were a period of unusual vitality in the history of occultism is an undeniable fact. The ubiquity of occultism is reflected not only in the works of such avowed occultists as Mead but also in many literary works which had their genesis at that time, including the two outstanding examples of modernism: *Ulysses* and *The Waste Land*. James Joyce's ridicule of the occult in *Ulysses* and the prominent position given to Madame Sosostris in T.S. Eliot's *The Waste Land* reflect the ubiquity of the occult at the time.[7]

2. A History of the "Occult Tradition"

This section must begin with a disclaimer. In the last section I pointed out that the claims made by occultists to an ancient lineage and historical continuity are fallacious—and this is a point worth stressing at the outset of my discussion of what I call, with reservations, "the occult tradition." The existence of such a tradition is itself highly debatable. "Tradition" means something handed down, implying a linear descent. But the doctrines, myths, and motifs of the occult tradition are highly eclectic and too various for any claims of homogeneity to be meaningful. The occult is a heterodox tradition constantly re-discovered by its adherents who simply borrow, steal, or re-invent religious ideas and practices that other eccentrics like themselves have kept current in all sorts of societies and publications.[8]

To understand many of the elements contributing to "the rising psychic tide," one needs some knowledge of the religio-magical cults of antiquity, particularly those of the Hellenistic age, the age of syncretism, during which many spiritual and religious groups competed—among them, Christianity. The drama of the first three Christian centuries out of which emerged such important movements as Hermeticism, Gnosticism, and Neoplatonism, as well as Christianity itself, was enacted within the framework of "the one universal, Hellenic culture and language" (Jonas 10). Hans Jonas divides Greek culture into four distinct historical phases: "(1) before Alexander, the classical phase as a national culture; (2) after Alexander, Hellenism as a cosmopolitan secular culture; (3) later Hellenism as a pagan religious culture; and (4) Byzantinism as a Greek Christian culture" (10). Alexander's conquest of the East (334-323 B.C.) brought about the first transition. The second transition was a development of the Greek-Oriental synthesis which already was taking place in the second phase; it was the consequence, however, of the impact made by the non-Greek forces, introduced from the East, which had for a time played a rather passive role. The "defeat" at the hands of a dominant Christianity of the spiritual movements which flowered during Hellenism ushered in the age of Byzantium, twelve centuries of Greek-Orthodox culture. It is the second and third of these periods that witness the genesis of occultism.

Having made clear the fictional nature of the claims made by occultists regarding the continuity of their tradition, I would now like to trace the origin of these claims. Looking back to pre-classical and classical Greece, we find, besides the orthodoxy of the Olympian gods and the state cults, various mystery cults sharing a number of doctrines and practices: (1) the doctrine of palingenesis; (2) the doctrine of salvation (*soteria*) through communion with the divine (the desire and belief in an afterlife where the reward for the fully purified soul is "to dwell with the god"); (3) certain observances such as strict ritual purity (*katharsis*); and (4) initiation rites. The initiates of these cults shared a sense of election and, even on earth, claimed to have been rewarded with an *epopteia*, or enlightenment, that is, direct communion with the divine.

The best known, and the most characteristic, of the mysteries of ancient Greece are those of Eleusis. The origin of the rites of Eleusis, celebrated every four years in honour of Demeter and Persephone, go back to the time before the arrival of the Hellenes. The cults of "Demeter Eleusinia" existed in Greece before the local ritual of Eleusis developed into the mysteries. Beginning as agrarian rites designed to maintain and increase the fertility of the land, the mysteries were later modified and (especially after the introduction during the sixth century of Orphic and Dionysian elements) became charged with metaphysical meanings, most especially the immortality of the soul. The *mystai* or initiates were promised Persephone's protection in the world beyond the grave — thus eschatology was added to traditional fertility rituals.[9]

The Eleusinian myth is preserved in the Homeric *Hymn to Demeter*, dated between 650 and 550 B.C. This hymn narrates the abduction of Koré or Persephone, Demeter's daughter, by Hades. After an unsuccessful search for Koré, Demeter, disguised as an old crone, comes at last to Eleusis. Engaged by the local prince as a nurse to the baby prince Demophon, she tries to make the baby immortal by immersing him in fire. Discovered in the act, she reveals her divinity, orders a temple to be built in her honour and, by causing the land to be barren, blackmails Zeus into restoring her daughter to her, at least for half the year. Having eaten a pomegranate seed while in the underworld, Koré must spend the other half of the year with her husband Hades. Following the return of her daughter, Demeter restores life to the crops and reveals the mysteries to the Eleusinian princes.

The Eleusinian initiation rites were secret, and we have only scraps of information about them — at least, the ἄρρητον, the *arrheton* or ineffable secret that formed the heart of the rites, remains unknown to us. Though much information about the mysteries has reached us by way of both literary and artistic sources, their meaning and significance still escape us. George E. Mylonas's remarks on the secrecy of the mysteries are instructive:

> It is amazing indeed that the basic and important substance of the secret rites was never disclosed, when these Mysteries were held at Eleusis annually for some two thousand years, when a multitude of people

from all over the civilized world was initiated, and when their content was transmitted orally from Hierophant to Hierophant over so many generations (226).

There were two stages to the Eleusinian Mysteries: the Lesser Mysteries, a preliminary ritual which had a predominantly purificatory character (*katharsis*) and took place in the month of Anthesterion (February-March); and the Mysteria, or Greater Mysteries, which took place in the month of Boedromion (September-October). On the first day of the Greater Eleusinia the *ephebé* (youths) of Athens went to Eleusis, brought back the *hiera*, or sacred objects, and placed them on the Eleusinion, at the foot of the Acropolis. The following day the *mystai* (initiates) took a ritual bath in the sea and fasted for three days. At that point they marched in procession (*pompé*) from Athens to Eleusis, guided by the statue of Iacchos—Iacchos is the mystic name for the ecstatic Dionysus who early on became associated with the cult of Demeter. Arriving at Eleusis toward dusk, the *mystai* descended into the sanctuary, a "dark subterranean passage" (*Katabaskion to skoteinon*—hence *katabasis*), broke their fast by partaking of the *kykeon* (a mixture of barley, spices, and water), and enacted the search for Koré by torchlight. The central rite, which is clear only in its outline, involved, first, the *dromena*, during which for a whole night the *mystai* underwent terrifying darkness, and then came a climax full of illumination, when the *anaktoron*, or inmost sanctum, was opened and a great fire burst forth. At the same time, the *Hierophant* or High Priest[10] shouted that the goddess had given birth to a sacred child, Brimo, and showed the initiates the great mystery, an ear of corn cut in silence. A year after initiation (*myesis*), the *mystes* (initiate) could attain the degree of *epopteia* (the stage of "having seen" the mystery) by participating in a sort of liturgical drama (*drama mystikon*) whose subject is usually thought to have been the acting out of the sexual union of Demeter and Zeus (an *hieros gamos*), with the priestess of Demeter and the Hierophant as protagonists. Following his initiation the *mystes* became an *epoptes*, one who "has seen." Whatever its exact nature (and there is much controversy as to the exact nature of the Eleusinian rites[11]), the *myesis* had a tripartite character: *katabasis/dromena/epopteia*, of which I will have more to say in a subsequent chapter.

As noted in the previous chapter, Pound alludes to the rites of Eleusis a number of times in his prose writings (especially in *Selected Prose* but also in *Guide to Kulchur*) as well as in *The Cantos*. It is believed that Pound knew Plutarch's description of Eleusinian initiation (*Light* 50); but he probably also learned about Eleusis from Thomas Taylor's *The Eleusinian and Bacchic Mysteries: A Dissertation*, as well as from Mead's treatment of the subject.[12] Pound himself took for a fact the *hieros gamos* which some scholars have guessed was the principal rite of the Eleusinian *epopteia* — and this explains the prominence in his poetry of the motifs of divine sexual coupling and transformation. In fact, we have Mr. Laughlin's testimony for Pound's knowledge of the terminology associated with the Eleusinian mysteries and his conviction of the centrality of the *hieros gamos*. During one of the peripatetic lessons during his "Ezuveristy" period, Mr. Laughlin says, Pound "explained the Eleusinian mysteries, about *dromena* and *epopte* [sic], and went on to the bizarre theories you will find in the postscript to his translation of De Gourmont's *Physique de l'amour*" (*Pound as Wuz* 6).[13] Furthermore, Mr. Laughlin also reveals that in Pound's mind the Eleusinian *dromena* corresponded to a sexual "orgasm": "the bust of 'marvelous light' is the *dromena*, which Pound suggested to me was an orgasm" (*Pound as Wuz* 85). Thus, Pound's understanding of the Eleusinian Mysteries shapes his understanding of the "celestial tradition" and is a theme of major importance, never too far from his mind. This theme is a subject which has repeatedly engaged Pound scholars.[14]

Developing alongside the older mysteries, Orphism and Pythagoreanism seem to have been parallel phenomena (at least during the sixth and fifth centuries B.C.), and the confusion between them is so complete that it is quite impossible to say definitively of any of the fragments surviving from that time that it is purely Orphic or purely Pythagorean. What is certain is that these mystery cults remained alive and that their influence can be discerned easily in the writings of the authors of the classical period, including Plato and the dramatists Aristophanes and Euripides. The attitude of the classical writers towards these cults is often mixed. For example, Aristophanes parodies the private mysteries of the Orphic type in the *Clouds*, while his more serious depiction of the other world in the *Frogs* is based on exactly the same ideas. This ambivalent attitude should be attributed to Orphism's decline to a point where the cult's ethical code was disregarded by those practising a lower, popular form in which interest had shifted from a concern for the moral condition of the initiates to the performance of quasi-magical rites. This decline would explain Aristophanes's attitude and, more importantly, Plato's, since in the latter's writings we find a strong Orphic-Pythagorean influence in opposition to his obvious contempt for what he perceives as Orphic charlatanism.[15]

Orphism, Pythagoreanism, and the mysteries persisted throughout the classical age. The Eleusinian mysteries even became part of the religious establishment of Athens. At the same time, certain developments prepared the ground for the religious and ideological syncretism which was to become one of the distinctive features of the aftermath of Alexander's conquest of the East. The people of the East, who had come under the control of successive despotic empires, had become politically passive and incapable of self-determination. The old political and intellectual centres of oriental civilizations, on the Euphrates and on the Nile, after having experienced centuries of intellectual achievement, had finally arrived at a state of inertia. In addition, the practice of the Babylonian and Assyrian empires of uprooting and transplanting whole peoples had disengaged cultural and religious elements from their native soil (so that these elements became available to the cosmopolitan *agora*) and created a climate favourable to the mixing of the gods. To be accessible to the cosmopolitan *agora*, the substance of local cultures had to be transformed into abstract doctrines comprehensible to people with different cultural backgrounds. Among the most important of these transformations were those of Jewish monotheism, Babylonian astrology, and Iranian dualism. These doctrines, having already been formulated on the eve of the Hellenistic age, became great forces in Hellenistic syncretism.

The first period, one of Greek dominance and oriental submersion, is marked by the maturing of oriental systems and cults through Greek conceptualization of Eastern thought. The greatest gift of the Greek culture to the world is the λόγος (*logos*), in its dual meaning of language and reason. During Hellenism, the Greek language and Greek intellectual systems became so dominant that the East seems to have observed forced silence or have become totally inarticulate. However, the truth is that "anyone who had something to say had no choice but to say it in Greek, not only in terms of language but also in terms of concepts, ideas, and literary form, that is, as ostensibly part of the Greek tradition" (Jonas 18). The Greek *logos* became the formal instrument used to transform oriental thought into concepts available to all peoples, regardless of ethnic background. Oriental thought, non-conceptual by nature, was thus given the opportunity to re-introduce itself to the world in terms the world could understand.

The first phase of Hellenism came to an end approximately at the time of Christ's birth. The second phase, in which Hellenism is transformed from a secular into a religious oriental culture, coincided with the first three centuries of the Christian era. This second phase was characterized by the re-emergence of the East in a syncretism in which the gods and cults of the East assumed great prestige. The elements of this syncretism have three main sources: the oriental mythological heritage, the figures and symbols of the Bible, and the doctrines and terminology of Greek philosophy. All the elements were available and any system or cult could select any combination of them to create its own synthesis.

Out of this syncretism a number of systems arose which, since they emerged from a common intellectual climate and common material, shared many common points. The main forms which arose from the Hellenization of oriental thought are the following:

> the spread of Hellenistic Judaism, and especially the rise of Alexandrian Jewish philosophy; the spread of Babylonian astrology and of magic, coinciding with a general growth of fatalism in the Western world; the spread of diverse Eastern mystery-cults over the Hellenistic-Roman world, and their evolution into spiritual mystery-religions; the rise of Christianity; the efflorescence of the gnostic movements with their great system-formations inside and outside the Christian framework; and the transcendental philosophies of late antiquity, beginning with Neo-pythagoreanism and culminating in the Neoplatonic school (Jonas 25).

Gnosticism is an extreme case of Hellenistic syncretism. Its provenance is a mixture of mythological and religious ideas whose roots are Greek, Oriental, Jewish, and Christian. As is the case with most such movements, the syncretism is artificial, the product of a conscious effort on the part of some of the most cultured and educated minds of the time. Jacques Lacarrière observes that "the Gnostics built a pure mental construction... upon an a priori vision of the universe" (18). Drawing its material from the most varied traditions, Gnosticism at first appears to be an artificial synthesis with no internal unifying power or distinct character of its own. But such is not the case. As Kurt Rudolph explains, "The gnostic expositions gain their thread of continuity or their consistence... through the gnostic 'myth.'... Its mythology is a tradition consciously created from alien material, which [, however,] it has appropriated to match its own basic conception" (54-55).

Most of the Gnostic documents were written in Greek which, besides giving them wider influence, also resulted in Gnosticism's strong links with the conceptual language of Greek philosophy. Nonetheless, careful consideration of Gnosticism reveals that although Greek philosophical thought provided much of the terminology, its basic structure or structures cannot be made tractable to philosophical interpretation. It is quite clear that Gnosticism is not a speculative but a mythological system; its affinities are not with philosophical systems but with religion (Lacarrière 60).

Such is the *morphé* of Gnosticism. What needs to be discussed now, however briefly, is the movement's main doctrines and its *mythos*. Jonas defines Gnosticism as a *"dualistic transcendent religion of salvation"*: dualistic because of the reality of irreconcilable opposites (God against the Demiour-

gos and his creation, good against evil, light against darkness, life against death, spirit against matter, soul against the body); *transcendent* because both God and salvation are "transmundane," beyond the material cosmos; and a *religion* because of the distinctively devotional nature of the second phase of Hellenism during which Gnosticism made its mark. The central doctrine of Gnosticism, like that of all mystery religions, is soteriological and eschatological; that is, it concerns itself with humankind's redemption or deliverance (*soteria*) from the material or "polluted" world to the higher world of pure being (*pleroma*).[16]

The soteriology of Gnosticism is based on the idea of γνῶσις, *gnosis* or "knowledge." Radically different from rational knowledge, *gnosis* is esoteric or mystical knowledge made available to the elect through revelation. The ultimate goal of the gnostic is the knowledge of God and the salvation of humanity. *Gnosis* is received either by coming into the possession of occult lore (revealed wisdom gained through ritual participation and instruction in secret names and magical catchwords) or by undergoing a mystical experience. And *gnosis* is the only form that salvation can take, both as a condition and instrument. Rudolph brings together the different meanings of *gnosis* in this way: "All gnostic teachings are in some form a part of the redeeming knowledge which gathers together the object of knowledge (the divine nature), the means of knowledge (the redeeming *gnosis*), and the knower himself" (55). Thus Gnosticism involves a mystical γνῶσις θεοῦ (*gnosis theou* or direct beholding of the divine essence), a πρᾶξις (*praxis*, human acts of self-modification which induce the proper disposition), and a γνώστης (*gnostes* or knower). *Gnosis* is a "happening" of divine activity and grace involving "knowing" God as well as "being known" by Him. Perhaps Jonas captures best the essence of the term *gnosis* when he says that "the ultimate 'object' of *gnosis* is God: its *event in the soul* transforms the knower himself by making him a partaker in the divine essence (which means more than assimilating him to the divine essence) [italics mine]" (35). It is worth pointing out here the similarity between this form of Gnosticism and the contemporary phenomenon of the charismatic or "born again" Christians who claim to have "met Jesus."

Gnosticism is elitist in the sense that *gnosis* is attained by a limited number of people (elitism is a tendency shared by all mystery religions). Thus in most gnostic sects people are divided into three categories: πνευματικοί (*pneumatikoi* or spiritual), ψυχικοί (*psychikoi* or psychic), and ὑλικοί (*hylikoi* or material). Only those belonging to the first class can attain *gnosis*. Christians belong to the second class because they possess πίστις (*pistis* or faith) instead of *gnosis*. At the bottom of the schema are the pagans, material men for whom there is no salvation.

The gnostic *mythos* is a cosmogonic-soteriological narrative which explains how a supremely transcendent God created the world which Gnosticism, being anti-cosmic, views as evil. The god is unknown (ἄγνωστος θεός), an alien, sometimes conceived as pure light, whose names serve to emphasize absolute transcendence (Unbegotten, Ineffable, Immeasurable, Unknowable . . .). From him proceed a number of beings in descending scale of dignity who in their totality make up the *Pleroma*, the "fullness of blessedness and perfection." The world came into being when Σοφία (*Sophia* or Wisdom), one of the lower powers in this gnostic emanationist system, fell from the *Pleroma*. The agent of creation is the Δημιουργός (*Demiourgos* or Archegenetor), usually represented as Sophia's son, who, ignorant of the Unknown God, acted unwittingly, though with no evil intent, and created the "hylic" cosmos — this *Demiourgos* is often identified with the God of the Old Testament. Sophia's fall disrupts the perfection of the Pleroma since it causes the loss of particles of Divine Light which are scattered in the hylic world of Darkness. Humans, who are composed of flesh (ὕλη, *hyle*), soul (ψυχή, *psyche*) and spirit (πνεῦμα, *pneuma*), were created by the *Demiourgos* and his Powers or Archons in order to enslave the Divine Light. Through their flesh and soul, humans are part of the *Heimarmene* or Universal Fate, the world of matter. But humans are also made of spirit which usually remains unconscious and ignorant of itself. *Gnosis* is the instrument through which the spiritual being is awakened and liberated from the captivity of the hylic world. As Jonas says, *gnosis* is "the reminder of origin, the promise of salvation, [and] the moral instruction" (81). The Divine Being that undertakes the work of deliverance of the Divine Light is the (Σωτήρ, *Soter* or Saviour). The Saviour's task includes the deliverance of the fallen Sophia and the ἀποκατάστασις (*apocatastasis*, the restoration of the *Pleroma*), that is, the gathering of the seeds or sparks of Divine Light. In terms of human beings, the real task of the *Soter* is the communication of the hidden *gnosis* which, preserved by the Gnostic tradition, can effect the delivery and the restoration of the *pneumatics* to the Kingdom of Light.[17]

One last point that needs to be raised here is the intense myth-making tendencies of the Gnostics. What distinguishes this myth-making is that its shape is determined by a functional need to serve the purposes of a preconceived gnostic value system. Thus, "it must be noted that this new mythology, despite some genuinely 'first' creations, was a secondary one in that it supervened upon an older mythological tradition and constructed its new object-system out of the consciously reinterpreted elements of a complex heritage" (Jonas 262). This point is of great importance because it demonstrates the a priori principle employed by many of the occult system-makers: first, they formulate a particular framework or value system; then, they proceed by searching, discovering, and incorporating into the original system elements from various cultural heritages which appear to them to be analogues to those elements belonging to the original framework; finally, they use the resulting syncretic sub-structure as proof of the legitimacy of the original structure.

That Pound was familiar with Gnosticism is beyond doubt. His acknowledgement in his 1916 note to *The Spirit of Romance* (91) of his debt to Mead's Gnostic interpretation of the legend of Simon Magus and Helen of Tyre is the most explicit sign in a series of acknowledged debts to gnostic tradition.[18]

The Gnostic depreciation of the cosmos and its creator aroused the ire of the founder and corypheus of the Neoplatonic School, Plotinus (205-70), who presided over an academia in Rome and possibly had a private mystical practice. Neoplatonism, whose cradle was the great intellectual city of Alexandria, in contrast to Gnosticism, is a legitimate development of Greek philosophical thought in general and of Plato's speculations in particular. Plotinus's philosophical ideas have been preserved in the *Enneads* ("Sets of Nine"), Porphyry's edition of his lecture notes.

There are certain common elements shared by the Gnostic and Neoplatonic schools, such as the wholly transcendent and Unknowable God and speculative emanationism. But there are some fundamental differences as well, particularly with respect to the Gnostic obsession with evil. The title of Plotinus's treatise, *Against the Gnostics, or against those who say that the Creator of the World is evil and that the World is bad* (*Enneads* II.9), reveals the reasons for his objections to this group and also suggests his belief in the unity of all beings in the Universe. According to Plotinus's system, there are three mystic and transcendent realities (he calls them *hypostases*): the Godhead which he calls "the One" (τό Ἔν) or the "Good" (τό ἀγαθόν), Spirit or Intellect (νοῦς), and Soul (ψυχή). Beneath these is the cosmos, including humans, made of emanations from the One. In Plotinus's philosophy everything emanates from the One and shares in its goodness; thus, the body and the natural world are not evil but only less good than the "things" above them, by virtue of their distance from the One. Humans can return to the One by a mystical experience involving the unity of the perceiving spirit (νοῦς), the spiritual world (τά νοητά), and the spiritual perception (νόησις), thus uniting subject and object into "the One." This return to "the One" is described by Plotinus himself as ἔκστασις (*ekstasis* or ecstasy, to stand outside one's self), "a blow, a capture, a sort of ravishment, fulfillment, and of course inebriation" (see

O'Brien 24). This understanding of *ekstasis* transports us back to the pantheism of Greece.

Plotinus himself condemned magic as an effective but egotistical misuse of power. Despite Plotinus's warnings about magic, the theurgic side of Neoplatonism ultimately overwhelmed its philosophical side. Driven by the practice as well as the vision of Greek, Egyptian, and Chaldean mysteries, Plotinus's successors (including Porphyry, Iamblichus, and Proclus) transformed Neoplatonism from a philosophic system into a system of magic, demonology and, especially, theurgy. Iamblichus "turns the ideas of hypostases of Plotinus into gods and daemons, and leaves the door wide-open for magic and theurgy," while Proclus is said to have been "frequently visited by the gods in person, and was a great miracle-worker" (Inge 117).

Neoplatonism has, of course, been recognized as an influence of considerable importance for Pound. As James J. Wilhelm rightly notes, Pound's "philosophical training was very heavily influenced by the Neoplatonics" (*Dante and Pound* 137); and a number of other critics have noted the importance of Neoplatonism in the shaping of much of Pound's thought.[19] In addition, several critics have stressed the presence of Neoplatonic ideas in the thought of Blake, Wordsworth, Coleridge, Shelley, Keats, and Yeats—to name but a few. It has also been pointed out, by F.A.C. Wilson among others, that the imaginative tradition of Neoplatonism was made accessible to most of these writers through the writings of Thomas Taylor (1758-1835), and that it came to them in a form "contaminated" by other occult movements. But a discussion of the ties of these writers to Neoplatonism and the "wisdom tradition" in general would take us too far afield; therefore, the reader is referred to specialized studies in which these relations are discussed in detail.[20]

The teachings of Gnosticism and theurgic Neoplatonism can be seen behind many of the systems of Western occultism during the Middle Ages: alchemy, ceremonial magic, Albigensianism, and the Cabala. The first two of these were practical or theurgic. Albigensianism or Catharism is the best known in Western Europe of a number of gnostic sects, including the Paulicians of Phrygia and Thrace, and the Bogomils of the Balkans. It flourished between the tenth and thirteenth centuries in Southern France. The Albigensians derived their knowledge of Gnosticism from the Cathari. Though one of the accusations brought against them by the Church was that they were Manichaeans, this was not true; Manicheanism, in fact, disappeared completely in the West during the Middle Ages and had no direct successors there. The Cathari, like the Gnostics, were dualists in theology, ascetic in practice, and heretical in their intense criticism of and opposition to the Church.

Because the demands of Catharism were exceptional (extreme asceticism and austerity, rejection of marriage, of everything material, of all foods which were the product of sexual generation, of all material elements in worship, and of all involvement in things of this world), strict practice was confined to a small minority of adepts or "perfects." The central rite of the Cathari, and the dividing line between the "perfects" and the believers, was the reception of *consolamentum*, an initiation rite of spiritual baptism by the laying on of hands that admitted the recipient into the ranks of the perfect. The *consolamentum* was usually performed after a year's probation and thorough *catechesis* into Cathar teaching, accessible only to the Cathari or "perfect ones." Once received, the *consolamentum* remitted the recipient's sins and the consequences of the soul's imprisonment in the body, reuniting his soul with his spirit in heaven and releasing him from Satan's rule. Thus, the rite conferred a gnostic-like certainty of salvation in contradiction of orthodox Christian revelation. The self-detachment of the Cathari from the evil world is best exemplified by the *endura*, a ritual suicide by fasting, poisoning, or suffocation which ensured salvation — especially when preceded by *consolamentum*!

The Catholic Church attempted to convert or at least subdue the Albigensian heresy, but these attempts were at first unsuccessful. During the first half of the thirteenth century, the Church's persecution of the Albigensians took the form of crusades which destroyed the towns and culture of Provence and nearly exterminated the Provençal people. The most severe blow came with the fall of Montségur, the centre of Albigensian activity, in 1243. With the capture and burning of over 200 perfects at Montségur, the Cathari were effectively destroyed as an organized group.

The Albigensians form part of Pound's "celestial tradition," and he refers to them in some of his prose works as well as in *The Cantos*. The clearest statement of Pound's opinion on the subject of the Albigensian crusade appears in "Terra Italica" (*SP* 58-59). In this essay Pound rejects the accusation that the Albigensians were Manichaeans and states categorically that "this [accusation] I believe after a long search to be pure bunkumb" (*SP* 59) — instead, Pound thinks that the Albigensians derived their beliefs and rites from the cult of Eleusis.

Albigensianism is given an important place in Pound's conception of his highly syncretic version of the "celestial tradition," as Surette has shown in *A Light from Eleusis*. Pound's version of the "celestial tradition" was derived partly from Joséphin Péladan (1858-1918), the French Rosicrucian who believed that Georgius Gemistus Plethon, Marsilio Ficino,

Dante, and the troubadours were all Albigensians. Characteristically, Péladan says that "Gemisto Plethon and Marsilio Ficino are the official teachers of old Albigensianism, as Dante is the prodigious Homer" (qtd. in *Light* 38). Although I am anticipating the discussion that follows in this chapter, it is worth pointing out here that Péladan is expressing a position that was shared by other occult thinkers of his day. According to many occult thinkers of the late nineteenth and early twentieth centuries, the modern occult is essentially a continuation of a secret wisdom-tradition surviving underground and clearly traceable to Plethon and Ficino in Florence, and reputedly found in Provençal poetry and Dante. As Surette shows, this occult fantasy history was gradually adopted by Pound himself. Pound's adoption of the fantasy history explains, among other things, his understanding that the troubadours of Provence and their rituals descend from the Greek mystery cults of antiquity.

During roughly the same period that the extinction of the Albigensians was taking place, the Cabala, a complex system of secret mystical ideas and magical methods, was emerging as a distinct esoteric school in Southern France and in Spain. The term "Cabala" or "Kabbalah" means "tradition" in the sense of "reception." According to Cabalist legend, when God gave the Law to Moses he also gave him a second revelation as to the secret meaning of the Law. This esoteric tradition was said to have been passed orally by initiates from Moses down to the present. In Frances A. Yates's words,

> [the Cabala] was a mysticism and a cult but rooted in the text of the Scriptures, in the Hebrew language, the holy language in which God had spoken to man. Out of Cabalist studies of the Hebrew text there developed a theosophical mystique, nourished on elaborate search for hidden meanings in the Scriptures, and on elaborate manipulation of the Hebrew alphabet (*Occult Philosophy* 2).[21]

Like other occultists, Cabalists claim extreme antiquity for their doctrines and for their texts, even though the most important of all Cabalist works, the *Sefer ha-Zohar* (Book of Splendour), is a medieval work written in Aramaic in Spain by Moses de Leon between 1280 and 1286. Nonetheless, it is true that the material out of which the Cabala was formed is indeed old. Harold Bloom, in *Kabbalah and Criticism*, writes that Cabalist speculations and beliefs "appear to have been influenced by Gnosticism and Neoplatonism, and it seems fair to characterize the history of subsequent Kabbalah as being a struggle between Gnostic and Neoplatonic tendencies, fought out on the quite alien ground of Judaism" (15). The assimilation of the human race, the microcosmos, to the macrocosmos through the agency of the emanations or *Sephiroth* and the intense preoccupation with evil (a preoccupation also found in Gnosticism) form the kernel of the Cabalistic mysticism that spread from France and Spain to Italy. The Italian humanists of the Renaissance later fell under its spell in this Gnostic form.

The emanationist doctrine of Cabala closely resembles Neoplatonism. In the Cabala there are ten "Sephiroth" or divine emanations; these are arranged diagrammatically in the Tree of Life which joins the divine with the material world. Gershom G. Scholem, in *Major trends in Jewish Mysticism*, explains that,

> The consensus of Kabbalistic opinion regards the mystical way to God as a reversal of the procession by which we have emanated from God. To know the stages of the creative process is also to know the stages of one's return to the root of all existence. In this sense, the interpretation of *Maaseh Bereshith*, the esoteric doctrine of creation, has always formed one of the main preoccupations of Kabbalism. It is here that Kabbalism comes nearest Neoplatonic thought, of which it has been said with truth that "procession and reversion together constitute a single movement, the diastole-systole, which is the life of the universe." Precisely this is also the belief of the Kabbalist (20).

The Cabala does differ from Neoplatonism, nonetheless, since it revises the Neoplatonic idea of emanation as a process *out of God* into a process which takes place *in God* (Scholem 217-18).

Despite the historically close connection between Gnostic dualism and the Cabala regarding the relationship of the hidden and Unknown God and the Creator, Cabalist doctrine is not dualistic, since these two Gods are not seen as opposing forces but as aspects of one and the same power. Like the Gnostics, Cabalists do accept, and indeed show an obsessive concern with, the reality of evil. Unlike the Neoplatonists, for whom evil has no metaphysical reality, the Cabalists believe that evil manifests itself as a separation of two of the Sephiroth: *Din* (Judgment) and *Hesed* (Love). "The totality of divine potencies forms a harmonious whole, and as long as each stays in relation to all other, it is sacred and good," writes Scholem (237). Evil results when Din, the quality of God's stern judgment (the equivalent of the Platonic *Ananke* or Necessity), ceases to be tempered by *Hesed*, God's Covenant Love (the equivalent of Christian *caritas* or grace). When this happens, this quality breaks away from God completely and transforms itself into the radically evil. But even then it retains a spark of its divine origin and can be redeemed. Thus, even the demonic has its roots somewhere in the divine mystery.[22]

Many elements of speculative Cabalism were adopted by Renaissance occult movements, one of the greatest periods of occult efflorescence. The term which immediately comes to mind in thinking about the occult during this period is Hermeticism. Paul Oskar Kristeller discovered the importance of the Hermetic treatises of the *Corpus Hermeticum* while studying the provenance and development of Marsilio Ficino's Neoplatonism. The *Corpus Hermeticum* is a collection of texts attributed to the fictional Hermes Trismegistus. In a 1967 essay entitled "The Hermetic Tradition in Renaissance Science" (and later in *Giordano Bruno and the Hermetic Tradition*), Frances Yates affirmed that the core of Renaissance Neoplatonism is "Hermetic, involving a view of the cosmos as a network of magical forces with which man can operate" (225). According to Yates, the texts of Hermes Trismegistus, as understood by Ficino and later by Pico della Mirandola and Giordano Bruno, portray man as magus, "with powers of operating on the cosmos through magic and through the numerological conjurations of Cabala" (257). The "Hermetic tradition," allegedly reaching back to Hermes Trismegistus (Milton's "thrice great Hermes") who was, reputedly, at least as ancient as Moses, dates in fact (as A.J. Festugière showed in 1949) from the third period of Greek cultural history (second and third centuries of our era). The treatises, originating in Hellenistic Egypt, are written in Greek (except for *Asclepius* which exists only in a Latin version), and represent a fusion of philosophical writings dealing with the doctrine of the human race's metaphysical constitution and personal salvation through *gnosis* with the more instrumental and popular arts of astrology, alchemy, palmistry, numerology, and other forms of divination. The texts are an entirely derivative compendium of the common syncretic tradition of Hellenistic thought.

The appearance of the *Corpus Hermeticum* in the west followed the visit to Florence in 1438 of Plethon—a visit that inspired a revival of Neoplatonism in Italy. Plethon attended the Councils of Ferrara and Florence (1438-39) and seems to have made an impression upon Sigismundo Malatesta who later brought Plethon's ashes from Peloponnesus and reinterred them in one of the sarcophagi of his Tempio at Rimini. In the wake of Plethon's visit, Marsilio Ficino translated Plato and Plotinus into Latin and wrote commentaries aimed at harmonizing the Platonic and Chaldean traditions with Christianity. A Greek manuscript containing the fifteen treatises that constituted what would later be called the *Corpus Hermeticum* was brought to Florence by Leonardo da Pistoria, a monk. Leonardo, who had found the document in Macedonia, presented it to Cosimo de' Medici, the ruler of Florence and a great patron of letters. At the end of 1462 or the beginning of 1463, the ailing Cosimo asked Marsilio Ficino

(1433-99) to put aside his translation of Plato in order to translate the *Corpus Hermeticum* before his death. By April 1463 the translation was complete.

In fact, Ficino translated just four treatises, of which the most important are the *Poimander*, a philosophical treatise on cosmology, and the *Asclepius*, a description of Egyptian magical rites through which the powers of the cosmos could be used by man. Ficino himself thought of the *Corpus Hermeticum* as the origin for the wisdom tradition deriving from Plato. Later Pico noticed that the Hermetic writings shared with the Cabala such features as numerology and hierarchical categories, and tried to combine the two. Still later, Giordano Bruno, the Italian heretic and visionary, departed altogether from the Christian Hermetic direction formulated by Ficino and Pico and maintained that "the magical Egyptian religion of the world was not only the most ancient but also the only true religion, which both Judaism and Christianity had obscured and corrupted" (Yates, *Giordano Bruno* 11).

Despite its obvious importance, it must be made clear that Hermeticism does not constitute a distinct driving force in the Renaissance. Rather than becoming the fountain of a new world view, the Hermetic writings are used as rhetorical embellishment consciously couched in the Neoplatonic philosophical terms of the writers mentioned above and designed to give an aura of ancient wisdom and authority. Charles B. Schmitt argues that Hermeticism is one more ingredient in the syncretic amalgam of Renaissance philosophy:

> it was Hermeticism which became assimilated into Neoplatonism and seldom, if ever, was Hermeticism itself thought of, even by its Renaissance proponents, as an independent system of ideas. It was Neoplatonism which served as a strong trunk onto which ideas derived from Hermetic, Orphic, Zoroastrian, Neopythagorean, Cabalistic and other sources could be grafted during the Renaissance, continuing a tendency already begun in antiquity. Neoplatonism was the receptive body of knowledge susceptible to being bent in a number of ways to adapt itself to a rather remarkable range of syncretic formulations. It was, however, the Neoplatonic system of metaphysics and epistemology which provided a life-giving sap to hold it all together (206).

Schmitt's sensible analysis of Hermeticism must be taken into account in any discussion of this movement. This analysis should not, however, take attention away from the *Corpus Hermeticum*, whose significance as a philosophical text is twofold: first, it provided excitement and impetus to the whole occult movement because it seemed to furnish a link with ancient sources of wisdom; and second, in true occult manner, it generated a vast number of analogies which could be used to validate already formulated occult structures.

I have been discussing the tradition of secret *gnosis* or knowledge which allegedly descended through the ancient mysteries and Orphism to Plato, to the Neoplatonists and the Gnostic schools, and to the Cabala and Hermeticism. This is a tradition which counts among its members Renaissance magi such as Ficino and Pico, the medieval alchemists, sixteenth- and seventeenth-century occultists, as well as Robert Fludd, Thomas Vaughan, Sir Thomas Browne, and Thomas Taylor in England. There seems to be a continuous poetic tradition as well to which Henry Vaughan, Blake, Coleridge, Shelley, Keats, and Yeats belong. The example of Thomas Taylor (1758-1835) as a transmitter of this tradition is instructive. Taylor translated into English the works of Plato, the Neoplatonic commentators Plotinus and Proclus, and a variety of other texts of Greek religious philosophy. Though his translations have now been superseded, it has been argued that in his day they made accessible his own version of the "occult tradition" to Blake, Wordsworth, and Keats. Shelley could read Greek but was probably also familiar with Taylor's translations. Taylor's influence also extended to America through Emerson and the New England Transcendentalists. And of course, Taylor's work influenced Yeats and George Russell (A.E.), and Theosophical scholars such as Mead. Pound also seems to have been familiar with Taylor's work.[23]

Going underground during the seventeenth century, the speculative Hermetic-Cabalistic occult tradition emerges in such secret mystical groups as Rosicrucianism. The origin of the Rosicrucians dates from the publication between 1614 and 1616 of three anonymous treatises purporting to emanate from an occult brotherhood. Of most interest is the first of these publications, *Fama Fraternitatis*, which is presented as a message from certain "adepts" who propose a radical change aiming at effecting universal moral renewal and perfection. *Fama* tells the story of the founder of this secret Brotherhood, Christian Rosenkreuz, a German youth who journeys to Egypt, Fez, and Spain, is initiated into the mysteries of occult sciences and, upon returning to his native country, surrounds himself with assistants to form the nucleus of the Rosicrucian fraternity. The founder of Rosicrucianism is said to have been born in 1378 and to have lived for 106 years. Modern scholarship regards the Rosicrucian Brotherhood as a hoax, and has shown that this Brother C.R. is a fictitious character. The real author of these treatises is probably Johann Valentin Andreae, a Lutheran pastor with socialist interests.

Frances A. Yates claims, in *The Rosicrucian Enlightenment*, that Rosicrucianism was originated by a group of Lutherans whose hopes centred on the Protestant Elector Palatine "as the politico-religious leader destined to solve the problems of the age" along lines suggested by Hermetic and Cabalistic speculative ideas. In the treatises published by this group, a theosophy, or pansophia, was developed. It was hoped by the proponents of this theosophy that it would be used as a non-sectarian basis for universal harmony which would be acceptable to all people, regardless of personal religious views, and which would lead to a peaceful resolution of all religious and intellectual conflicts. As Yates writes,

> The [Rosicrucian] manifestos would appear to be proclamations of enlightenment in the form of an utopist myth about a world in which enlightened beings, almost assimilated to spirits, go about doing good, shedding healing influences, disseminating knowledge in the natural sciences and the arts, and bringing mankind back to its Paradisal state before the Fall (207).

The Rosicrucian movement, then, included a vision of universal and general reformation, an emphasis on philanthropy, a programme for the reconciliation of science and religion to be carried out by an elite group of adepts, as well as an esoteric approach to religion and a proclivity for initiation and legitimation through alleged ancestry from ancient mystery cults.

The hopes of the Rosicrucians were defeated in the horrors of the Thirty Years War (1618-48). The Rosicrucian Brotherhood itself seems not to have existed at all until the eighteenth century. There were, nonetheless, many people who became interested in it during the seventeenth century and some who claimed to be initiates themselves. Michael Maier (1566-1622), who wrote books on spiritual alchemy, wrote *Atlanta Fugiens* in 1618 in which he traced the Brotherhood's spiritual ancestry to Egyptian sages, Persian Magi, and Indian Brahmins, and hinted that behind all this was the figure of Apollonius of Tyana. On the continent many others, including the young Descartes and later Leibniz, were attracted to Rosicrucian ideas. In England the cause and ideas of Rosicrucianism were taken up by a number of people including Robert Fludd (1545-1637), the Paracelsist physician who wrote *Utriusque Cosmi Historia* (1617), a Cabalist-alchemical account of the macrocosm and microcosm. Another Englishman who seems to have been attracted to Rosicrucian ideas is Edmund Spenser. In *The Occult Philosophy in the Elizabethan Age*, Yates discusses the mystical politics of *The Faerie Queene* and asserts the influence of Bruno's and Francesco Giorgi's blend of Neoplatonism and

Christian Cabalism on Spenser's work. Francis Bacon (1561-1626) denied the theory of human beings as the microcosmos but was, nonetheless, interested in occult ideas. His posthumously published *New Atlantis* (1627) presents a dream of an ideal religious and scientific society which is clearly based on the myth of Christian Rosenkreuz and his benevolent order. John Heydon, described by Yates as a strange character, "an astrologer, geomancer, alchemist, of a most extreme type," published *The Holy Guide* in 1662, largely an adaptation of Bacon's *New Atlantis* (*Rosicrucian Enlightenment* 189). *New Atlantis* is read by Heydon as if it were practically identical with *Fama*; this reinforces the opinion that Bacon's work is based on the Rosicrucian manifesto.

Pound's familiarity with John Heydon is, of course, well known. He quotes from Heydon's *The Holy Guide* several times in the "Ur-Cantos," refers to him in *Gaudier-Brzeska* (1916), includes him as one of the company of luminaries belonging to the "celestial tradition" (*GK* 225), and "rediscovers"him in the later cantos (especially in canto 91).[24]

The Rosicrucian movement in turn probably exerted an influence on Freemasonry. Speculative Freemasonry, which spread rapidly through the Continent after the formation in 1717 in London of the Grand Lodge of England, shares many characteristics with Rosicrucianism, since both are self-conscious reform movements and both combine claims to ancestry from an "ancient wisdom," and esoteric and ethical doctrines, with an emphasis on good works. But unlike Rosicrucianism, Freemasonry is not interested in reforms in art and science nor in the occult sciences of alchemy and magic (Yates, *Enlightenment* 218).

The masonic movement probably has its roots in the periodic gatherings of operative stonemasons engaged in the building of churches and cathedrals in England. During the eighteenth century masonry placed great importance upon secrecy (the result, it seems, of the desire to guard the secrets of the craft) and upon its putative lineages from ancient mystery cults, preserved and transmitted through the Knights Templar and the Rosicrucians.

The legendary or fantasy history of Freemasonry, which has been preserved in fourteenth- and fifteenth-century manuscripts found in England, identifies the art of building with geometry. In these medieval records, of which the most noted is the so-called *Regius Manuscript* (ca. 1390), it is alleged that masonry was founded in Egypt and entered England at the time of Athelstan. Geometry is said to have been discovered by Hermes Trismegistus (who is identified with Euclid) in order to deal with the floods of the Nile river. Thus, like many of the occult movements, Freemasonry traces its origin to an Egyptian past preserved in Hellenistic writings. The ancient wisdom of Hermes is said to be enshrined in the Solomonic Temple. The medieval Knights Templar are seen in masonic mythology as the keepers of the oriental wisdom of this Temple. Jacques de Molay, the Templar Grand Master who was arrested on 13 October 1306 on orders from King Philip IV and after a much delayed trial burned at the stake on 19 March 1314, belongs to this tradition.

Pound refers to de Molay three times in *The Cantos*, connecting him with the Albigensians who died at Montségur and with Scotus Erigena, the medieval philosopher, theologian, and early Greek scholar who was accused of Manicheanism and, according to Pound, was exhumed three hundred years after his death.[25] Pound also suggests that de Molay and the Knights Templar were persecuted because they practised an enlightened, non-usurious form of economics (canto 87). In fact, modern scholarship has shown that they amassed great wealth because they were usurious, and that they were destroyed so that their enormous wealth could be expropriated by King Philip IV.[26] Of course, the King's excuse for destroying them was that they were heretics, Gnostics and Manicheans in particular, who practised sodomy and idolatry, and denied Christ.

The eighteenth century saw the emergence of two new occult systems, which were later to provide the foundations of nineteenth-century Spiritualism: Mesmerism and Swedenborgianism. Franz Anton Mesmer (1734-1815) studied medicine in Vienna, joined the German Rosicrucian Order of the Golden and Rosy Cross, and founded the Order of Universal Harmony. Influenced by Paracelsus, Mesmer was interested in magnetic therapy and developed the concept of "animal magnetism." He thought that there was a subtle, universal force pervading all bodies (the fluid of animal magnetism), and believed that nervous disorders were caused when the rhythm of the bodily fluid was not in harmony with the universal rhythm. This universal fluid was seen by Mesmer as being responsive to the human mind; thus, the human mind could use this force to affect the behaviour of others and cure illnesses. In addition, Mesmer's concept could be employed to awake the powers of perception which lay dormant in all humans and which can transcend space and time. Thus Mesmer achieved two things: first, he discovered hypnotism and the related psychosomatic medicine; and second, he formulated a system which could be used to explain "scientifically" such "arts" as telepathy, clairvoyance, and psychokinesis.

Mesmer's concepts had a strong influence on Spiritualism, as did the mystic visions of Emanuel Swedenborg (1688-1772), the Swedish philosopher, scientist, and clairvoyant. As a scientist Swedenborg made considerable contributions to metallurgy and mining engineering. But between

1743 and 1745 he had several visions during which he claims to have engaged in dialogue with angels and spirits. As a result, there is a transition in his work from plain scientific and philosophical concerns to concerns with revelation. Swedenborg's voluminous theological writings are presented as inspired, since he attests to having conversed with a man who identified himself as God, showed him the spirit worlds of heaven and hell, and instructed him to write about the spiritual sense of the Bible.

Swedenborg's attempt to explain spiritual concepts with the exactitude of scientific discourse led him to the formulation of the doctrine of correspondences that shares many points with the emanationist systems of Neoplatonism and the Cabala — not to mention Hermetic analogy and macrocosm/microcosm. According to Swedenborg, every natural object is the effect of a spiritual cause and, thus, there exists a correspondence between the visible cosmos and the spiritual cosmos: the first is a reflection of patterns existing in the second. The natural world, then, when properly understood, can reveal the spiritual world; this is a theory of an actual correspondence of every physical fact to some eternal truth.

Pound was introduced to Swedenborg while still in the United States (possibly by Katherine Ruth Heyman — as I argue in Chapter III), studied Swedenborg's writings during his stay with Yeats at Stone Cottage (1913-14), and again returned to this mystic in the 1950s. He also refers to Swedenborg in his prose writings and in *The Cantos*. In a 1956 letter to Olivia Rossetti Agresti, Pound spells out his interest in the "secret history" of speculative occultism and, in particular, observes Gabriele Rossetti's linking of speculative masonry, Swedenborg, and Dante — something which Pound himself has been doing, he writes, for "fifty years"! (BRBL, letter dated 7 December 1956).

Pound's linking of speculative masonry and Swedenborg and his strong interest in these matters raise a particular problem and justify, I think, the following brief digression. In a letter to William Bird, dated 18 March 1933, Pound denigrates the masons and their secrets. He is quite sarcastic about them, saying that he finds it very hard to believe in "these GRRREAT minds" (Pound MSS II Correspondence, Lilly Library). Elsewhere Pound has explicitly denied sharing the occult interests of Yeats and Orage. It is useful to remember that the occult movement encompasses a wide variety of warring factions which vie for credibility by trying to discredit each other. It is not clear what prompted Pound's outburst against the masons in his letter to Bird; in the case of Yeats and Orage, it is obvious that Pound disapproves of their particular interests in theurgy and Gurdjieffianism respectively. The factionalism of the occult goes some way towards explaining Pound's statements against particular factions of the occult, since, on the one hand, he often draws on a body of occult opinions, concepts, and beliefs which fit his own while, on the other hand, he dismisses those concepts (and their adherents) that do not fit his own particular version.

The accounts of journeys to the world of departed spirits and angels which are contained in Swedenborg's works, especially in *Spiritual Diary* and *Heaven and Hell*, make him the immediate predecessor of Spiritualism, a movement which originated in the United States and became very popular during the middle of the nineteenth century. The source of this movement's popularity must be sought in the promise to provide empirical evidence of life after death and the possibility of communication with the spirits of the departed. Best known as communication by way of a "passive" medium with the dead through such phenomena as rappings, automatic writing, telekinesis or materialization, Spiritualism has a more reflective and philosophical side. The popular side is represented by the Fox sisters, while the second is represented by Andrew Jackson Davis's Harmonical philosophy.

Davis (1826-1910), a shoemaker turned clairvoyant, is the most important American spiritualist writer. He experienced a series of mystical visions and wrote an account of them, published in 1847 in *The Principles of Nature, Her Divine Revelations and a Voice to Mankind*. Fundamentally Swedenborgian, this work promotes a pantheistic-tending idealism, looks upon nature as a "dispensation of types foreshadowing the natural world," and calls for a special sense of perception needed to unlock nature's system of symbols (Moore, *In Search of White Cows* 11-12). Modern practical Spiritualism dates from 1848 when a series of spiritualistic phenomena (mysterious rappings) broke out at the home of the Fox family in Hydesville, in upstate New York. From there Spiritualism flourished and spread all over the world.

Spiritualism is, in the context of Pound's thought, important not so much in itself but as the immediate forerunner of Theosophy. Speaking in particular about the impact of Theosophy on the London scene, Warren Sylvester Smith points out that although it would be unfair to equate Theosophy with Spiritualism, nevertheless "Theosophy could not have made a serious bid for attention among Londoners — or elsewhere — if a revival of Spiritualism had not preceded it" (142). Before we turn to Theosophy we need to make clear the fact that Spiritualism does not really belong to this discussion because, unlike the other forms of the occult discussed here, it places no special emphasis on secret or esoteric wisdom and secret initiation rites. These features have no place in Spiritualism, since the participant in a séance needs no preparatory instructions nor is the goal of the experience palingenetic.

Generally speaking, the term Theosophy is used to denote those forms of religion and philosophic thought primarily concerned with the knowledge of the hidden mysteries of the Divine nature.[27] This insight may be gained through supernatural revelations or private speculation. Theosophical thought focusses on the acquisition of knowledge through understanding of the mysteries of the divinity itself, or of the created universe. The roots of Theosophy, at least in terms of Western thought, are to be found in Neoplatonism, Hermeticism, and the Cabala. In terms of individual writers and thinkers, the speculative mysticism of such men as Plotinus, Paracelsus, Böehme, Eckhart, the Cambridge Platonists, and Swedenborg may be said to be Theosophical.

Modern Theosophy is the child of the dialogue between Spiritualism and those who dissented from the most fundamental of spiritualist beliefs, that is, the reality of communication with the still-living spirits of the dead. Theosophists warned about the dangers of desiring to commune with spirits around the séance table. Against the false Spiritualism of the spiritualists the Theosophists purported to endorse a "True Spiritualism [which] should envisage the phenomena of the divine spirit of men in their highest manifestations, the cultivation of which the ancients and the East has given man his most sacred and vital knowledge" (qtd. in Kuhn 96). In a letter to her sister (ca. 1875), Helena Petrovna Blavatsky, the real force behind Theosophy and herself a former spiritualist medium, states that one of the purposes of her own movement is "to show certain fallacies of the Spiritualists. If we are anything we are Spiritualists, only not in the modern American fashion, but in that of the Ancient Alexandria with its Theodidaktoi, Hypatias and Porphyries" (qtd. in Kuhn 96). The distinction Madame Blavatsky is making here is between the popular Spiritualism of rappings on furniture and slate writing and the higher Spiritualism of Theosophy. In addition, like so many of these groups, Theosophy too looks back to the Hellenistic age and in particular to Alexandria for its roots.

Modern Theosophy began with the foundation of the Theosophical Society in New York in 1875 by Madame Blavatsky and Colonel Henry Olcott. The professed objects of the Society were the following: (1) to form a nucleus of the Universal Brotherhood of Humanity without distinction of race, creed, sex, caste, or colour; (2) to encourage the study of Comparative Religion, Philosophy, and Science; and (3) to investigate the unexplained laws of nature and the powers latent in man. Thus Theosophy aimed at combining an ethical goal with the quest for the fulfillment of the seventeenth-century Rosicrucian programme of bridging science and religion by studying and cultivating powers latent in man. Madame Blavatsky used the Theosophical Society to advance what she perceived as her goal in life: the gift of "Ancient Wisdom" to modern man.

The founding text of Theosophy was Blavatsky's *Isis Unveiled* (1877) which, like her other major work, *The Secret Doctrine* (1888), was dictated to her, she claimed, by the Mahatmas, said to be hidden masters or adepts living beyond the Himalayas. Blavatsky claimed that these Mahatmas were the guardians of a secret, ancient wisdom and that she had been chosen by them as their intermediary through whom they desired to instruct those in the West who were ready to receive this wisdom. The "invention" of the Mahatmas gave Blavatsky's synthesis the pretence of historical continuity which all occultists claim for their systems — and which is, in this as in other cases, a mere fiction.

In spite of her very uncritical and often bogus scholarship, Blavatsky's works are remarkable surveys of religion and occultism through the ages. For her synthesis, she relied primarily on her reading in, and knowledge of, Pythagorean, Gnostic, Neoplatonic, Hermetic, Cabalistic, Rosicrucian, and Masonic texts as well as her knowledge of esoteric writers such as Fludd, Fabré d'Olivet, and Eliphas Lévi, together with Hindu and Buddhist material. Blavatsky's eclectic mind, influenced by the new familiarity the West was gaining with Asian religions, reconstructed the Ancient Wisdom, formulating in a continual process of synthesis "A Master-Key to the Mysteries of Ancient and Modern Science and Theology" (this is the subtitle of *Isis Unveiled*). Again, it must be emphasized that Theosophy is an orientalization of the Western occult tradition, a syncretistic movement similar in many ways to the Hellenistic syncretism which also got much of its inspiration from the East. Of course, in the case of Theosophy, the inspiration came from the Far East and, especially, India; in the case of the syncretistic movements of Hellenism, the inspiration came from the Near East.

Isis Unveiled and *The Secret Doctrine* are seemingly without a central thesis. But there is a position which emerges gradually and by its very nature has given a multitudinous and fragmented character to the works. Robert S. Ellwood, Jr. describes this position as follows:

> Behind the religions of the world lies a "monomyth," in Joseph Campbell's later term. The monomyth concerns the making-up of the universe and the individual human by the conjoining of three principles: matter, an invisible energizing spirit, and immortal consciousness. It tells us that true seership and magic are possible if based on knowledge

of those principles. It also recounts the spiritual evolution of the universe (117).

The similarity between these Theosophical positions and all those manifestations of the occult which emerged periodically from the great river whose central spring can be located in Hellenistic Alexandria is easily discernible. Thus Theosophy claims that the world consists of matter or *hyle* and spirit or *nous*, the energizing, subtle force which is closest to the ultimate source of everything, that is, God. Consciousness represents the link between *hyle* and *nous*. In addition to these we find in Theosophy all the other principles one would expect to find in such a speculative occult system: there is a secret tradition preserving the ancient wisdom; a God who is unknowable, transcendent, and the source of being, a source from which humanity is far removed; the cosmos emanates from God (doctrine of correspondence); the human soul is the divine spark, a fragment of the divine substance; the cosmos is permeated by a subtle bodily substance (immanentism); and, finally, the object of human life is to return to the divine source, accomplished through repeated incarnations.

The Theosophical belief in the close intermingling of matter and spirit led to the Theosophists' claims that the movement was scientific: the purpose of "occult science" was to explore the correspondences between the diverse parts of a universe thoroughly permeated by the *nous*. This approach led to a confusion of theological speculation and scientific concepts. Despite the reiterated emphasis on Theosophy's empirical foundation, when Theosophists speak of science they have in mind a "Higher Science," described by theosophist William Kingsland as follows:

> There exists ... a Higher Science, which is also Religion in its truest sense, and which deals with the hidden forces in nature at which physical Science stops short, but which are more than suspected by the majority of mankind, because every form of Religion whatsoever is an acknowledgment of a *something*, which underlies, and is superior to, the phenomena of Nature (qtd. in Oppenheim 196).

Theosophists maintain, then, that science is incomplete without religion, since the former is limited to the investigation of those phenomena which can be measured and observed by the physical senses or can be rationally inferred, while the latter looks at the real spiritual force behind these phenomena.

The attractiveness of the Theosophical synthesis is understandable when one reflects upon Peter Kuch's analysis of the solutions Blavatsky's books offered to the late nineteenth-century:

[Blavatsky's] synthesis was . . . boldly offered as a means of solving the major problems thrown up by the Nineteenth century debates on Science, Religion, and Philosophy. Science and Religion were reconciled by declaring that evolution took place in both the physical and the spiritual worlds, and that Darwin and Huxley were in harmony with the Ancients and with the Buddhist scriptures. Contemporary discoveries in thermodynamics, electromagnetism, and physics were related to the occult and to research being conducted in Spiritualism. The faith-corroding problems raised for traditional Christianity throughout the century by Higher Criticism—especially works like Feuerbach's *Das Wesen des Christentums* (1841) and Renan's *La vie de Jésus* (1863)—were solved by advancing a theory of exoteric and esoteric interpretation, and by expounding the Bible in terms of the Kabbalah and the Vedas. The widespread belief that a knowledge of Eastern literature was necessary for true self-understanding, a belief evident in the popularity of translators such as Edward Fitzgerald and Edwin Arnold, in the monumental labours of Max Müller, and in the pervasive influence of Schlegel, Hegel, Schopenhauer, and Schelling, all of whom drew heavily on the *Upanishads*, was adopted as one of the fundamental tenets of Theosophy. In short, it offered itself, as the sub-title of *Isis Unveiled* declared, as "A Master-Key to the Mysteries of Ancient and Modern Science and Theology" (9).

On their way from New York to India in 1878, Madame Blavatsky and Colonel Olcott stayed in London for two weeks. Blavatsky had already been to London as a young woman in 1844 and was to return and spend the last years of her life (1887-91) there. The London branch of the Theosophical Society was formed shortly after the original one in New York. During their visit in 1878, Blavatsky and Olcott were warmly received by the London Theosophists. The trip to India and the setting-up of the Theosophical World headquarters in Adyar were the natural outcome of the movement's efforts to blend the philosophies of East and West.

In India Blavatsky attracted a lot of attention, especially as a result of the psychic phenomena which came to be associated with her and which she attributed to the invisible Mahatmas. It was to investigate these phenomena and the charges of fraud which had been brought against Blavatsky that the Society for Psychical Research (the SPR had been formed in London in 1872 in response to the growing interest of Englishmen in psychic phenomena) sent Richard Hodgson, a Cambridge-educated lawyer, to India. Hodgson, in a 200-page report, concluded that the charges of charlatanry against Blavatsky were true and the messages from the unseen Mahatmas were in her own handwriting. Blavatsky was shown to have been a mystery monger, a charlatan, and a cheat. But even the SPR's conclusion that Blavatsky had "achieved a title to permanent remembrance as one of the most accomplished, ingenious, and interesting impostors in history" was not enough to convince Theosophists worldwide. They refused to admit that the report was true (Oppenheim 178).

At the end of March 1885 Blavatsky literally had to be smuggled out of India, and she eventually transferred her operations to London, where she was able to regain her energy and re-establish her power and fame. She again attracted many important people to her, including Yeats who, as we have already noted, joined Blavatsky's Esoteric Section of the London Lodge in 1888.

Theosophy is at least partly responsible for "the rising psychic tide" which Pound encountered upon coming to London in 1908. In this discussion of the occult tradition the emphasis has been placed upon what we should call "metaphysical occultism"—which is very different from theurgy or the practice of occult arts. Even so, the manifestations of the occult with which we have dealt share many characteristics, and it is often hard to distinguish one from another. In summary, at the summit of the occultist cosmology is an utterly transcendent Principle (or God), the source from which emanated the cosmos, including humankind; humanity's soul is of the same substance as the divine Absolute and its goal is to return to its origins; union with the One can be achieved only by those initiates who come into the possession of a hidden *gnosis* or knowledge handed on secretly by oral tradition and discoverable in fragments which belong to this tradition; the *gnosis* has as its source an ancient wisdom which was ultimately revealed to humanity by God; finally, the whole occult "system" is based on the homo-analogical principle, or doctrine of correspondence. These are characteristics which are shared by all the metaphysical occult groups discussed here.

It is worth repeating that while the occult is identifiable in a general way as a heterodox mixture of a relatively small set of doctrines, there is no orthodoxy and no way of drawing sharp boundaries between the various schools. It is also important to remember that any given occultist may draw indiscriminately on any combination of the traditions identified in this chapter—and that many disputes amongst fellow occultists are sparked by the fact that their more or less freely invented a priori systems often reflect individual tastes and rarely resemble each other.

Either in *The Cantos* or in his prose writings Pound makes mention of virtually every one of the occult movements outlined in this discussion, except Mesmerism. But before we examine Pound's relation to some of these movements and their ideas, we must first discuss, more fully than we have done at the beginning of this chapter, Pound's early friends and contacts and their relation to "the rising psychic tide."

Notes

1. In an interview with Pier Paolo Pasolini Pound said: "... I gave a series of lectures at the Polytechnic Institute about troubadour poets. In the audience there was a friend of Yeats' who, years later, became my mother-in-law. This lady introduced me to Yeats" (Anderson 334).
2. Collection of American Literature, Beinecke Rare Book Library, Yale University, Pound Collection; hereafter cited as BRBL.
3. See books by the following: Ellmann, Moore, Wilson, Harper, Flannery, Hough, Kuch, Bachchan, and Senior. There are also numerous articles on the subject, too many to list here. It should also be noted that Yeats's fascination with the occult is well documented in his own writing; the clearest example of this fascination is probably his unfinished novel, *The Speckled Bird*. Of course, mainstream critics such as Ellmann, and more recently Hough, identify the occult elements in Yeats's "education" but argue for a division between his occultism and poetry. Considering the accumulation of evidence that points to the prominence of occult themes and imagery in Yeats's poetry, Ellmann's and Hough's position is no longer defensible.
4. Regarding the word's origin, in the *Encyclopedia of Religion* we read that "The French term *occultisme* was perhaps first used by Eliphas Lévi (1810-75), whose work is sometimes somewhat misleadingly identified with the beginnings of occultism itself. The English equivalent, *occultism*, was apparently first used by A.D. Sinnett in 1881" (XI.38).
5. The laudatory remark about Mead's article on "Occultism" is Robert Galbreath's ("The History of Modern Occultism" 730).
6. Hynes elaborates on this statement in this way: "Within a few years of 1880 the following organizations were established in England: the Democratic Federation, the Hermetic Order of the Golden Dawn, the National Anti-Vaccination League, the National Anti-Vivisection Society, the Society for Psychical Research, and the Theosophical Society. These movements, ranging from socialism to spiritualism, had one thing and only one thing in common—they were all opposed to conventional Victorian ideals" (135).
7. For Joyce and the occult see Tindall, "James Joyce and the Hermetic Tradition" and *The Literary Symbol*, Goldfarb, Gilbert, Scott, and Herr; for Eliot see Senior, Goldfarb, Gibbons, and Surette, "*The Waste Land* and Jessie Weston: A Reassessment." It should also be noted that, besides Eliot and Joyce, many major artists, including of course Yeats, as well as Stringberg, Hesse, and D.H. Lawrence, have at one time or another and in varying ways incorporated occult material into their art.

It is of some interest that the occult elements of modernism did not escape the keen eye of Marshall McLuhan. In a 28 February 1953 letter to Pound McLuhan writes: "Last year has been spent in going through rituals of secret societies with fine comb. As I said before I'm in a bloody rage at the discovery that the arts and sciences are in the pockets of these societies. It doesn't make me any happier to know that Joyce, Lewis, Eliot, yourself have used these rituals as a basis for art activity" (*Letters, Marshall McLuhan* 235). Though I do not know what Pound's response to this letter was, I have no doubt that McLuhan's observations would have been met with scorn.

8. For an excellent discussion of the debatable nature of the occult tradition see Hough (esp. 9).
9. My information about the Eleusinian mysteries comes from the article on "Eleusis" in *Encyclopedia of Religions*, Mead's articles, and books on the subject by Funnell, Mylonas, and Kerényi.
10. ἱεροφάντης, from ἱερός (holy) and φαίνω (to appear); literally, the one who makes the holy things appear.
11. Both Mylonas and Kerényi reject the notion that the *hieros gamos* was part of the original Eleusinian mysteries (see Mylonas [311-16] and Kerényi [*Eleusis* passim]). Nonetheless, there is no question that Pound was convinced that the *hieros gamos* was the culmination of the mysteries, an idea he could have picked up from a number of sources, including Mead's studies on Gnosticism.
12. See Mead's discussion of the Eleusinian Mysteries in *Thrice-Greatest Hermes* (passim) and in "Notes on the Eleusinian Mysteries."
13. For more on Pound's "bizarre theories" see Oderman (esp. 25-49). In a conversation that took place in London, Ontario in March 1986, Mr. Laughlin told me that in private Pound had claimed a link between "orgasm" and "illumination."
14. See, for example, Surette's *Light*, as well as studies by Miyake, Laurie, Elliott, Davis, Sicari, Dennis as well as Laughlin (*Pound as Wuz* 83-86).
15. For example, in the *Republic* Plato shows his contempt for those who take part in the trade of pardons or indulgences. On the other hand, in *Phaedro* and *Theocritus* Plato discusses the Orphic doctrine of deification. As Hough observes, "Above all, Plato, though contemptuous of the ritualist and superstitious side of Orphism is in the mystical and mythological part of his teaching deeply penetrated by Orphic and Pythagorean influence" (24).
16. An explanation is in order here. Gnosticism in its original, Hellenistic forms is dualistic. For example, Robert A. Segal's definition of Gnosticism as it appears in the Nag Hammadi manuscripts is well taken: "Gnosticism here is the belief in a radical, or antithetical, dualism of immateriality and matter. More specifically, it is the belief in radical dualism in man, the cosmos, and god; the primordial unity of all immateriality; the yearning to restore that unity; the present entrapment of a portion of immateriality in man; the need for knowledge to reveal to man that entrapment; and the need for a savior to reveal to him that knowledge" (14). However, it is important to remember that modern occult theory provides for a monistic and not a dualistic cosmos. Mead, Upward, Orage, Blavatsky, and all the other modern occultists are monists. Today it is Christianity and its Aristotelian sources that are dualistic. At the extreme end of dualism is Manicheanism where ψυχή = ἀγαθόν (Spirit = Good) and ὕλη = κακόν (Matter = Evil). The occult today sees spirit as the "subtle body" — that is, occultists believe that the universe consists of one sacred substance; in Indian philosophy, on the other hand, matter is seen as illusory. Both the Western occult and the Indian occult are monist.
17. Around this basic *mythos* the Gnostics built a complex speculative system marked by antinomian and anti-cosmic tendencies. Perceived as a Christian heresy, Gnosticism was attacked by the Christian Fathers. This attack was instrumental in preventing Christianity from being sucked into the vortex of syncretism from which, however, it had already absorbed a variety of elements. In addition, the consciously defensive stance of Christianity against the "Gnostic Heresy" is reflected in the formation of the Christian canon (New Testament) and the rigid dogmatism of the Church.

18. For further details see Surette, *Light* (esp. 60-64); Christine Brooke-Rose, *A ZBC of Ezra Pound* (206, 214); Elliott, "Light as Image" (passim) and "The Word Comprehensive: Gnostic Light in *The Cantos*"; and my discussion of Mead and Gnosticism in Chapters III and IV. Other writers, especially many of the Romantics, have been identified as having been familiar with Gnostic texts and ideas. On Blake criticism and Gnosticism, see Paul A. Cantor (esp. 195). For a detailed study of Shelley's knowledge and use of Gnosticism, see James Rieger, *The Mutiny Within*. Gnosticism has been the inspiration for a few modern writers as well. Anatole France (1844-1924), Aleksander Blok (1880-1921), Michail Bulgakov (1891-1940), Albert Verwey (1865-1937), and Hermann Hesse (1877-1962) are the most important of these. As well, C.G. Jung (1875-1961) was very impressed by Gnostic imagery and even wrote a Gnostic work, *Septem Sermons ad Mortuos* (written in 1915-16), inspired by Basilides's speculations. For a discussion of Jung and Gnosticism see Hoeller.
19. The best and most complete study of Pound's Neoplatonism is Libera's 1971 dissertation. See also studies by Jackson, Emery, and Elliott. There are passing references to Pound's Neoplatonism in most of the other major books on Pound. Neoplatonism has been, of course, an accepted field of research—unlike occultism. In the present study, Neoplatonism is seen as part of the "occult tradition." This approach is justified not just by such scholars of the occult as Yates, but also by Pound's own writings. For example, it is absolutely clear that Pound sees Gemistus Plethon's bringing of Platonism to Italy as the major event in the transmission of the occult tradition from east to west (see chapter entitled "NEOPLATONICKS ETC" in *Guide to Kulchur* and my discussion of Plethon in Chapter IV).
20. See Tuveson on Wordsworth, Beer on Coleridge, Raine and Harper on Blake and Yeats, Rogers and Welburn on Shelley, Blackstone on Keats, and Wilson on Yeats. Anya Taylor's excellent bibliographical essay "The Occult and Romanticism," demonstrates the prominence and range of Neoplatonic ideas in the work of the Romantics. For a hostile reaction against the "occult school of criticism," see Harold Bloom's review essay entitled "Myth, Vision, Allegory." Bloom denies that there is any occultism in Blake at all, asserts that Yeats was "a delighted charlatan who at least half-believed his own charlatanry," and finds no value in most of the studies mentioned above.
21. Yates adds that "Cabala was basically a method of religious contemplation which could, rather easily, pass into manipulation of religious magic" (2). Pound, in *A Visiting Card*, seems to share Yates's understanding of Cabala's potential of turning into magic. While speaking about the presence of Hebraic and Hellenistic elements in the Church, he writes:

> ... Not a jot or tittle of the hebraic alphabet can pass into the text without danger of contaminating it.
>
> Cabbala, black magic, and the whole caboodle. Church against Empire, Protestantism against the unity of the Mother Church, always destroying the true religion, destroying its mnemonic and commemorative symbols (*SP* 320).

See also Pound's reference to Cabala in "The Art of Poetry" (*SP* 362).
22. So far as I know, Boris de Rachewiltz was the first to notice the importance of Cabalistic concepts for Pound (181). Using de Rachewiltz's remarks as her starting point, Angela Elliott examines *The Cantos* and finds many parallels between Cabalistic teachings and Pound's religion ("Pound's 'Isis Kuanon': An Ascension Motif in the

THE OCCULT TRADITION   57

Cantos," and "Light as Image" passim). Elliott's discussion of a number of cantos in terms of what she calls a "mystical guideline" ("Light as Image" 77) also seems to be derived from her understanding of the Cabalistic notion of the various stages involved in "the mystical way to God," a notion that shares much with Neoplatonic thought. For an interesting discussion of Cabalistic elements in the poetry of Yeats and Pound, see McDowell and Materer, "Gyre as Vortex: W.B. Yeats and Ezra Pound."

23. For discussions of Taylor's importance, see Raine's books on Blake; Rogers's on Shelley; Blackstone's on Keats; and Wilson's on Yeats. For Pound and Taylor see Libera's dissertation, Miyake, Terrell's "Mang-Tsze, Thomas Taylor, and Madam ῞Υλη" as well as my discussion in Chapter IV of this study.

24. In canto III of the Ur-Cantos Heydon is described as a "Worker of miracles, dealer in levitation, / In thoughts upon pure form, in alchemy, / Seer of pretty visions ('servant of God and secretary of nature')." He is mentioned in *Gaudier-Brzeska*: "And John Heydon, long before our present day theorists, had written of the joys of pure form . . . inorganic, geometrical form, in his 'Holy Guide'" (127). For further discussion see Baumann's article on Heydon in *New Approaches to Ezra Pound*, Surette's *Light* (263-67), and Materer's "Ezra Pound and the Alchemy of the Word." Although I do not agree with his suggestion that Pound's request for a copy of Heydon's *The Holy Guide* can be taken as a sign of his reawakened interest in the occult, Materer's glossing of Pound's comparison between Heydon and Apollonius of Tyana in canto 91 ("Heydon polluted. Apollonius unpolluted") is sensible and, I think, correct:

> When Pound compared Apollonius of Tyana to Heydon in Canto 91 . . . , Baumann thinks that Pound refers to the scholarly edition of his work received by Apollonius but not Heydon. Actually, Pound is saying that Heydon himself is "polluted" or "desensitized" in comparison with Apollonius. This is clear at the conclusion of 92:
>> After Apollonius, desensitization
>>   & a little light from the borders. . . . (622)
> John Heydon the alchemist is not a Poundian hero such as Apollonius but does represent "a little light from the borders." He thus finds his place in Pound's equivalent of Dante's *paradisio* (118).

Materer quotes a letter from Pound to William French, dated 30 August 1954, where Pound's attitude to Heydon and Apollonius is made clear: "part way thru Heydon/Rosy Cross a.D 1662 already corrupted in part/tho gt/scholar/by contrast Apollonius of Tyana, even in fragmentary account of Philostratus is UNcorrupted/" (118).

25. As Terrell explains, "it was not Scotus whom they dug for, but a disciple of his, Amaury de Bène" (*Companion*, I.143).

26. See G. Legman's *The Guilt of the Templars* (passim).

27. In *The Key to Theosophy*, the founder of Theosophy H.P. Blavatsky has this to say about the term "Theosophy":

> Theosophy is Divine Knowledge or Science. . . . "Divine Wisdom," θεοσοφία (Theosophia) or Wisdom of the gods, as θεογονία (theogonia), genealogy of the gods. The word θεός means a god in Greek, one of the divine beings, certainly not "God" in the sense attached in our day to the term. Therefore, it is not "Wisdom of God," as translated by

some, but *Divine Wisdom* such as that possessed by the gods. The term is many thousand years old. . . .

It comes to us from the Alexandrian philosophers, called lovers of truth, Philaletheians, from φιλ- (phil) "loving," and ἀλήθεια (aletheia) "truth." The name Theosophy dates from the third century of our era, and began with Ammonius Saccas [the teacher of Plotinus] and his disciples, who started the Eclectic Theosophical system (1-2).

III

POUND'S OCCULT EDUCATION

1. AMERICAN BEGINNINGS: KATHERINE RUTH HEYMAN AND H.D.

I have already remarked that even though critics of modern poetry are beginning to recognize that Ezra Pound worked in the same esoteric tradition as Yeats, there is still a relative dearth of current scholarly comment on his relation to the occult. Given the emphasis placed by Yeats scholars on the renewed interest with which Yeats was pursuing his occult studies and experiments during the early period of his association with Pound (1909-16), it is surprising to find that most Pound scholars have sought to isolate Pound's work from any taint of occult influence, ignoring this aspect of his life.[1]

Those critics who do deal with Pound's occultism usually locate the roots of this interest in his London years (1908-21). As already indicated earlier, many of his London friends — Yeats, Mead, Upward, and Orage, as well as Dorothy and Olivia Shakespear — had strong connections with various occult groups and could not but have communicated their interests to Pound. The published correspondence between Pound and John Theobald and that between Pound and Dorothy Shakespear reveal clearly Pound's interest in the occult during the years preceding the genesis of *The Cantos*.

William French claims that Pound's interest in "things occult" faded after the early London years and was not rekindled until the late 1950s. Despite the support of Boris de Rachewiltz and, to a certain extent, Noel Stock, this story does not stand up. On the contrary, Pound's interest in the occult never waned, as is clear from his correspondence with John Theobald and Patricia Hutchins. As pointed out in Chapter I, "Terra Ital-

---

The notes to Chapter III are found on pp. 92-100.

ica" (1931-32) and *Guide to Kulchur* (1938) also testify to Pound's continued interest during the 1930s. But this continuous and unbroken interest in the occult originated much earlier than Pound's London years; it dates back, in fact, to his years as an undergraduate.[2]

The beginnings of Pound's familiarization with esoteric ideas had its roots, then, in his earlier years in Philadelphia, as well as in his reading and in his contact with at least one of his early friends, Katherine Ruth Heyman, who seems to have exerted considerable influence upon the young Ezra. The balance of this chapter presents a biographical sketch of Pound and two of his friends in Pennsylvania, Miss Heyman and Hilda Doolittle (H.D.); and then it provides the evidence for Pound's occult interests and examines the nature of his contacts with six members of the occult circles of London: Yeats, Olivia and Dorothy Shakespear, Upward, Orage, and Mead. Since the occult London milieu of the time is complex, it will be necessary to discriminate between the varieties of occultism Pound encountered and to identify those with which he became involved.

Although Pound's biographers have discussed Pound's Pennsylvania years in nearly exhaustive detail, the occult interests of Miss Heyman and H.D. are either completely ignored or underemphasized.

In the spring of 1906 Pound received his M.A. from the University of Pennsylvania and in June of the same year was made a Harrison Fellow in Romantics; he used the five-hundred-dollar stipend to finance a trip to Europe and spent much of the summer of 1906 reading in the British Museum. During that summer he wrote a poem based on the life of Bertold Lomax, "English Dante scholar and mystic, [who] died in Ferrara 1723, with his 'great epic,' still a mere shadow, a nebula crossed with some few gleams of wonder light. The lady of the poem an organist of Ferrara, whose memory has come down to us only in Lomax' notes" ("Note" to "Scriptor Ignotus," *CEP* 26). Pound dedicated his poem to Katherine Ruth Heyman, an American concert pianist he had met either during his days at Hamilton College or later in Philadelphia. In "Scriptor Ignotus" Pound adopts the persona of Lomax addressing his beloved:

> "When I see thee as some poor song-bird
> Battering its wings, against this cage we call Today,
> Then would I speak comfort unto thee,
> From out the heights I dwell in, when
> That great sense of power is upon me
> And I see my greater soul-self bending
> Sibylwise with that great forty-year epic
> That you know of, yet unwrit
> . . . .

> Will I make for thee and for the beauty of thy music
> A new thing
> As hath not heretofore been writ.
> Take then my promise!" (24-26).

Though it cannot be claimed with any degree of certainty that Pound is thinking of *The Cantos* here, we know he had been entertaining ideas about writing a long poem himself since his years at Hamilton College. At least this is what he would like us to believe, for when Donald Hall asked him in 1960 about the genesis of *The Cantos*, he replied, "I began the *Cantos* in 1904 or 1905. The problem is to get a form—something elastic enough to take the necessary material. It had to be a form that wouldn't exclude something merely because it didn't fit" (23). It takes a rather naive person to believe that in 1904 or 1905 Pound had conceived of *The Cantos* in their present form (or that he knew what he wanted to say but was struggling with the form of his poem), and his reply to Hall's question should be seen as part of his enduring capacity for self-dramatization. It is conceivable, nonetheless, that even at such an early stage Pound had intimations of grandeur and envisioned himself in the tradition of great epic poets capable of composing what he described in an early letter as a "cryselephantine poem of immeasurable length which will occupy me for the next four decades unless it becomes a bore" (Tytell 127).

Pound's fixing of the date of his inception of his own "great forty-year epic" ca. 1904-1905 is important in this context because the date coincides with the time of his first acquaintance with Miss Heyman. As Leon Surette speculates, Miss Heyman was perceived by Pound as his Beatrice, just as the lady organist in "Scriptor Ignotus" became Lomax's Beatrice (*Light* 7). Surette notes that Pound's claim to have begun *The Cantos* in 1904 or 1905 is not supported by the biographical and manuscript evidence and that it simply implies an unspoken analogy: "as Dante's *Commedia* was in a manner begun when he saw Beatrice at the age of nine, so the *Cantos* were begun when Pound met Miss Heyman at the age of nineteen" (7). Surette goes on to say that the news that the poem was inspired by Miss Heyman is not likely to "throw any light at all on the poem even if much more were learned about Pound's relationship with the lady than is currently known" (7). It is here that I part company with Surette, since I believe that there is an important connection to be made between Miss Heyman's role as Pound's muse and the nature of the poem; that is, I think an important connection can be drawn between the precise nature of Pound's relationship with Miss Heyman and the shape of his epic poem.

I have argued that Pound's epic is best understood as a poem of initiation. The obscure and hermetic nature of the poem itself embodies the initiation for the reader: the author plays the role of the mystagogue or hierophant presenting a description of a mystery in the hope that this presentation will exert upon the reader the same effect as an actual revelation or mystical experience. It is because I view *The Cantos* in these terms that I think that the early influence of Miss Heyman is of such importance.

Miss Heyman (1874-1944) is described by Charles Norman as "the older woman every young man meets" (7). She was the daughter of the noted Jewish violinist Arnold Heyman and his Christian wife; Pound and Miss Heyman probably met in Philadelphia around 1904 or 1905, possibly through a young painter named William Brooke Smith (1884-1908) for whom Pound had great respect (*L* 165) or else a bit earlier, during Pound's final year at Hamilton College.[3] Pound seems to have fallen in love with her. The affair is usually seen as having been platonic, but the evidence is not conclusive. How close the two were at the time is emphasized by the fact that she gave Pound a diamond ring, which belonged to her mother, "to keep until we're very old together."

It is of some interest that Miss Heyman's appearance in Pound's life is also noted by Hilda Doolittle in her autobiographical novel HERmione (completed in 1927 but not published until 1981). The scathing portrait of Miss Stamberg (as Miss Heyman is called in the novel) reveals a narrator (H.D.) full of envy and bitterness. "Hermione" (H.D.) clearly feels the pangs of jealousy over the sudden emergence of this older woman who holds "George Lowndes" (Pound) under her spell and fascinates him in a way H.D. herself could not (HERmione, esp. 108-109).

Miss Heyman was already well established as a concert pianist when Pound first met her. The young Pound "fell completely under her spell, a not uncommon experience where she was concerned, for hers was a forceful, dynamic and imperious personality" (Norman 27). Music was only one of Miss Heyman's enthusiasms; the other one was the occult — and as we shall see, these two enthusiasms were closely interconnected in her mind.

The person who knew Miss Heyman best during her later years in the United States is Faubion Bowers; he "studied piano with Miss Heyman and became so good a friend that he inherited all her papers at her death in 1944" (Terrell, "KRH and the Young E.P." 50). Writing about the second of her enthusiasms, namely the occult, Bowers says that she "swallowed everything magical" and that

> Long before drugs made . . . correlations between the senses common place, and decades before Zen, I Ching stick tossings, table-tipping, ouija boards, Tarot cards, astrology and the like became so *very* fashionable among our young, Kitty [Miss Heyman] was a passionate convert and a militant proselytizer to and for all things recondite (61).

Besides Faubion Bowers's testimony and what can be gleaned from her unfinished "Memoirs," Miss Heyman's book, *The Relation of Archaic to Ultramodern Music* (1921), gives us the best insight into her mind and reveals her occultist bent. She came to be known as the "high priestess of the Scriabin cult," and her devotion to the Russian composer Alexander Scriabin "continued to the end of her life and past the general decline of the composer's reputation, [and] was about equally divided between his music and his theosophy" (Adams 9). In her book, Miss Heyman "interprets music in occultist terms (e.g. 'The tone E is mana-consciousness')," and it becomes absolutely clear that her attachment to Scriabin was based "nearly as much on his mystical beliefs as his music" (Adams 17).[4] Miss Heyman did not meet Scriabin until 1913, but her reaction to him was prepared for and prompted, no doubt, by her dabblings in the occult. She certainly had ample opportunity to communicate her occult enthusiasms to Pound — enthusiasms that go unremarked in Pound biographies.

After the period of their initial acquaintance ca. 1904-1906, Miss Heyman reappears in Pound's life in 1908 in Venice, rescuing him from poverty and offering him an alternative to the poet's life he was about to embark upon. Pound actually considered throwing the proofs of *A Lume Spento* into the waters of the Grand Canal; and, in a diversion from a life devoted to the Muse of Poetry, he had a brief stint as Miss Heyman's European concert tour manager.

Giving up his role as impresario, Pound arrived in London in September 1908 and, as he wrote to Iris Barry, had an introduction or two from Miss Heyman and, indeed, "entered London more or less under her wing" (L 95). It is of some consequence that Pound's introduction to London, a city teeming with occult groups at the time, was through an occultist. Miss Heyman herself arrived in London on 24 March 1909 and is mentioned by Patricia Hutchins as being one of those whom Pound numbers as a frequent visitor to his Kensington flat (69-70).[5] When Pound went to New York in 1910, Miss Heyman was there and he visited her in her studio. Her esoteric interests were still strong since, as Charles Norman writes, "Miss Heyman was now interested in Buddhism, and he [Pound] may have met in her company the founder of the first Buddhist church in New York" (Norman 63). Back in London in 1913, she composed a musical setting for Pound's "Apparuit." Although their intimacy tapered off after the 1910s, they did remain friends until her death in 1944. The last time they met was in New York during Pound's 1939 visit to the United States.

There are two early poems dedicated to Miss Heyman and she also appears in the *Pisan Cantos*.[6] The Heyman link, interesting in itself, is also important in connection with Pound's relationship with H.D. As we have seen, H.D. was disturbed by the appearance, in 1904 or 1905, of Miss Heyman who, at least for a while, monopolized Pound's attentions. Using as her source H.D.'s *End to Torment*, Barbara Guest claims, correctly I think, that "Heyman had been the 'older woman' who had introduced Pound to Freud, Swedenborg, Balzac's *Séraphita*, Yoga, [and] all the 'culture' Pound had brought back to Hilda" (11).

End to Torment is an intensely personal memoir of H.D.'s and Pound's years in Pennsylvania and London, and it provides us with some hard information regarding the kinds of books these two were reading during their stormy engagement (ca. 1905-1907). H.D. wrote *End to Torment* from March to July 1958 in anticipation of Pound's release from St. Elizabeths. In the event, he was freed while the manuscript was still in progress.

There are two separate references in *End to Torment* to the kind of books Pound encouraged H.D. to read during their Pennsylvania years. The first reference begins with an idyllic recollection of listening to Ezra reading William Morris in an orchard under blossoming apple trees:

> It was Ezra who really introduced me to William Morris. He literally shouted "The Gilliflower of Gold" in the orchard.... It was at this time that he brought me the *Séraphita* and a volume of Swedenborg—*Heaven and Hell*? Or is that Blake? He brought me volumes of Ibsen and of Bernard Shaw....
>
> He brought me the Portland, Maine, Thomas Mosher reprint of the Iseult and Tristan story.... There was a series of Yogi books, too (dated 18 March 1958; *End to Torment* 22-23).

The occasion in *End to Torment* for the second reference is her recollection of reading Marcel Schwob's *The Children's Crusade*:

> *The Children's Crusade* by Marcel Schwob....
>
> I made that last entry yesterday. It flashed into my mind, a book that I have not thought of, for perhaps 50 years. It was one of little *de luxe* reprints of the Portland, Maine, Mosher series that Ezra brought me at the time of the avalanche of Ibsen, Maeterlinck, Shaw, Yogi books, Swedenborg, William Morris, Balzac's *Séraphita*, Rossetti and the rest of them (11 May 1958; *End to Torment* 45-46).

These two entries, which are separated by approximately a seven-week period, establish the character of the books Pound was bringing H.D. at this time. In the second entry H.D. undertakes to place the time of her reading of Schwob's book and to recollect "the avalanche" of books Pound brought her. The edition of the Marcel Schwob book which H.D. mentions is a translation by H.C. Green published in Portland, Maine in 1905. This book, about which H.D. had not thought "for perhaps 50 years" (1905-57), places the "avalanche" of books in, or shortly after, 1905, that is, at just the time that Miss Heyman entered Pound's life.

Pound greatly influenced H.D.'s reading around 1905, initiating her later involvement with Spiritualism and the occult in general.[7] There is an irony involved here in that the woman whom H.D. despised for capturing Pound's attention influenced the direction of her own life. More to the point, it is clear that H.D.'s occult education began during the early years of her acquaintance with Pound rather than as the aftermath of various psychic experiences she underwent during the early 1920s—as she herself claims.

The books H.D. mentions also establish Pound's early exposure to then fashionable occult literature. Among Pound scholars, only J.J. Wilhelm has discussed the character of the literature; but he fails to note at least two important points. First, he ignores Balzac's *Séraphita*, a mystical novel including an explication of Swedenborg's Theosophy; and second, Wilhelm fails to deal adequately with H.D.'s cryptic yet specific reference to "Yogi books."

As already noted in the discussion on Swedenborg's place within the "occult tradition," his Theosophical writings were one of Pound's enduring interests. We find him studying Swedenborg's writings during his stay with Yeats at Stone Cottage (1913-14), and again during the St. Elizabeths years. He refers to him in his prose writings and in *The Cantos* (e.g., GK 73-74; *The Cantos* 77/472, 89/590, 93/631, and 637). In his unpublished correspondence with Olivia Rossetti Agresti, the granddaughter of Gabriele Rossetti and Dante Gabriel Rossetti's niece, Pound spells out his interest in the "secret history" of speculative occultism and, in particular, remarks on Gabriele Rossetti's linking of speculative Masonry, Swedenborg, and Dante—something which Pound himself has been doing, he writes, for "fifty years":

> Want to know more of yr/ grand-dad? Political exile?? escaped from fury and bigotry of vatican??? not a mason but student of masonry? Interested to see he hooks D/ [Dante] to Swedenborg, as I have done for 50 years, but can't recall having found in the VERY small amount of criticism or Dante-studien that I have looked at.

Prefer text to comments. Of course the Dant-Swed hook-up may have filtered thru footnotes, but I can't recall anything but my own observations of the two writers (letter of 7 December 1956; BRBL).[8]

Pound did not have any direct knowledge of Gabriele Rossetti's work until he received a copy of *La Beatrice di Dante* from Olivia on 6 December 1956. Rossetti relied heavily on speculative Masonry and elaborated a "secret history" which was an unacknowledged source for much of the historical speculation of Joséphin Péladan and Luigi Valli—writers we know Pound read.[9] More to the point for this discussion, Pound's fixing of the date he first made the initial link between Swedenborg and Dante (ca. 1906) agrees with the date given by H.D. for the "avalanche" of books that came to her from Miss Heyman by way of Pound.

As already noted, Wilhelm fails to distinguish between Yogi and Yoga—a distinction worth pursuing here. Wilhelm writes that "They also read books of Yoga, because, even though Pound preferred the rational ethics of Confucius to the mystical immersion of Buddhism, he nevertheless was aware of the powerful way that Hindu wise men could exert control over their bodies" (106). Besides the point about the "Hindu wise men" which makes no sense in this context, Wilhelm is probably quite wrong in reading H.D.'s "series of Yogi books" as "books of Yoga." Why is it that H.D. says "Yogi" and not "Yoga" books? I think that it is likely that what H.D. is referring to here is not books on Yoga in general but rather a specific series of books brought out by the Chicago, Illinois-based "Yogi Publication Society." More specifically, she is referring to a particular author published by this Society, Yogi Ramacharaka (a pseudonym), a number of whose books appeared in the first decade of this century, including *Fourteen Lessons in Yogi Philosophy and Oriental Occultism* (1903).[10] In fact, Pound refers to this writer in a footnote to his 1908 sonnet "Plotinus" (*CEP* 296) and to one of his books, *Hatha Yoga* ("And the copy of 'Hatha Yoga'"), in his poem "Moeurs Contemporaines" (*P* 180). William French has reported that Pound "himself recommended Ramacharaka's series of 'little blue Yoga books' to the Frenches during their studies with him at St. Elizabeths in the 1950s" and that Dorothy "already had the references to the Ramacharaka books written in her pocket address-book when she passed them on to Wm French in 1953 as noted in the Yale Beinecke correspondence" (French and Materer 47). Yogi Ramacharaka is also listed, at the back of *Fourteen Lessons*, as the writer of many other books on similar subjects, including *Science of Breath, Philosophers and Religions of India*, and *Advanced Course in Yogi and Oriental Occultism*—interestingly, the latter is a text which Pound and Dorothy Shakespear are reported to have been reading in 1910 (Tytell 57).

It is possible that Pound is indebted to Ramacharaka's books for some of his occult ideas. For example, in *Fourteen Lessons* he could have encountered the concept of the "subtle body," that is, belief in an order of existence which is not incorporeal but of an order of corporeality which cannot be perceived ordinarily. If this is so, he could have encountered this concept long before he read Lodovico Maria Sinistrari's *De Daemonialitate, et Incubis et Succubis,* or Mead's *The Doctrine of the Subtle Body in Western Tradition*. It is upon these and similar sources that Pound draws when he describes the *nous* as a "sea crystalline and enduring, ... bright as it were molten glass that envelops us, full of light" (*GK* 44) or when he begins canto 91 with these two verses: "that the body of light come forth / from the body of fire" (610).

I want to reiterate that Pound's and H.D.'s initiation into things occult took place on American soil during their youth and that this interest endured for both of them. Of course, this introduction was developed in later years by further research and further acquaintance with occultists—among them Yeats, who introduced Pound into London occult circles. Pound was attracted to Yeats as much by his occultism as by his fame as an established poet, as Colin McDowell and Timothy Materer observe:

> When Pound sought out Yeats as the greatest living English poet, with the ambition of "learning how Yeats did it," he was not merely impressed by Yeats's poetic technique. Echoes of Yeats in his early poems, as in "The Tree," with its echo of Yeats's "He Thinks of His Past Greatness," are of mystical themes as well as diction and rhythm (345).

An example of the close connection in Pound's mind between Yeats the craftsman and Yeats the occultist is found in "Note Precedent to 'La Fraisne,'" written before he met Yeats (1909). Following some comments on the phenomenon of *ekpyrosis*, Pound links the tales of spirits he has found in Yeats's *The Celtic Twilight* with *De Daemonialitate, et Incubis et Succubis*, a Latin occult text written by the Franciscan theologian Lodovico Maria Sinistrari (1622-1701).[11] Pound's comment on the relationship between Yeats's fairies and Sinistrari's daemons is instructive: "Also has Mr. Yeats in his 'Celtic Twilight' treated of such, and I because in such a mood, feeling myself divided between myself corporal [*sic*] and a self aetherial 'a dweller by streams and in woodland,' eternal because simple in elements" (*CEP* 8). It is important to emphasize that Pound made the connection between the Sinistrari text and Yeats's poetry before he had met Yeats. He had read Sinistrari's book before setting out for Europe. Perhaps this is also one of the books to which he was introduced by Miss

Heyman. During the first winter with Yeats in Stone Cottage (1913-14), Pound wrote to his father asking him for his edition of Sinistrari: "Yeats is doing various books. He wants my *Daemonalitas*. Will you try to find it along with the other thing I asked for. 'Daemonalitas' by the Rev. Father Sinistrari of Ameno. Paper cover, not very large" (*EP/DS* 305). Homer Pound did send his son's copy and Yeats read it and made some use of it in one of the two essays he wrote to accompany Lady Gregory's compilation of Irish folklore (*Visions and Beliefs in the West of Ireland* 340).

In connection with H.D., it is of some significance to note that Pound nicknamed her "The Dryad" (meaning semi-divine, "subtly bodied" creature — usually a tree spirit), a nickname which she used to sign her letters to him to the very end.[12] The nickname is often, and rightly, mentioned in connection with one of the poems in Hilda's Book, "The Tree," which was later published in *A Lume Spento* (1908) and appears at the head of *Personae: The Collected Shorter Poems of Ezra Pound*:

> I stood still and was a tree amid the wood
> Knowing the truth of things unseen before
> Of Daphne and the laurel bow
> And that god-feasting couple old
> That grew elm-oak amid the wold
> . . . .
> Naethless I have been a tree amid the wood
> And many new things understood
> That were rank folly to my head before . . . (*End to Torment* 81)

This mystical theme is repeated in Pound's essay on "Psychology and Troubadours," an essay we should remember was first delivered before Mead's Quest Society in 1912 and published later that year in the Society's journal, *The Quest* IV (October 1912). He speaks there of myth as a "delightful psychic experience," and says that he is personally acquainted with people to whom such experiences occur (*SR* 92) Though Pound does not tell us who these people are, it is entirely possible that he is thinking of such friends as Yeats, Upward, and Mead. In any case, there is a strong similarity between the kinds of experiences described in "The Tree" and in "Psychology and Troubadours," supporting the argument that Pound was familiar with this type of esoteric experience since at least as early as the time of the composition of "The Tree" (1905-1907).

The congruity between Pound's views before and after his Kensington "initiation" strongly indicates that he brought his occultism with him to London, and did not encounter it there for the first time. Pound's contact with occult speculation dates from his undergraduate years, and was merely intensified and broadened by his London contacts ca. 1908-21. The persistence of his occultism throughout his career is less surprising in the light of the evidence that his entrée to London literary circles was his occultism.

2. POUND'S CATECHESIS IN LONDON (1): YEATS AND THE SHAKESPEARS

Arriving in London from Venice in 1908, Pound encountered what Mead has called the "rising psychic tide." Leading figures in this tide were Yeats, Upward, Mead, Laurence Binyon, Ernest Rhys, Rabindranath Tagore, and Orage. Florence Farr, her friend Olivia Shakespear, and Olivia's daughter, Dorothy, were marginal hangers-on.

As already noted, it was Yeats who attracted Pound to London. As their friendship developed, Pound naturally met Yeats's numerous occult associates. Yeats's own occult learning is an amalgam of the ideas of numerous occult groups and individuals. By the time he and Pound met in May of 1909, Yeats's occult education had reached an advanced stage: he was pursuing, with more vigour than ever before, his interest in theurgy or practical magic. Pound is on record as dissapproving of Yeats's psychic experiments.[13] Critics usually take this disapproval as evidence of Pound's rejection of the occult. But, as will become clear, it is only theurgy and Spiritualism that Pound rejects.

A representative example of Pound's ambivalent attitude toward Yeats's occultism is a November 1913 letter to his mother, written just prior to the Stone Cottage winter of 1913-14. Pound writes: "My stay in Stone Cottage will not be in the least profitable. I detest the country. Yeats will amuse me part of the time and bore me to death with psychical research the rest. I regard the visit as a duty to posterity" (*L* 25). Notwithstanding this initial dislike of psychical research and theurgy, Pound later admitted that Yeats "improves on acquaintance" (letter of 21 November 1913; *EP/DS* 276).

In his reminiscences about their activities during the Stone Cottage winter of 1914-15, Pound modified his disapproval of Yeats's psychic research. But writing on the "'Noh' Plays," Pound is still careful to voice his reservations so as not to appear persuaded of the validity of Yeats's practices and beliefs.

> I dare say the play, Suma Genji, will seem undramatic to some people the first time they read it. The suspense is the suspense of waiting for a supernatural manifestation — which comes. Some will be annoyed at a form of psychology which is, in the West, relegated to spiritistic séances. There is, however, no doubt that such psychology exists. All

through the winter of 1914-15 I watched Mr. Yeats correlating folk-lore (which Lady Gregory had collected in Irish cottages) and data of the occult writers, with the habits of charlatans of Bond Street. If the Japanese authors had not combined the psychology of such matters with what is to me a very fine sort of poetry, I would not bother about it (*T* 236).

The writers Yeats was reading included Avicenna, Paracelsus, Agrippa, and Swedenborg. F.A.C. Wilson observes that "All these sources of information seemed to corroborate his [Yeats's] own developing philosophy, as did also the detail of the Japanese Noh plays which he was then first reading: as the authorities accumulated, it is interesting to note, his findings won the grudging assent of Ezra Pound" (*W.B. Yeats and Tradition* 145). Pound is still distancing himself from the "habits of charlatans of Bond Street," but he is now willing to suspend his hostility toward such things and attend closely to the occult psychology because, first, the poetry of the Japanese plays is very fine, and, second, the *telos* of the exercise is the beatific vision (or "new beauty" [*T* 237]). The strident tone of his letter to his mother, quoted above, has disappeared in favour of what appears to be "grudging assent."

The impression which emerges from this and similar examples is of a student of the occult trying to find his bearings, a student who is discerning and discriminating but far from eager to advertise his interest in occultism. Pound's usual stance is that of an interested and informed outsider who never became a member of any of the occult groups which proliferated in Edwardian London. Although he was present at many of the gatherings of people interested in esoteric matters, especially those held by Yeats and his occult friends, Pound did not see himself, nor was he seen by them, as "belonging."

The Yeats-Horton correspondence of the middle-1910s provides strong evidence of Pound's participation in Yeats's occult friendships. It reveals that occult subjects were discussed during Yeats's "Monday Evenings" and also that the correspondents included Pound in their conversations and cared enough about him to make prophecies about his future. Horton includes a characteristic note to Pound in his letter of 3 March 1913 to Yeats: "You'll do, only climb higher, ever higher and thus forget the burden" (Harper, *W.B. Yeats and W.T. Horton* 119). Three years later, on 6 September 1916, after having attended Yeats's Monday Evening on the 4th, Horton writes a letter in which he is very critical of Yeats's actions and ambitions:

> I was & am very sorry for Ezra because beneath all his many wrappings I see the Real Man who sorrows deeply over the antics & perverse lucubrations of his distracted charge. Watching & listening to Ezra I could see, as it were, a something slimy crawling over everything that is beautiful & noble & of good report & leaving behind him an unquestionably *glittering* but at the same time foul track of slime. I am sorry for him because of what he must go through, for *Love-in-Death is approaching who will open his eyes & those of his Moon & other satellites.*
> What is astonishing is that you do not see what Ezra is to you. . . .
> Ezra was your guest last Monday as were others so I did not think it right & proper to say anything but at the same time I cannot allow my attitude to be mistaken. I gather from you that one cannot be a Poet & a Hero; in other words to be a Hero you must be a Zero. Well I prefer the Heroic Zero to the Olympian Poet on his sham Olympus. . . .
> What you or Ezra or anyone else believes or says matters not one tittle to me but I do know we are all in the hands of the Living God & sudden & quick & drastic will be the Event.
> I have a word for Mrs Shakespear. *Sundry of her accounts are being made up, the balance is being struck — she will soon know on which side it is to be* (Harper, *W.B. Yeats and W.T. Horton* 128-29).

The references to Pound in this letter establish his participation in Yeats's occult friendships. But this is not the principal lesson to be drawn from the episode: the letters also make clear that Pound had nothing in common with Horton, or most of the rest of the fools and tricksters who made up much of the London occult. That he knew many of them personally and understood the nature of their practices and beliefs explains his frequent — and misleading — outbursts against their scandalous and outrageous ways.

Horton's letter includes the strange but typical "prophecy" about Olivia Shakespear. Lionel Johnson's first cousin and a novelist in her own right, she is the "Diana Vernon" of Yeats's autobiographical writings and had a love affair with the poet which lasted less than a year (1895-96), after which they remained close friends. Olivia participated in the occult movements of the period and even co-authored two plays with Florence Farr, the accomplished actress and occultist, who for a time headed the Order of the Golden Dawn. The two plays, which have occult subjects, were published together as *The Beloved of Hathor and the Shrine of the Golden Hawk* (1902).[14] Pound and his future mother-in-law were introduced in January 1909, likely by the Australian poet Frederic Manning, Olivia's nephew, and Pound was invited to the Shakespear home at number twelve Brunswick Gardens in early February.

The Ezra Pound-Dorothy Shakespear correspondence provides several examples of Olivia Shakespear's occult interests. She acted as Yeats's ambassador to Pound in the business of getting the information necessary for casting Pound's horoscope; she was an expert in drawing occult symbols; and she translated a seventeenth-century occult text, *Le Comte de Gabalis* (Paris, 1670), by the Abbé de Montfaucon de Villars, which Yeats and Pound had been reading earlier at Stone Cottage (*EP/DS* 108, 181, 293, 294, 302, 303, and 334).[15]

In her letters and notebook Dorothy Shakespear discusses palmistry and astrology, and she mentions a number of books which she is reading, ranging from Evelyn Underhill's *Mysticism* (which was hot off the press when she read it) to Conybeare's translation of Philostratus's *Apollonius of Tyana* (a text from which Pound later drew heavily for cantos 91 and 94) and Sinistrari's *Demonology; or, Incubi and Succubi* (*EP/DS* 31-32, 188-89, 305). The degree of Dorothy's, and Pound's, involvement can be measured by what is for this account the most important passage in their correspondence — a letter in which he attempts to clarify, for Dorothy's edification, the difference between "real symbolism" and aesthetic or literary symbolism:

> ... What do you mean by symbolism? Do you mean real symbolism, Cabala, genesis of symbols, rise of picture language, etc. or the aesthetic <symbology> symbolism of Villiers de l'Isle Adam, & that Arthur Symons wrote a book [*Symbolist Movement in Literature*] about — the liteway [sic] movement? At any rate begin on the "*Comte de Gabalis*," anonymous & should be in catalogue under "Comte de Gabalis." Then you might try the Grimoire of Pope Honorius (IIIrd I think).
>
> There's a dictionary of symbols, but I think it immoral. I mean that I think a superficial acquaintance with the sort of shallow, conventional, or attributed meaning of a lot of symbols *weakens* — damnably, the power of receiving an energized symbol. I mean a symbol appearing in a vision has a certain richness & power of energizing joy — whereas if the supposed meaning of a symbol is familiar it has no more force, or interest of power of suggestion than any other word, or than a synonym in some other language.
>
> Then there are those Egyptian language books, but O.S. [Olivia Shakespear] has 'em so they're no use. De Gabalis (first part only) is amusing. Ennemoser's History Of Magic may have something in it — Then there are "Les Symbolistes" — french from Mallarmé, de l'Isle Adam, etc. to [Remy] De Gourmont, which is another story (letter of 14 January 1914, *EP/DS* 302).

Pound's preference for "occult" over "aesthetic" symbolism is quite clear in this letter. It severely tests the arguments of those who deny Pound's interest in esoterica. Michael H. Levenson, for example, in his persuasive revisionist account of modernism, *A Genealogy of Modernism*, argues that both Pound and Ford criticized Yeats's symbolism and opposed its technique of "suggestion" and "invocation" as well as its straining after the ineffable. Levenson, having carefully traversed the terrain between the time of the acceptance for publication of the imagist anthology (summer of 1913) and the outbreak of the war the following summer, observes that

> Ford criticized the poetry of Yeats because it forsook immediate perception in favour of imaginative wanderings through mystical arcana. Pound, too, liked to compare art to science (the "arts, literature, poesy, are a science just as chemistry is a science") and in one of his early manifestos he insisted that "the natural object is always the *adequate* symbol." The pursuit of transcendence is thus summarily abandoned (110).

Levenson insists that "to symbolist 'evocation,' Imagism opposed precision, hardness, clarity of outline. To symbolist transcendence, Imagism opposed the natural world" (120). But as we have seen, Pound does not reject the "real symbolism of vision" nor the possibility of transcendence. Moreover, Pound's use of scientific terminology and scientific analogies, which one finds in his prose, belongs to the tradition of "occult science."

The letter to Dorothy reveals that Pound was clear about the difference between literary symbolism, as represented in Arthur Symon's *Symbolist Movement in Literature*, and "real" or esoteric symbolism. He understood literary or aesthetic symbolism as a mixture of occultism, spiritualist mysticism, and magic couched in a language of emotional reverberation and suggestiveness. And even though he had no trouble with the first component, his own modernist needs dictated that a precise language be used in his poetry. Therefore, in his work he rejected the symbolist technique of suggestion in favour of a "sort of hyper-scientific precision" (*SR* 87) but without rejecting the symbolist metaphysical mysticism. Clearly, this is what Pound means in his "Vorticism" article where he rejects the "mushy technique" of symbolism but not its transcendentalism. In the same essay he approves wholeheartedly of a "belief in a sort of permanent metaphor [which] is, as I understand it, 'symbolism' in its profounder sense. It is not necessarily a belief in a permanent world, but it is a belief in that direction" (*GB* 84). In short, while attacking and rejecting aesthetic symbolism, he approves of "real" symbolism.[16]

The dialectic, during Pound's early London years, between Yeatsian symbolism and his own need for a language which would be precise and free of symbolism's "mushy technique" was the measure of Pound's modernism. When he says that "I went to London because I thought Yeats knew more about poetry than anybody else. . . . I went to study with Yeats and found that Ford disagreed with him," he is thinking in terms of technique (Hall 47). His *catechesis* under Yeats was an education in the occult through Yeats's occult friends. Pound rubbed shoulders with many occultists: during the meetings of the Quest Society in Kensington Town Hall and later in a large studio in Clareville Grove, South Kensington; in Paris during the spring of 1911 when Yeats and Pound were often together; during Yeats's "Monday Evenings"; and perhaps during visits to John M. Watkins's bookstore at Cecil Court where people came for *"tea, talk,* and *theosophy"* (Harper, *Yeats and the Occult* 309).

3. Pound's Catechesis in London (2): Upward and Orage

The intellectual climate that nurtured Pound's interest in the occult was shaped by many a strange yet now obscure or forgotten figure. Some of these receive not even a footnote in Pound's writings; but he does reserve special praise for one of them: Allen Upward (1863-1926), an English barrister, amateur sinologist, amateur religious historian, author of several detective stories, poet, playwright, publicist, civil servant, and volunteer soldier. Upward's participation in the various occult groups of the time brought him in close contact with many of Pound's own acquaintances. He was a friend of Mead, with whom he studied the Chaldean thaumaturges. He was even more friendly with Orage, whom he first met in 1900. Upward contributed regularly to *The New Age*. He knew all the members of the Pound circle in the early 1910s, and his poetry was included in the first *Des Imagistes* anthology. Finally, he belonged to Yeats's circle of esoteric companions and even participated in psychic experiments with Yeats (Knox 71, 73).

Pound discovered Upward's work in *Poetry* and, as Upward wrote later, he "rose up and called me an Imagist. (I had no idea what he meant.)" ("The Discarded Imagist" 98). They first met at a gathering of Mead's Quest Society in 1911. Upward and Pound became lifelong friends, and we have evidence that they spent some time together discussing the ideas we find in Upward's *The Divine Mystery*. Upward is named or alluded to in at least five of Pound's letters to Dorothy (*EP/DS* 257, 259, 264, 270, 323). The most important of these are Pound's references to a contemplated visit with Upward (Tuesday, 23 September 1913) and an account of that visit (Wednesday, 2 October 1913). The first letter appears to have been written after Pound spent the weekend with Upward and Orage:

> [Allen] Upward of the chinese poemae is quite an addition. He is off for greece possibly in a months [sic] time. I may go down to the I. of Wight with him for a visit before then. *Il pense* that IS an addition. He seems to [know] things that ain't in Frazer, at least he talked sense about sun worship & the siege of Troy, & he has been "resident" in Nigeria and divers other joyous adventures so far as I can make out....
>
> I week-ended with the N.Age [*New Age*] and caught a drenching gold-n-me-'ead. As to fungi, Upward also talked about fungi—(and Francis Bacon) (*EP/DS* 259).

This letter, like the one which follows, underlines Pound's admiration for Upward's powerful and original mind: "I would have writ before but I went to Ryde to visit [Allen] Upward. *Il pense*. It is a rare phenomenon. He has just finished 'The Divine Mystery,' digested golden bough with a lot more of his own intelligence stuck into it" (*EP/DS* 264). Besides the recognition that Pound found Upward's work more penetrating than Sir James Frazer's *The Golden Bough* (he seems to have gotten from Upward what Eliot, for example, got from Frazer), we see here that Pound and Upward had the opportunity to discuss ideas they shared. Many years after Upward's suicide in 1926, Pound was still fond of his work and took pride in declaring that, in fact, he was the "sole reader of all Upward's books, now surviving" (*L* 296). Nor did he ever stop praising Upward's originality or emphasizing the fact that Upward never got the recognition he deserved. "He ought to get credit as autodidact. And a lot more than he has had," writes Pound in a letter dated 10 April 1958.[17]

There is no real need for an extensive recounting of Pound's possible debt to Upward, since this has already been done by a number of Pound scholars.[18] But while a number of critics have discussed Pound's adoption of such Upwardian concepts as those of the "fluid universe" and the "Divine Man," they have failed to notice that Upward's ideas are those of the London Spiritualist groups, mediums, and ghost hunters. Even Bryant Knox, who in "Allen Upward and Ezra Pound" provides many important details, fails to emphasize Upward's occult interests. Though Knox mentions that Upward and Mead were good friends, the detail about Upward's and Yeats's psychic experiment is buried in a note (73).

For our purposes, Upward's significance lies in his occult reading of religious history. His two most important works from that perspective are *The New Word* (1910) and *The Divine Mystery* (1913). In his 1914 review of *The New Word*, Pound is emphatically positive in his estimation of

Upward's ideas: "what Mr. Upward says will be believed in another twenty or fifty or a hundred years, just as a lot of Voltaire's quiet thrusts are now a part of our gospel" (*SP* 409). *The New Word* is a sardonic analysis of contemporary thought. Upward's real purpose in this book, however, is to show that the true source of knowledge is primitive language. Employing etymological clues, he demonstrates how certain words still preserve once living beliefs.

While the aim of his etymological game is the undermining of those concepts which have been widely viewed as forming the backbone of modern thought, Upward does not stop there. Another central concern of his is to demonstrate the falsity of the standard textbook definition which assumes that "The universe is made up of matter." Rejecting both the materialistic as well as the idealistic viewpoint as inadequate, he proposes that we see matter as a knot of energy, a network of forces which cannot be broken down into components such as matter and energy.

This concept is captured in the book's central image of the waterspout (he called this image a "whirl-swirl") which Upward puts forth as a model for the real world.

> Consider this idea [of the waterspout]. Consider this inner strength, coming and going, turning and returning, millions of beats in every tick of secular time, while, throbbing through the network woven by their meeting, the over-strength comes and goes faster than flashes in a diamond.
>
> It is no longer a mere word. It is a magic crystal, and by looking long into it, you will see wonderful meanings come and go. It will change colour like an opal while you gaze, reflecting the thoughts in your own mind. It is a most chameleon-like ball. It has this deeper magic that it will show you, not only the thoughts you knew about before, but other thoughts you did not know of, old, drowned thoughts, hereditary thoughts; umbering ancestral ghosts that haunt brain; you will remember things you used to know and feel long, long ago. What do you see in the magic crystal? . . . (*The New Word* 201).

The "whirl-swirl" is a point of conduct between man and the *theos* and thus not a mere word but the *logos*. This *logos*, or magic crystal ball, represents a form of *gnosis*, since man's relation to the universe, and god in particular, is seen here as the coming together of interpenetrating energies manifested through this union, energies which otherwise have no independent existence. The Upwardian conception of matter as a knot of energy, and of man and the divine as two interpenetrating strengths, and his often skeptical drawing upon science for examples to illustrate the true picture of the world, all belong to the occult thought of his time. Evidently, these concepts held great appeal for Pound. In particular, it is possible that the "great crystal" image of the later cantos is derived from Upward. What is more, Upward's concept of the waterspout and his penchant for scientific analogies parallel Pound's concept of the vortex and use of scientific metaphors.

A receptacle and container of all knowledge or wisdom, the waterspout is a symbol of the vital universe, of a universe energized by "some power still working to mould our planetary fates" (308). This last quotation is from Upward's *The Divine Mystery*, a book Pound reviewed for *The New Freewoman*, paying it the highest possible compliment by calling it "the most fascinating book on folk-lore that I have ever opened. I can scarcely call it a book of 'folk-lore,' it is a consummation. It is a history of the development of human intelligence" (*SP* 403). In this book Upward concerns himself with the origins and development of religions and argues for their evolution from primitive fertility rites through stellar to solar worship and the parallel evolution of the Divine Man, who passes through the phases of the Wizard, the Magician, the Genius, the Seer, the Priest and the Prophet, all of whom are prototypes of the Χρηστός (Chrestos), the anointed one. According to Upward, the universe is made up of vital forces and "the secret of genius is sensitiveness" to these forces. The "genius" acts as an antenna, or a barometer, registering the changes in the cosmic atmosphere and is, as Upward says, "the archetype of all Heroes in all Mysteries." When this conception of the human race and the universe is put together with the depiction, in *The Divine Mystery*, of the history of human religion as a journey from darkness to Helios or Sun ("primitive man turns from his worship of the dead, and of the earth and of various fears, to a worship of the life-giving Helios" [*SP* 404]), we can begin to see Upward's impact on Pound's ideas and art and appreciate the appeal that Upward's concepts held for Pound.

Upward's ideas were formed in the process of comparing the doctrines and beliefs—often cranky and ill-educated—of London Spiritualist groups, mediums, and ghost hunters with those found in primitive magic-lore. Behind this search for analogies is Upward's belief in the existence of "some power still working to mould our planetary fates," a power which is responsible for all religious manifestations, including Christianity. While Upward's trafficking, similar to Yeats's, with the rogues and fools of London occult groups provided him with the evidence for the continued operation of this power during his time, the rest of his evidence certainly came from his study of synoptic Hellenistic tradition—that is, the same body of speculative, "metaphysical" occultism with which Pound also became familiar during his London years.

Upward committed suicide in late 1926. In an early 1927 article which appeared in *The New Age*, Philip Mairet praised his genius in this way: "The man who wrote 'The Divine Mystery' and the 'New Word,' and who contributed to THE NEW AGE such series of articles as 'The Order of Seraphim' and 'The Planetary Origin of Man,' was one of the greatest spirits in modern letters" ("Allen Upward and His Order of Genius" 162). An occultist himself, Mairet is the author of the biography of A.R. Orage (1873-1934). The latter is another of Pound's occultist friends of the period—a fact that has also largely escaped the attention of Pound scholars.[19]

Orage, the editor of the weekly paper *The New Age* (1906-22), is almost never discussed under any topic other than economic theories.[20] Although everyone is aware of Orage's occult as well as his economic connections, no attention has been paid to the possibility that Pound shared Orage's occult interests. Partly responsible for this is Pound's dismissive remark about Orage's mysticism: "I had no interest in Orage's mysticism and am unqualified to define it. I was thankful he had it simply because it kept him in action" (*SP* 446). This denial is typical of Pound's public stance on the occult and it is, most likely, an honest enough statement, since his dislike for Indian mysticism is at least as well known as Orage's predilection for it.[21] In a letter to John Theobald, written over three decades after his London period, Pound mentions that at the time he had been reading an Indian classic at Orage's prodding. In this letter, dated 28 March 1957, Pound says that "Orage drug me thru 1 1/2 vols of *Mahabharatt* and then I stuck" (*EP/JT* 25). Thus, regarding Pound's statement about Orage's mysticism, we can be certain that Pound was, indeed, more than qualified at the time (1935) to pass judgment. It is also certain that *The New Age* offices on Cursitor Street and the A.B.C. restaurant in Chancery Lane across the street where Orage and his circle often gathered must have witnessed many a discussion on occult subjects.[22]

Orage's biographical details are interesting in themselves; but an examination of them also points to the ubiquity of the occult at the turn of the century. Born in 1873 in the Yorkshire village of Dacre near Bradford, Orage was trained as a schoolmaster at Culham College near Oxford and, in 1893, began his twelve-year long teaching career at Leeds. During this time he met his future wife, Jean Walker. A keen Theosophist, she clearly encouraged Orage's natural bent for mystical and esoteric study. Orage became a member of the Leeds branch of the Theosophical Society around 1896. His two best friends of the period, Holbrook Jackson, a lace manufacturer and a Fabian, and A.J. Penty, an architect who at the time was studying the medieval guild system, introduced him to Nietzsche and to socialism, respectively. With these two friends, who were also Theosophists, Orage formed the highly successful Leeds Art Club, which organized exhibitions of paintings, drawings, arts and crafts, and lectures on religious, philosophical, social, and economic subjects. The three associates also arranged open meetings in the Leeds Museum (attended by such important figures as Yeats, G.B. Shaw, Edward Carpenter, and G.K. Chesterton). The Leeds Arts Club also housed the local Theosophical and Fabian Societies, and members of the first were likely to be members of one or both of the other societies. His participation in these clubs reflects Orage's interests at the time. Jackson's comments about Orage's syncretist zeal are even more pointed: "He wanted a Nietzsche circle in which Plato and Blavatsky, Fabianism and Hinduism, Shaw and Wells and Edward Carpenter should be blended, with Nietzsche as the catalytic. An exciting brew" (qtd. in Webb, *The Harmonious Circle* 200).

At the end of 1905 Orage left Leeds for London, where he mixed with the Theosophical and Fabian crowd while trying to survive as a journalist. By July 1905 he was a member of the committee of the British section of the Theosophical Society and, at about the same time, he was Acting Secretary of the Society for Psychical Research. Between the end of 1905 and the end of 1907 he published a series of articles in the *Theosophical Review*, many of which attracted criticism because of Orage's skepticism and refusal to compromise his critical faculty by becoming the slave of Tibetan Mahatmas or their representatives. During the same period Orage also published three small books on philosophical and religious subjects: *Friedrich Nietzsche: The Dionysian Spirit of the Age* (London: T.N. Foulis, 1906), *Nietzsche in Outline and Aphorism* (London: T.N. Foulis, 1907), and *Consciousness, Animal, Human, and Superhuman* (London and Benares: The Theosophical Press Society, 1907).[23]

In May 1907 Orage and Jackson purchased *The New Age*, a weekly magazine founded in 1893 by Frederic R. Atkins, and which at the time was in grave financial difficulties. The money for this venture was donated by Shaw and a Theosophical friend, Lewis Wallace, who also became a frequent contributor under the pseudonym "M.B. Oxon." Although the magazine was opened to his occult friends (for example, Wallace and Florence Farr), Orage—who became the sole editor in January 1910 when Jackson left—never used it to advance his own Theosophical ideas and was able to build for it a solid reputation as a paper of avant-garde political, economic, and cultural ideas.

Pound was introduced to Orage by F.S. Flint in 1911 and by the end of that year he had become a regular contributor to *The New Age*.[24] Orage and Pound seem to have had a divergence of opinion on literary matters, so there must have been other things they agreed upon. For example, in the letter to his mother in which he discusses, among other things, his upcoming stay at Stone Cottage with Yeats and the recent publication of Upward's *Divine Mystery*, Pound writes: "I am fully aware of *The New Age's* limitations. Still the editor is a good fellow—his literary taste—is unfortunate" (*L* 25-26).[25] Beatrice Hastings, in her vindictive memoir *The Old "New Age": Orage and Others* (1936), claims that Orage, too, did not think highly of Pound's literary taste, his individual style, nor the cultural ambience of his pieces: "Orage . . . said, so late as Oct. 1913, nearly two years after Pound's debut: 'Mr. Pound's style is a paste of colloquy, slang journalism and pedantry. Of culture in Nietzsche's sense of the word, it bears no sign'" (qtd. in Surette, "Economics and Eleusis" 60). That Orage could have been critical of Pound's style is probable. But despite Pound's later denial of interest in Orage's "mysticism," the evidence suggests that the two men did share a number of interests and that their relationship was not simply that of editor and contributor.

In a letter to Dorothy, already quoted in connection with the Pound-Upward friendship, we have seen that Pound and Orage spent at least one weekend together (20-21 September 1913). This establishes that they did see each other away from *The New Age* offices. Against the claim for the absence of "Nietzschean" culture in Pound's writing, one simply has to look at *Patria Mia* (first serialized in *The New Age* in eleven installments between 5 September and 14 November 1912) to realize that Pound did, indeed, echo some of Orage's Nietzschean ideas.[26]

Another common interest, dating from a little later (1917), is the Social Credit economic theories of Major Douglas. There are other points of common interest, but here let it suffice to note that I endorse Leon Surette's observation that "We will never understand the strange and potent mix of Orientalism, radical underconsumption economics, mythography, right-wing politics, and poetry that make up Pound's career without a fuller knowledge of the kind of education Pound received in *The New Age* offices at 38 Cursitor Street" ("Economics and Eleusis" 60).

In his "Obituary: A.R. Orage," which appeared in the *New English Weekly* (15 November 1934), Pound points out that "the small dissident minority who profess to get some profit from my writings owe debt, above whatever they realise, to the man whose weekly guinea fed me when no one else was ready to do so, and that for at least two years running" (*SP* 437). Orage and his *New Age* circle fed and kept feeding Pound during his London years in more ways than the one he shows gratitude for here. Among all the other people Pound may have met in Orage's company was a foreigner who played a large part in the editor's own occult education between 1915 and 1921. This was Dmitri Mitrinovic (1884-1948?), an attaché at the Serbian embassy in London, introduced to Orage by Paul Selver in 1915. Mitrinovic was a friend of Wassily Kandinsky and was well versed in the arts, ancient and modern, as well as the occult tradition. Inspired by the old Slav Messianic vision of a united Christian Europe, he proclaimed world salvation and dressed it up with trappings borrowed from all sorts of occult systems and religions. Orage was very receptive to these ideas, even though the "prophet's ascendancy over his mind was never complete" (Mairet, *A.R. Orage: A Memoir* xi). Orage and Mitrinovic collaborated on a series of articles on "World Affairs" which appeared in *The New Age* from 19 August 1920 to 13 October 1921 under the pen name of "M.M. Cosmoi." The theme of these articles, as it was announced by Orage on their first appearance, was "the development of world consciousness under the guidance of the European mind" (Mairet xvii). Mitrinovic's occultism, like so many other brands of occultism flourishing at this time in London, was a very mixed bag — but Pound himself would certainly not have been impressed by Mitrinovic's Christianizing of paganism.[27]

This phase of Orage's life coincides with his interest in psychoanalysis as well as his conversion to Major Douglas's economic theories, a conversion for which he had been prepared by his Leeds association with Penty. Beginning in 1912, *The New Age* devoted increasing attention to psychoanalysis and, at Orage's initiative, a "psychosynthesis" group was formed which included Havelock Ellis, David Eder, James Young, Maurice Nicoll, J.A.M. Alcock, and Rowland Kenney. This group's regular meetings, at least at the beginning, were sometimes attended by Mitrinovic. This was a rather mixed group of men who were genuinely interested in psychoanalysis and leaned, at the same time, toward the occult. A brief look at one of these individuals, Dr. Eder, whose interests are also representative of the rest of the group, reveals the strong ties between psychoanalysis and the occult.

Dr. Eder was a Freudian pioneer and a close associate of Freud, a member of the Arts Group of the Fabian Society, and a member of *The New Age* circle. His cryptic but obviously favourable review of Aleister Crowley's *Konx Om Pax* which appeared in *The New Age* (February 1908), his close ties with Mead's *Quest* group, and his attendance of Ouspensky's lectures in 1921 leave no room for doubt about the attraction which he felt for the occult (Webb, *The Quest Anthology* 473).

The psychoanalysts and the occultists shared a number of interests. Among these was the interest in the interpretation of symbolism and myth. As well, most of these people saw psychoanalysis as the harbinger of a golden age; and although their approach was different from those of more traditional occult groups, their basic concern with ushering in a New Age is something which is at the heart of all occult movements.

Orage's own involvement with Mitrinovic in the mid- and late-1910s prepared him for G.I. Gurdjieff and P.D. Ouspensky, Gurdjieff's missionary in London. Orage's Gurdjieff phase lasted for ten years and took him first to Gurdjieff's Institute at Fontainebleau in France (1922-23) and later to New York, where he remained until 1930 as the American head of Gurdjieff's movement.[28] Pound himself visited Fontainebleau for a day sometime in June 1921.[29] Orage returned to London to establish the *New English Weekly* (first issue 21 April 1932) and made a point of inviting contributions from Pound, then living in Italy. Orage also continued to discover new literary talent (such as Dylan Thomas) until his death in 1934.

4. "ECHOES FROM THE GNOSIS": G.R.S. MEAD AND POUND

Of those who contributed to Pound's occult education, G.R.S. Mead contributed the most. Pound's letters to his parents (1909-14), Dorothy Shakespear (1909-14), Margaret Cravens (1910-12), Patricia Hutchins (1953-60), John Theobald (1957-58), and Margaret Anderson (1917 and 1953)[30] establish beyond doubt that he paid considerable attention to Mead's work, that he was interested in the subjects that were Mead's trademark, and that he and Dorothy were regulars at Mead's lectures.[31]

Pound must have met Mead at one of Yeats's "Monday Evenings," which Mead attended about twice a month.[32] Pound's earliest reference to Mead is in a letter to his mother, dated 17 September 1911: "I wrote yesterday on Friday so there's not much more. I have spent the P.M. with G.R.S. Mead. Edtr. of 'The Quest' who wants me to throw a lecture for his society which he can afterwards print. 'Troubadour Psychology,' whatever the dooce that is" (BRBL).[33] Though as usual Pound attempts to obscure his deep interest in his Theosophist friend by suggesting that nothing special has occurred since his last letter, his interest in and curiosity about Mead are clear; moreover, the uncertainty in the last sentence indicates that it was Mead who suggested the title, and possibly the subject, of Pound's essay "Psychology and Troubadours." The same uncertainty or uneasiness is discernible in a letter from Dorothy to Pound dated two days after Pound's letter to his mother: "Don't *you* be 'nebulous to the Nth' about yr. Troubadour psychology — or [G.R.S.] Mead won't be pleased. Say you're a reincarnation so you know. Are you? do you?" (letter of 19 September 1911, *EP/DS* 61). Dorothy's reference to reincarnation indicates a playful skepticism that Pound himself maintained throughout his occult studies – in contrast to Mead's credulity.

References to Mead appear frequently in Pound's letters to his parents. "I find Mead very interesting," he writes in December 1911; and on 21 February 1912 he is even more flattering, finding Mead "about as interesting – along his own line – as anyone I meet" (BRBL).³⁴ A letter from Dorothy to Pound, also dated 21 February 1912, shows that she herself and at least one of her friends shared Pound's interest in Mead: "I was deeply interested in [G.R.S.] Mead – so, I think, was G. [Georgie Hyde-Lees]" (*EP/DS* 87).

Pound's unpublished letters to his parents also strongly suggest that his attendance at Mead's Quest Society lectures was regular. In March 1912, he writes to his mother saying that "Mead's lecture on 'Heirotheos' was very good" (BRBL);³⁵ in a letter dated 5 November 1912, he announces to his parents that "Mead's lectures begin this P.M."; and in another dated four weeks later (3 December 1912) he says: "I'm going out to Mead's lecture. And so on as usual. This being Tuesday" (BRBL).³⁶ Even when Pound was away from London, he could rely on Dorothy for information about Mead's lectures, since there was apparently an understanding between them that Dorothy's Tuesday evenings would be spent listening to Mead (*EP/DS* 276).

Three other letters indicate that Dorothy was at the time reading Mead's books, including *The World Mystery* and *Fragments of a Faith Forgotten* (*EP/DS* 102, 114-15, 160). In her letters to Pound, Dorothy discusses Mead's works in a way which assumes Pound's familiarity with them. In a 22 May 1912 letter, for example, Dorothy writes about Mead's *The World Mystery*:

> I have been intensely excited over another of [G.R.S.] Mead's – "The World-Mystery." It is full of interesting things, and I have "correlated" several to vaguenesses of my own! Also a footnote fit for Walter [Morse Rummel], about a "dodecagonal pyramid" with a door of many colours – the pyramid "in a sphere of the colour of night" – . . . .
>
> I find Renan an excellent antidote to G.R.S. Mead & his numbers & Mysteries (*EP/DS* 102).³⁷

The key phrase here is "intensely excited over another of Mead's," since it indicates Dorothy's familiarity with several of Mead's works and suggests Pound's parallel interest.³⁸

About four weeks later, Dorothy is still studying *The World Mystery*. In a postscript she tells Pound of a visit by the Meads and mentions an exciting new finding:

> The Meads here at tea yesterday: they both have so much, & such pleasant, personality. . . .
> P.S. . . .
> I feel quite interested — having found an incantation in Mead beginning "iao, aoi, oia" . . . (letter of 16 June [1912], EP/DS 114-15).

The incantation, "AOI," found by Dorothy in Mead and brought to Pound's attention in this letter, was later used in *The Cantos* (79/490).[39]

More than forty years after his initial acquaintance with Mead, the London milieu of the first two decades of the century in general, and Mead in particular, remain an enduring interest for Pound. His letters to John Theobald and Patricia Hutchins confirm this interest. The letters to Theobald contain many references to things occult and to the activities of Jiddu Krishnamurti,[40] Madame Blavatsky, and Mead. One such reference appears in Pound's reply to Theobald's inquiry about whether "Mead [was] one of the Psychical Research [SPR] investigators that made trouble for Blavatsky?":

> GRS Mead / BlavatskiTe {no suspicion of a k} "Echoes from the Gnosis," possibly 40 vols/
> Quest Society and Quarterly, Q.S. lectures at least monthly for part of the year/ < London 19? to '14 >.
> . . . .
> I don't think Mead mucked with the psychical research gang/ that was another subject of satire/ . . . (EP/JT 29 and 32).[41]

In Pound's letters to Hutchins, most of which date from about the same period as those to Theobald, he stresses the special ambience of Kensington, and returns repeatedly to Mead and the Quest Society lectures at the Kensington Town Hall. As can be gathered from Hutchins's *Ezra Pound's Kensington: An Exploration, 1885-1913*, parts of which Pound would have seen in manuscript, she did not pay much attention to Pound's emphasis on the occult ambience of Kensington. In his letters Pound appears to become increasingly upset over Hutchins's failure to include Upward and Mead in her account or to document the activities of the Quest Society at the Kensington Town Hall, where not only Pound and Jessie L. Weston, but also T.E. Hulme and Wyndham Lewis came and even lectured.[42] Pound's irritation is clear in a letter from Italy, dated 15 June 1959, which effectively ends his direct correspondence with Hutchins: "I put a LOT of work telling you KENSINGTON, its inhabitants to which you paid not the least bloody damn bit of attention."

Mead had a decent reputation in Edwardian England. Modern studies on Gnosticism and the origins of Christianity still mention him.[43] But even though his most important books were reissued in the 1960s, he is little known. The chief source for what we know of him is a memoir he wrote and published in *The Quest* some eight years before his death in 1933. This essay, which recounts the early history of the Quest Society and outlines a major shift in the periodical's future course, is aptly entitled "'The Quest' — Old and New: Retrospect and Prospect."[44]

Born in 1863, Mead was educated at King's School, Rochester, England, and at Cambridge (M.A., 1885). He entered Oxford to study philosophy and later attended the French University of Clermont-Ferrand where he seems to have studied Spiritualism! (Nethercot 345-46). He joined Blavatsky's Theosophical Society in 1884 and in 1889 gave up the teaching profession to become her private secretary — in which capacity he remained until her death two years later (1891). He subedited Blavatsky's monthly magazine, *Lucifer*, which he renamed *The Theosophical Review* upon becoming editor. The impossible task of correcting and revising *The Secret Doctrine* fell to him. In 1890 Mead was appointed General Secretary of the European section of the Theosophical Society, a position from which he resigned in 1897 in order to devote himself more fully to his writing. When Colonel Olcott, the co-founder of the Theosophical Society, died in 1907, the presidency was offered to Mead; but he declined because he "much preferred continuing [his] studies, editing, writing books and lecturing... to continual travelling and organization" ("'The Quest' — Old and New" 295). When problems divided the society in 1909 because of what Mead calls the "miserable, unpalatable episode" of C.W. Leadbeater's sexual scandals,[45] Mead led a schism, and some seven hundred members resigned with him.

At one time Mead's followers expected him to set up a rival "Neo-theosophic tin tabernacle" to carry on the pretence and charlatanry of the original group; but he wanted no part in any of this because, as he categorically states,

> I had never, even while a member [of the Theosophical Society], preached the Mahatma-gospel of H.P.B. [Blavatsky], or propagandised Neo-theosophy [Mead's term for Besant's movement] and its revelations. I had believed that "theosophy" proper meant the wisdom-element in the great religions and philosophies of the world ("'The Quest' — Old and New" 296-97).

The second sentence of this passage represents Mead's understanding of the term "Theosophy" and states a position which can be supported by his writings as a whole. Mead's distancing of himself from Blavatsky's theories and practices, and his skepticism regarding the validity of Neo-

Theosophical psychic phenomena are similar to Pound's own distancing of himself from everything smacking of the practices and beliefs of the "Bond Street charlatans."

Mead founded "The Quest Society" with one hundred and fifty ex-Theosophists and another one hundred outside recruits, and its journal *The Quest* in order "to promote investigation and comparative study of religion, philosophy and science, on the basis of experience" and "to encourage the expression of the ideal in beautiful forms" (Mead, "On the Nature of the Quest" 29-30).[46] Mead and his society abjured "all 'magical' and 'occult' pretensions that seek the 'will to power' and are essentially 'anti-social.'" *The Quest* would accept articles examining "the history and criticism of such 'occult' subjects, but never [articles concerned] with their advocacy" ("'The Quest'—Old and New" 307). The distinction Mead makes here is between theurgic practices and psychical phenomena on the one hand and speculative occult philosophy on the other. This is a distinction which Pound would also make while favouring, like Mead (and unlike Yeats), the latter.

Although the later volumes of *The Quest* include essays on Freudian psychoanalysis and other contemporary topics, it was mythology, religious mysticism, and the study of Christian origins that remained closest to Mead's heart. Among the contributors were the following: A.E. Waite, Fiona Macleod, Algernon Blackwood, Arthur Machen, Ernest Rhys, Denis Saurat, Rabindranath Tagore, W.B. Yeats, A.E. (George Russell), Laurence Binyon, Alfred Noyes, Edward Carpenter, F.C. Conybeare, Arthur Symons, Evelyn Underhill, Jessie L. Weston, Raymond A. Nicholson, G. Scholem, Martin Buber, and Ezra Pound. Many of these names are well known in their respective fields.

Undoubtedly Pound would have read many issues of *The Quest* during his years in London.[47] Volume 4 is of particular interest because it contains Pound's essay "Psychology and Troubadours." This volume includes articles by Mead himself ("The Meaning of the Gnosis in Higher Hellenistic Religion"), Weston, Tagore, Underhill ("The Mystic as Creative Artist"), and a poem by Yeats ("The Mountain Tomb"). An article of possible interest to Pound is Arthur E. Bailly's "Dante and Swedenborg: Two Other-World Explorers." Even more significant are some of the reviews, of which two are of Pound's new volumes of poetry, *The Sonnets of Guido Cavalcanti* and *Ripostes*. There are reviews of F.C. Conybeare's Loeb Classical Library edition of *Apollonius of Tyana*, Edouard Schuré's *The Great Initiates*, Edmund G. Gardner's *Dante and the Mystics*, and three reviews of Evelyn Underhill's books, among them one of *The Mystic Way*.[48]

Pound's clearest statement of his debt to Mead is his footnote on Mead's lecture on Simon Magus and Helen of Tyre. It is dated 1916 and acknowledges Pound's debt to "a recent lecture by Mr. Mead on Simon Magus [which] has opened my mind to a number of new possibilities" (*SR* 91). Accordingly, Pound sees the legend of Simon and Helen of Tyre as a "clearer prototype of 'chivalric love'" than anything he himself has discovered for use in his own essay. Even though the text of the "recent lecture" remains unknown, its arguments must have been those Mead makes at length in *Simon Magus: an Essay* (1892) and in more condensed form in *Fragments of a Faith Forgotten* (1900). We may safely assume that it was Mead who introduced Pound to the history of this Gnostic allegory of the soul; but Pound would certainly not agree with Mead's interpretation of the legend's sexual symbolism. Mead is explicit, for example, in his warning to the readers of *Simon Magus* not to interpret the legend literally, "for nothing but sorrow will follow such materialization of divine mysteries" (*Simon Magus* 75). Pound's note makes clear that he absorbed both the sexual and the theological dimensions which the Simon legend shares with Gnosticism in general; it is clear, as well, that Pound did not share Mead's prudishness regarding the sexual symbolism inherent in the legend and parts ways with Mead at this point.

Other opinions, ideas, images, and historical personages important to Pound have been traced to Mead.[49] But more important than the discovery of the exact sources of some of Pound's ideas in Mead's writings is that the general substance of Mead's occult thought is reflected in Pound. In particular, Pound's conception of the "celestial tradition," his formulation of a fantasy history, and his theory of "palingenesis" or soul-making (outlined most clearly in the section entitled "Religio" of *Selected Prose* and in *Guide to Kulchur*) correspond quite closely to Mead's occultist formulations.

The most consistent argument in Mead's writing is for the existence of a living esoteric tradition whose origins are to be found in Orphism and the ancient mystery cults of Greece and Egypt. In *Orpheus*, for example, Mead argues that Orphism lies behind all the mystery religions of antiquity—Pythagoreanism, Eleusis, and Mithraism are among those mentioned. Mead writes, as he says, "as a man convinced of the persistence of the Mysteries" through the ages, a belief Pound shared:

> In the construction of my skiff I have mainly combined the researches of Lobeck, who was a scholar and no mystic, with the writings of Taylor, who was half scholar, half mystic, and cemented all together with some information derived from H.P. Blavatsky, who was a mystic and no scholar. I write as a man convinced that the Mysteries have not gone

from the earth, but still exist and have their genuine adherents and initiators (*Orpheus* 195).

Pound, too, writes "as a man convinced that the Mysteries have not gone from the earth," that the "light from Eleusis" is the "inextinguishable source of beauty [which] persisted throughout the Middle Ages maintaining song in Provence, maintaining the grace of Kalenda Maya" (*SP* 53 and 58).

Though Pound incorporates or superimposes his own variations, in *The Cantos* and elsewhere he appeals to a "celestial" or esoteric tradition very much like the one we find in Mead. This tradition includes secret societies such as the Albigenses and the Templars — both of which preserved, according to both Pound and Mead, the true light of *gnosis* or wisdom. Pound appeals to this tradition in canto 90 (605) and elsewhere, presenting his own syncretist variation (for a fuller discussion see Chapter V). The associations presented there establish the outline of a "tradition" which turns out to be Pound's rediscovered, fictional "tradition," rising from the ancient rites of Delphi, Dodona, and Mithras through the medieval manifestations of the tradition in the Albigenses, the Knights Templar, and Erigena to its later appearances in John Heydon and Swedenborg. Even with the help of Mead's more comprehensive accounts of the tradition, Pound's associations often remain obscure; but the obscurity is part of the intention, since this is a secret tradition meant to be understood only by those who have undergone the proper initiation.

The clearest formulation of the supposed esoteric tradition is to be found in Mead's three-volume work, *Thrice-Greatest Hermes: Studies in Hellenistic Theosophy and Gnosis* (1906).[50] This book is "intended to serve ultimately as a small contribution to the preparation of the way leading towards a solution of the vast problems involved in the scientific study of the Origins of the Christian Faith" (*Thrice Greatest Hermes* I.xiii). Mead's study includes a discussion of the name Trismegistus, of the ancient tradition of wisdom contained in the Trismegistic (that is, Hermetic) literature, and of those texts that have survived under the general title of Trismegistic literature. He also discusses the history of the text. The unique manuscript was discovered by Michael Psellus in the eleventh century during a revival of Platonic studies in Byzantium. Gemistus Plethon visited Florence in 1438, bringing a Neoplatonic doctrine with him, and prompting the acquisition by Cosimo Medici of a Greek manuscript from Macedonia. Cosimo had Marsilio Ficino translate the text into Latin so that he could read it before he died. Ficino then articulated for the West Plethon's idea of a tradition of Wisdom to which Zoroaster, Hermes Trismegistus, Orpheus, Pythagoras, and Plato all belonged. The story of the passage of the importation of Greek thought into Italy and the revival of Hellenism appears in both *Guide to Kulchur* and *The Cantos*.[51] Pound attaches great importance to this story whose probable source was Mead.[52] Mead insists that there is "an unbroken line of tradition in which Gnosis and Mystery-teaching have been handed down through pre-Christian, Pagan and Jewish, and through Christian hands" (*Thrice-Greatest Hermes* III.213). Pound also believed in an unbroken tradition which he traced back to Eleusis (See "Terra Italica," *SP*, esp. 58-59).

Mead's major books, including *Fragments of a Faith Forgotten* and *Thrice-Greatest Hermes*, were published prior to Pound's arrival in London in late 1908. But his arrival did coincide with the serial publication between 1907 and 1909 of *Echoes from the Gnosis*, a multivolume series written by Mead and intended for the general reader. These slight volumes were part of a proselytizing campaign designed to draw people to Theosophy, and the topics under discussion represent a helpful outline of Mead's interests during the fifty-odd years of his career as an author.

There are two major interests apparent in *Echoes from the Gnosis*: palingenesis and the origins of Christianity. Mead claims that the *gnosis* of God is the "Perfect Perfection" which, unlike "the birth or *genesis* into matter, . . . [is] the essential birth or palingenesis, the means of re-becoming a pure spiritual being" (*The Hymns of Hermes* 51). These two concerns are constantly present in Mead's writing, regardless of whether he is focussing on Gnosticism (as in *Fragments of a Faith Forgotten*) or the spiritual significance of sacred dances in pagan and Christian rituals (as in *The Sacred Dance of Christendom*).

Echoes from the Gnosis itself deals with a variety of subjects, ranging from *The Gnosis of the Mind* to *The Mysteries of Mithra* and *The Chaldaean Oracles*. A total of eleven volumes were published under the general title of *Echoes from the Gnosis*, and there were other volumes which were projected but never appeared.[53] Pound was at least aware of this series, for he wrote to John Theobald nearly forty years after the series came out: "I think Mead must hv done 'nigh onter' 40 vols, of *Echoes*, and the *Quest* 1/4 ly must have run at least ten years??" (letter of 11 June 1957, *EP/JT* 36).

Speaking about symbols in volume 6, Mead says that "The true interpretation of symbols depends upon the capacity of the learner [*mystes*, initiate, neophyte] to make them alive, and to see them from as many points of view as possible. All true symbols should first of all be made solid, then made interpenetrable, then made alive, in-breathing and out-breathing" (*A Mithriac Ritual* 51-52). This idea is not far from Pound's contrast of symbolism to imagism: "Imagisme is not symbolism. The symbolists dealt in 'association,' that is, in a sort of allusion, almost of allegory. . . . [T]he imagiste's images have a variable significance, like the signs *a*, *b*, and *x* in algebra" (GB 84).

The idea of the vortex—which we have already seen in Upward—is also found in Mead's volume 8, where he speaks of "Vortices, Voragines, Whirl-swirls, Aeons, [and] Atoms" in discussing the ultimate mystery or "Paternal Depth" (*The Chaldaean Oracles*, I.54-58). In volume 9, Mead discusses the form gods take in a way which is echoed by Pound in "Religio, or the Child's Guide to Knowledge" as well as in various places in *The Cantos*: "In themselves the Gods have no forms, they are incorporeal; they, however, assume forms for the sake of mortals, as Proclus writes: 'For though we [the Gods] are incorporeal: *Bodies are allowed to self-revealed manifestations for your sakes* . . .'" (*The Chaldaean Oracles*, II.68-69; see *SP* 48-49). The idea of *hieros gamos* or sacred marriage which pervades Pound's prose and poetry is also found in these volumes, notably in volume 11 (*The Wedding-Song of Wisdom* 80-84). Many of these concepts can be found in several other sources and are, in any case, the common stock of many occult texts; but Mead's works conveniently illustrate Pound's conformity to such occult views, and he did at least know of them.

There is a consistent and unswerving programme or structure which guides Mead's work as a whole and which parallels the structure of occult history articulated in *The Spirit of Romance*, some of the early essays in *Selected Prose*, and in *Guide to Kulchur*. The same structure is latent in *The Cantos*.[54] There is a strong parallel or affinity between the fundamental metaphysical ideas of Pound, the theosophical synthesis of Mead, and the occult history which represents "what has really survived in European minds after several centuries of trituration of the ideas of the cabalists and hermetists of the Middle Ages and the Renaissance" (Saurat 69).

In all of Mead's works, a number of tantalizing bits exist which Pound might be echoing in *The Cantos*. His most important work next to *Thrice-Greatest Hermes* is probably *Fragments of a Faith Forgotten*, a study of the origins and development of Gnosticism and the origins of Christianity in the light of theosophical belief in the One Ur-religion, the common source of all wisdom-traditions, and the "undivided Light" of the initiation.[55]

Mead's works on Gnosticism provided Pound with a composite model of initiatory ritual structures. His *Doctrine of the Subtle Body* possibly provided the poet with an account of the form and nature of palingenesis, the soul's ascension from the body's dense matter in a second birth to another realm, a region of light. Published in 1919, *Subtle Body* contains an introduction and three essays which had already appeared in *The Quest* in 1909 and 1910.[56] In these Mead undertakes to summarize the ancient conception of *sensorium*, "the notion that the physical body of man is as it were the exteriorization of an invisible subtle embodiment of the life of the mind" (*The Subtle Body* 1). Although Pound's palingenetic imagery does not derive from Mead, the palingenesis expressed in *The Cantos* (especially in *Rock-Drill* and *Thrones*) conforms to Mead's discussion of the "radiant body." Mead describes palingenesis as an ascension of the soul from the hylic cosmos to an aetheric, crystalline brightness of the "radiant body" — and this is echoed in *Guide to Kulchur* ("sea crystalline and enduring, of the bright as it were molten glass that envelops us, full of light" [44]). This is also the movement traced in many parts of *The Cantos*, including cantos 17, 23, 47, and 90-91.

I began the discussion of the reflection of Mead's ideas in Pound's writing with an example of an idea that Pound said he got from Mead. I would like to end this discussion with an example of an unacknowledged borrowing, first noticed by Sharon Mayer Libera. In 1895 Mead published a new edition of Thomas Taylor's *Selected Works of Plotinus*, adding his own "Foreword" to Taylor's "Introduction." There Mead refers to the "rising psychic tide" of the period, and to the need for a universal spiritual fellowship. He suggests that the previously irreconcilable conflict between religion and science has produced a generation which longs and searches for reconciliation, and he concludes that the study of man's psychic nature is necessary for this reconciliation. He concludes that Plotinus, the most discerning philosopher of mysticism, therefore deserves a new hearing. Mead's closing remarks are of particular interest for the student of Pound:

> And that Plotinus was not a mere theorist, but did actually attain unto such a state of consciousness, is testified to by Porphyry. Plotinus also treats of this in the last book of the "Enneads," but, as he says, it can hardly be described (διο καὶ δύσφραστον τό θέαμα). Thus we reach the borderland of philosophy as we understand it. Beyond this region lie the realms of pure mysticism and the great unknown. And if any one can lead us by a safe path to those supernal realms, avoiding the many dangers of the way, and in a manner suited to western needs, Plotinus is a guide that can be highly recommended (xxxiv).

The role of Plotinus as psychopomp in canto 15, as Libera explains it, is Pound's adaptation of Mead's suggestion in the above passage:

> Pound bestows on Plotinus precisely the role of guide in Canto 15; there Plotinus leads Pound out from the Hell of London just as Virgil led Dante through the *Inferno*. Plotinus shows Pound a solid path through the hellish muck and brings him to a mystical vision of the sun at the threshold of the region of the saved. Thus, in a true sense, Pound

followed Mead's recommendation of Plotinus as a guide ("Ezra Pound's Paradise" 30).

Many of the echoes of Mead's work in *The Cantos* and in Pound's prose are just that: echoes for which it is difficult to find the exact source. More important than direct borrowings is the discovery that Theosophical ideas are constantly in the background of Pound's thinking, formulating his world view. Pound found in Mead the following: the "celestial tradition"; the belief in the persistence of the light from Eleusis through the middle ages and its resurfacing in the songs of Provence and Italy; the desire for a "pagan revival," leading to the gathering of the forgotten fragments of ancient mystery rites so as to recapture a polytheistic consciousness which is now all but lost to modern man; the expectation for the dawn of a "New Age"; and palingenesis.

How, then, can we reconcile the mild ridicule directed by Pound towards "Old Krore" [Mead] in *Guide to Kulchur* and *The Cantos* with his serious interest in "things occult"?[57] I think that Pound's vacillations and evasions constitute attempts to put some distance between himself and the foolishness and charlatanry of those around him (including Yeats and Mead) who were participants in the psychic experiments and tricks common in occult circles of the period. In his own mind he could — or he believed he could — always distinguish between the merits and the absurdities of mysticism and occultism. When Pound speaks, therefore, about myth in terms of "delightful psychic experience" and says that he knows people to whom such experiences occur, he is telling us that he is familiar with the occult community of London and that "These things are for [him, too,] *real*" (*SR* 92).

Notes

1. Even James Longenbach, who manages in *The Stone Cottage* to uncover much about Pound's occult activities and friendships, maintains that it is only the penchant for deliberate obscurity and eclecticism that Pound takes from the occult. Angela Elliott, on the other hand, correctly remarks that in focussing on the aesthetic level instead of the religious significance of Pound's work the critic risks missing that work's principal meaning (157). Elliott's remarks have been anticipated by Clark Emery who, so far as I know, was the first to stress the significance of the religious element in *The Cantos*. Here is one of Emery's typical remarks: "In short, since, in Pound's opinion, a culture without a religious faith is impossible and since the *Cantos* represents a guide to culture, the work must be considered a religious poem" (110).
2. As already mentioned, Stock remarks that Pound was "much interested in the subject [occult and old religions] before he arrived in London" (*Poet in Exile* 21).
3. James J. Wilhelm speculates that Pound and Miss Heyman may have met in Utica, New York or thereabouts: "My ... siftings through press clippings at the Lincoln Center branch of the New York Public Library disclosed some interesting details. In

1904, when Pound was studying in the 'cultural wasteland' of northern New York State, Miss Heyman, triumphantly returning from Europe, gave a celebrated concert in Utica, where Pound went on weekends to get away from nearby Hamilton College. It is almost certain that he met her then because of an inscription in the Thomas L. Beddoes' book of that period (if he did not meet her earlier through his mother's musicales or W.B. Smith)" ("Addenda and Corrigenda for *The American Roots of Ezra Pound*" 242).

4. Stephen J. Adams also notes that Miss Heyman's book, *The Relation of Archaic to Ultramodern Music* (1921), was an expanded version of a 1916 lecture series and thus is closer to the period of her friendship with Pound. He adds that, "Readers of Pound will find it full of echoes and references, direct and indirect, to Pound and Poundian currents of thought.... Her entire approach of finding precedents for modern techniques in the archaic and exotic (skipping over everything between) is Poundian, and more novel then than now" (16).

5. Patricia Hutchins, using a letter from Pound dated 27 September 1957, writes that "When asked who used to come there [Kensington flat] Pound wrote, 'Actually in the front room, Florence Farr reading Tagore, D.H. Lawrence missing train for Croydon,' and spending the night in 'sort of armchair convertible to cot.' Then again, 'Let's see, actually IN the room, Aldington, H.D., Brigit [Patmore], once or twice [Paul] Selver, Skip Cannell and Kitty on the ground floor' [as temporary tenants perhaps] ..." (69). The important point for this part of the discussion is that Pound remembered Miss Heyman's presence in his London residence almost fifty years later.

6. In fact, Pound's *A Quinzaine for This Yule* is dedicated to Miss Heyman (the dedication runs: "To the Aube of the West Dawn"). "Nel Biancheggiar," a poem included in *Quinzaine*, was first published in the London *Evening Standard and St. James's Gazette* (8 December 1908), under the title "For Katherine Ruth Heyman. (After One of Her Venetian Concerts)." Also contained in this collection is "Aube of the West Dawn. Venetian June." Both of these poems can be found in *The Collected Early Poems of Ezra Pound*. Besides the dedication of these early poems to her, Pound also mentions Miss Heyman in the *Pisan Cantos* (76/461).

7. For more information see Guest (225) and Friedman's *Psyche Reborn: The Emergence of H.D.*, especially chapter 6 ("Initiations: Biographical Roots of Occult Influence"). Although she mentions the list of mystical books in *End to Torment*, Friedman does not stress Pound's place in H.D.'s occult education. She thinks that certain psychic experiences which H.D. claimed to have had at Corfu (ca. 1920) "probably provided [her] with the greatest impetus to begin serious study of esoteric traditions in the twenties. W.B. Yeats, with his poetic blend of theosophy and myth may have had some influence on H.D. But Madame Blavatsky and the Theosophical Society, major influences on Yeats's occult interests, held little or no attraction for H.D. as she first delved into the occult. Probably more significant than Yeats's example was the general interest in occult phenomena among literary people in London during the twenties" (160). As shown by my discussion, I think that Pound is a much more probable source for H.D.'s "delving" into the occult than either Yeats or any other London "literary people" of the period.

8. It is possible that when Pound says that "the Dant[e]-Swed[enborg] hook-up may have filtered thru footnotes" he is thinking of an essay by Rev. Arthur E. Beilby

entitled "Two Other-World Explorers: Dante and Swedenborg," which appeared in the same volume of *The Quest* as his "Psychology and Troubadours."

9. Surette, in "The Birth of Modernism," a work-in-progress, provides a detailed account of Rossetti's and Valli's place within the history of western occultism.

10. In *A History of White Magic*, Gareth Knight identifies Yogi Ramacharaka as W.W. Atkinson, a successful writer of the New Thought movement (with his *Secrets of Mental Magic*), "who also wrote a series of books on popularised forms of yoga under the pseudonym of Yogi Ramacharaka" (168). Atkinson was associate editor of *New Thought*, a Chicago-based periodical, and wrote a number of other New Thought books, including *Thought-Force in Business and Everyday Life* (1900) and *The New Law of the New Thought* (1903), both published by the Chicago, Illinois-based "The Psychic Research Company." William French and Timothy Materer, in "Far Flung Vortices & Ezra's 'Hindoo' Yogi," also comment on "Yogi Ramacharaka"; they point out that Pound refers to Ramacharaka's books in his footnote to the "Plotinus" sonnet (41).

11. In his "Note Precedent to 'La Fraisne,'" Pound quotes from Janus of Basel: "'When the soul is exhausted of fire, then doth the spirit return unto its primal nature and there is upon it a peace great and of the woodland...'" (*CEP* 8). This is one version of the emanationist theory of *ekpyrosis*; another version of the same theory appears, as noted in Chapter I, in *Guide to Kulchur* (124).

The Sinistrari text was discovered in 1872 by Isidore Liseux, a French bibliopole, and was originally printed with a French translation in 1875; the Latin text was reprinted by Liseux in 1879 with an English translation. Pound summarizes Sinistrari's argument: "Referendum for contrast. 'Daemonalitas' of the Rev. Father Sinistrari of Ameno (1600 circ). 'A treatise wherein is shown that there are in existence on earth rational creatures besides man, endowed like him with a body and soul, that are born and die like him, redeemed by our Lord Jesus-Christ, and capable of receiving salvation or damnation.' Latin and English text. pub. Liseux, Paris, 1879" (*CEP* 8).

Montague Summers has also translated *Demoniality* into English. He says that the first English translation "is something worse than indifferent. Nonetheless, probably as being the only available English version of an important treatise, the book has become excessively rare" (v).

12. A further point is that the name "Dryad" he chose for H.D. is probably taken from the occult works brought to him by Miss Heyman. In his introduction to his translation of Sinistrari's *De Daemonialitate*, Montague Summers notes that Sinistrari's title suggests that the creatures being described in his book, which have a corporeity "far more tenuous and subtile than the body of man," are also called incubis or succubis. Summers goes on to say that "the demi-gods of Greece and Rome, satyrs, fauns, pans, nymphs, oreads, *hamadryads*, and all the vast company of nature-deities, were, in truth, these incubi and succubi" (xxvi, italics mine). It is tempting to suppose that Pound dubbed H.D. "dryad" on the authority of Sinistrari's text that we know he read at about the same time.

13. For a thorough treatment of Yeats's influence on Pound with regards to occultism see Longenbach (esp. *Stone Cottage* 48-50, 226-36, and 240-46).

14. For more information see Josephine Johnson's *Florence Farr: Bernard Shaw's 'New Woman.'*

15. It was Pound who persuaded Olivia Shakespear to translate parts of *Le Comte de Gabalis*, which he then published in the *Egoist* from 16 March to 1 June 1914. For

the importance of this text for Pound, as well as for his reading of other occult texts during the period under discussion, see Longenbach's *Stone Cottage* (87-92).
16. In "The Secret Society of Modernism" (as well as in "The Order of Brothers Minor" and *Stone Cottage*), Longenbach examines many of the same issues presented here. Though we are in general agreement as to what Pound means by "symbolism," Longenbach concludes, as already mentioned in the Preface, that "It is finally not the subject matter but the elitist attitude of occult literature that was most important for Pound" (117). I, on the other hand, argue that the subject matter was also important to Pound.
17. Unpublished letter to Patricia Hutchins, Patricia Hutchins Collection, British Museum, Add. 57725. My remarks to the Pound-Hutchins correspondence are based on notes taken by Leon Surette in 1987.
18. With different emphasis, the following Pound critics have done this job: Schneidau (118-26); Davie (63-72); Bush (91-102); Surette, *Light* (192-95); Knox; Moody; Bell (225-29); Levenson (68-74); and Elliott, "The Word Comprehensive: Gnostic Light in *The Cantos*." With the exception of Schneidau, Surette, and Elliott, these scholars follow Davie's example and focus on Upward's espousal of many views which parallel Pound's London aesthetics.
19. The details about Orage's life in the following discussion are taken from Mairet's *A.R. Orage: A Memoir*. For an excellent discussion of Orage during his New Age period see John Finlay's *Social Credit: The English Origins*. As indicated by the title of his book, Finlay is more interested in economic theory; but he does not fail to give a rather full picture of the intellectual milieu of Orage's circle which does not skirt its occult provenance.
20. James Webb alludes briefly to the connection between Pound's economic and occult interests, and Leon Surette goes much further in explaining the link between underconsumption economics and Theosophy which would be part of the intellectual milieu Pound found in *The New Age* circle (Webb, *The Occult Establishment* 116-17; Surette, "Economics and Eleusis"). Pound's occult friends who stimulated his interest in myth and those who stimulated his interest in economics — the *Quest* and the *New Age* groups respectively — were in fact not two distinct sets but rather a single set. That is, they were all occultists.
21. In *A.R. Orage: A Memoir*, Philip Mairet speaks of Orage's attraction to Theosophy in these terms: "Orage, like many others of his generation, was fascinated by the 'Secret Doctrine' — that cosmic chaos of colossal symbols lit by auroral glimmerings of magic. But theosophy also gave him the Bhagavad Gita and introduced him to the Mahabharata — vital and permanent influences in his mental life . . ." (16).
22. Patricia Hutchins relates one instance of Pound's presence in Orage's *The New Age* offices during 1912 when he was a newcomer to Orage's circle (108-109).
23. The best study to date on Orage and Nietzsche is "A.R. Orage," in *Nietzsche in England 1890-1914: The Growth of a Reputation* by David S. Thatcher. Thatcher notes the occult provenance of Orage's beliefs and remarks that "for Alfred Richard Orage Nietzsche was above all a mystic whose affinities with the mystical tradition were beyond all question" (219). Though he sees Pound as a participant in the social, political, and cultural ambience of Orage's New Age circle, Thatcher has almost nothing to say about Pound and Nietzsche.
24. Regarding Pound's introduction to Orage, Robert Schultz writes that Pound met Orage upon his return from a trip to Italy and Germany and goes on to say that "it is

probably Hulme who introduced him to A.R. Orage, editor of *The New Age*. The Introduction probably took place at one of Hulme's 'Frith Street evenings,' held in the home of Mrs. Ethel Kibblewhite in Soho" (461). For biographical details of Pound's London years see Robert Schultz, "A Detailed Chronology of Ezra Pound's London Years, 1908-1920, Part One: 1908-1914" and "Part Two: 1915-1920." Of course, either one of these men (Flint or Hulme) could have been the one who performed the introductions. Both of them belonged to the "Secession Club" (which also included F.W. Tancred, Florence Farr, Edward Storer, Joseph Campbell, and occasionally T.D. Fitzgerald). In addition, both Flint and Hulme wrote for Orage's *The New Age*. Regardless of who made the introductions, Orage invited Pound to contribute to his periodical and thus "The Seafarer" (30 November 1911) and the series of essays entitled "I Gather the Limbs of Osiris" (30 November to 22 February 1912) appeared in *The New Age*; these were followed by many others, and this magazine was instrumental in ensuring Pound's survival (he was one of the few paid contributors) during some rather difficult years in London.

25. This difference in literary taste is even more unmistakably pronounced in Pound's "Obituary: A.R. Orage": "During 21 years, I think that Orage never admired a single author whom I admired, and that, in my own work, he liked only that part which differentiates me from the living writers whom I have respected or eulogised. The sole exception was, during the last year or so, Carlos Williams. I mean that our 23 years' friendship [1911-34] was a friendship of literary differences and never one difference concealed" (*SP* 437-38).

26. For an exposition of Pound's echoing of Orage's Nietzschean ideas see Surette's "Economics and Eleusis."

27. Though Pound would not have been interested, someone else, whose name is closely connected with Pound's and Orage's, was attracted to Mitrinovic's brand of occultism. I am referring to Major Douglas. When, in the early 1930s, Mitrinovic founded the New Britain movement ("pledged to a functional society, guilds, social credit, the welfare system, a European Federation, Rudolf Steiner's Threefold Commonwealth, and a restored Christianity"), Major Douglas was one of the people involved.

28. Orage influenced a number of groups during his stay in New York. In terms of literary criticism, his influence was important upon the Waldo Frank group (which included Hart Crane, Kenneth Burke, Gorham Munson, and Jean Toomer) and the editors of *The Little Review*, Margaret Anderson and Jane Heap. Most of these people visited Fontainebleau. I have found no evidence of such visits by Crane and Burke.

29. Letter to his father dated 28 June 1921 (BRBL). And later, in a letter to his mother he talks about Orage's submersion in "the Gurdjieff Ouspensky hash," indicates that the two men had not met during the latter's stay at Fontainebleau (1922-23), and suggests that his parents could meet Orage in the U.S.A. (letter dated 4 February 1924 [BRBL]).

30. There are only two references to Mead in Pound's letters to Anderson (mentioned below); and Pound's letters to Cravens contain a few references to both Mead and Theosophy (see *Ezra Pound and Margaret Cravens* passim). The other correspondences mentioned here contain numerous references to Mead and occult subjects.

31. In "Light as Image" Angela Elliott covers some of this same ground. She aptly stresses the significance of Mead's studies in Gnosticism and Theosophical subjects as probable sources for Pound's own idiosyncratic understanding of these arcane

areas of research and experience (134 and passim). See also Elliott's reworking of this topic in "The Word Comprehensive: Gnostic Light in *The Cantos*."

32. For the relation between Yeats and Mead see Virginia Moore, *The Unicorn: William Butler Yeats' Search for Reality* (esp. 105-12).

33. Elliott was the first to note Pound's numerous references to Mead in his letters to his parents ("Light as Image" 133-34). The channels of communication between the two men were open, Elliott also notes, until at least 1928 (Mead died in 1933) when the theosophist wrote to Dorothy Shakespear, recommending to Pound Valli's *Il linguaggio segreto di Dante* (134).

34. The reference to Mead is preceded by one to Henry James: "Henry James and I glanced at each other across the same carpet, about 2 weeks previous[ly]." Clearly, Pound is trying to impress his parents with name-dropping, as he does in many of his letters dating from this period—that he includes Mead in the list of London personalities worth being acquainted with goes a long way toward proving his intense interest in the theosophist's work.

35. The letter continues in this fashion: "... Tho' I personally don't see why we shouldn't enjoy paradise when we get there instead of rattling the whole thing off & starting over again, however there by hyper-celestial heresies, & Heirotheos is certainly more visible than the Pseudo-Dionysus. Before embarking on these affairs, I advise you to fortify your mind with the simplicities of Aristotle & Aquinas."

36. Pound seems to have attended the lectures at Mead's invitation and to have been aware that he was the chief beneficiary of his exchanges with the editor of *The Quest*. In an 11 January 1913 letter to his mother he writes: "Mead has sent me a ticket for his lectures, as usual. I get rather the better of the exchange ..." (BRBL).

37. As Stephen J. Adams has informed me, Pound met Rummel in the United States before he reached London in 1908. Rummel, as Dorothy's recollection of him in this context shows, also had strong occult interests.

38. Pound's familiarity with Mead's works is also made clear in a 1913 letter to his mother in which he seems to be responding to a request from his father: "He [Homer] can get any number of Mead's translations and books from the library or he can subscribe to the Quest. I haven't any to send him" (BRBL).

39. The editors of *EP/DS* point to Mead's *The World-Mystery* as the source of the incantation (116); but other works by Mead, including *Pistis Sophia* (105 and 295-96), are alternate possibilities. Peter Hamilton Laurie was the first to recognize that Pound's source for "this possible Eleusinian mantra" may have been Mead ("The Poet and the Mysteries" 103-104).

40. Jiddu Krishnamurti is the Indian theosophist who founded the World Order of Star in England with Annie Besant and who was pronounced, in 1925, the new messiah, a claim he repudiated in 1928.

41. Pound's complex attitude toward Mead is also in evidence in his letters to Margaret Anderson. In a 7 May 1917 letter to Anderson he includes the theosophist's name and address in a list of people to whom the May copy of *The Little Review* should be sent: "G.R.S. Mead Esq. 47 Campden Hill Rd. London W.8. (ask him to send you 'The Quest' as an exchange, but dont believe anything he says in it. He gets one interesting article every five years. sometimes more often.)" (*Pound/The Little Review* 36). Despite the tone of condescension, this note suggests Pound's familiarity with the contents of *The Quest*. In a letter written some twenty-six years later, Pound identifies the "psychic tide" he had experienced during his London years: "London

BOMbarded with mystics, Blavatsky, Quest Society, Echoes from the Gnosis (GRS Mead) Wisdom of the East Series, [A.R.] Orage an the unreadable Mahabharatta, etc." (letter dated 20 September 1953; *Pound/The Little Review* 313). Interestingly, the tone of condescension is absent from another letter from the 1950s that deals with the same subject. In a letter to Olivia Rossetti Agresti he recommends Mead's *Apollonius of Tyana*: "Put Helen [Olivia's sister Helen Angeli] onto Apollonius of Tyana / if yu haven't time to read either Mead or Philostratus, re that most estimable and unkikified character" (letter of 17 August 1954, BRBL) As well, Giovanni Giovannini's letters to Pound ca. 1956 reveal Pound's continued interest in Mead. Here is a passage from a Giovannini letter dated 6 November 1956: "... Your last letter: I'm sorry we don't have Mead's Fragments of a Forgotten Faith (nor his The Gnostic John the Baptizer, or Quests Old & New, which discusses ancient Chinese mystical matters). Perhaps Yale may help. Yes he did do a Plotinus (which I happen to have): an ed. of selections of Thomas Taylor's trans. of P., with preface and bibliog. I'll bring it down. In case you don't know: T. Taylor among the Romantics was anima naturaliter neoplatonica et pagana, tried to revive heathen ritual and polytheism, was supposed to have deeply affected Shelley. Yeats seems to have been wrapped up in him at the turn of the century" (Giovannini mss., Lilly Library, Indiana University, Bloomington, Indiana).

42. It is of interest to note that Levenson mentions Hulme's and Lewis's participation in the Quest Society Lectures at the Kensington Town Hall without mentioning that this was one of the centres of theosophical activities at the time.

43. See the following studies: Rudolph, *Gnosis: The Nature and History of Gnosticism*; Jonas, *The Gnostic Religion*; and the article on "Gnosticism" in Eliade, ed., *Encyclopedia of Religion*.

44. Most of my information about Mead's biography and his view of the problems of the Theosophical Society at the point when he left to form his own group comes from this essay.

45. Charles Webster Leadbeater (1847-1923) was a British clergyman and occultist who played a major role in the history of the Theosophical Society. From time to time he was accused of engaging in homosexual activities involving young students.

46. In a footnote we find that this first article of *The Quest* is "the substance of an address delivered by the President [Mead] at the Inaugural Meeting of the Quest Society, at Kensington Town Hall, London, W., on Thursday, March 11, 1909" (29).

47. Some firm evidence of Pound's knowledge of *The Quest* articles is his later use in *The Cantos* of Mead's essays on Dance and Christendom. For a discussion of this see Colin McDowell, "'The Toys ... at Auxerre': Canto 77."

48. Pound used Conybeare's edition of Philostratus in writing canto 96, and he probably knew of this edition even before the appearance of the review in *The Quest* (July 1913), since Dorothy mentions it in a February 1913 letter (*EP/DS* 188). Conybeare often appeared in *The Quest*. Conybeare's Loeb edition is accepted as legitimate scholarship, but Mead's book on Apollonius (*Apollonius of Tyana*) is not. While Pound scholars have kept these works distinct, *The Quest* review suggests that they were almost a collaboration. Gardner's book, which would also have been of considerable interest to Pound, is praised by the reviewer for placing Dante's epic in the context of a mystical tradition and for coming to the conclusion that the end of Dante's mysticism is "to make spiritual experience a force for the reformation of mankind." This book, then, reflects Pound's own faith in a spiritual reformation of

humankind. Finally, Underhill's books might well have attracted Pound's attention, since we know that both Dorothy and T.S. Eliot admired her study, *Mysticism* (1911), reviewed in volume 2 of *The Quest*.

49. For example, see Hugh Kenner's *Gnomon: Essays in Contemporary Literature* for a discussion of the importance of Mead's *Apollonius of Tyana* (1901), a critical commentary upon Philostratus's *Life of Apollonius of Tyana*, to Pound's treatment of the first-century A.D. sage in cantos 91 and 94 (295-96); Elliott's discussion of Pound's reliance on theosophical concepts of the "inner light" for the light imagery of *The Cantos* ("Light as Image" passim); Surette's discussion of Pound's absorption of Gnostic theology through Mead (*Light* 60-63); and Oderman's discussion of Pound's use of the concept of *augoeides*, which he borrows from Mead's *The Subtle Body* (1919), in the later cantos (72-75).

50. In *The Unicorn: William Butler Yeats' Search for Reality*, Virginia Moore argues that it was Yeats's "study" of Mead's *Thrice-Greatest Hermes* that consolidated his knowledge of the Western occult tradition.

51. See *Guide to Kulchur* 45, 160, 224, 263, and 313; and cantos 7, 23, 26, 83, and 98.

52. The centrality of the tradition and Pound's reverence for Plethon are most clearly expressed in *Guide to Kulchur* (224-25). The same tradition is wonderfully captured in the opening lines of canto 23, where Pound either mentions the names or uses quotations to allude to most of the Neoplatonists who appear in the above passage. (For an analysis of canto 23 see Chapter IV.)

53. These are the titles of the individual volumes: 1. *The Gnosis of the Mind*; 2. *The Hymns of Hermes*; 3. *The Vision of Aridaeus*; 4. *The Hymn of Jesus*; 5. *The Mysteries of Mithra*; 6. *A Mithriac Ritual*; 7. *The Gnostic Crucifixion*; 8. *The Chaldean Oracles*, I; 9. *The Chaldean Oracles*, II; 10. *The Hymn of the Robe of Glory*; and 11. *The Wedding-Song of Wisdom*. Among those volumes which were projected but never appeared are the following: "The Hymn of the Soul," "Some Orphic Fragments," and "The Words of Heraclitus."

54. For a detailed discussion of this structure (which I call *katabasis/dromena/epopteia*) as it appears in *The Cantos* see Chapter IV.

55. Among Mead's other works are the following: *Simon Magus: An Essay* (1892); *Orpheus* (1896); *Pistis Sophia: A Gnostic Gospel* (1896); *Apollonius of Tyana* (1901), a critical commentary upon Philostratus's *Life of Apollonius of Tyana*; *World Mystery* (1907); *Quests Old and New* (1913), a collection of thirteen papers, most of which had already been published in *The Quest*, dealing with the philosophy of the Far East, Gnosticism, and typical movements of contemporary thought; *The Gospels and the Gospel* (1902); *Did Jesus Live 100 B.C.* (1903); *The Theosophy of the Vedas* (1905); *The Gnostic John the Baptizer* (1924); and *The Sacred Dance of Christendom* (1926). Like other occultists, Mead was prolific and voluminous; unlike the majority of other occultists, however, he was also an erudite scholar of deep understanding.

56. For more details see my discussion of *The Subtle Body* in Chapter V.

57. Pound's mild ridicule of Mead always appears within the context of his ridicule of Madame Blavatsky. See *Guide to Kulchur* (225-26) and *The Cantos* (74/446). In one of his letters to John Theobald, Pound relates an anecdote involving Blavatsky, and again directs some mild ridicule toward Mead:

> ... Blavatsky, OBjective, as per sitting at table digging into juice beefsteak / disciples on carrot diet: "Ah, chilDren, my CHILdren, how many of you have succeeded ... in ... BEgetting vegeTARian children?"

Also her pulling Mead's leg to see whether M/ thinking or swallowing (11 June 1957, 36).

The editors of the Pound-Theobald correspondence observe that "Pound's anecdotes (e.g. Madame Blavatsky as a Gertrude Stein figure), rich in themselves, mask one of the enduring interests of his life, so evident in the visionary traditions invoked in *The Cantos*" (30).

IV

Palingenesis: *Katabasis* / *Dromena* / *Epopteia*

1. Palingenesis: *Katabasis* / *Dromena* / *Epopteia*

In the foregoing pages, I have endeavoured to accomplish the following tasks: (1) to describe some of Pound's ideas which may be termed occult; (2) to trace the general outline and describe the most important moments of efflorescence of the wisdom tradition of which the modern occult is essentially a development; (3) to discover the roots of Pound's occultism; and (4) to place Pound within the London occult milieu of the first two decades of the twentieth century. In the balance of this study, the results of the foregoing discussion are brought to bear on a small number of selected cantos (17, 23, 47, and 90-91) with a view to establishing the importance of Hellenistic "religious" thought to *The Cantos*. I propose to support the claim that *The Cantos* are structured on the model of a cultic initiation. This claim is based on the double-reading technique outlined earlier, and stresses the esoteric sense of the epic as opposed to the exoteric senses such as the motifs of journey, Odyssean *nostos*, Dantesquean dream-narrative, or periplum. Scholars have put forward one or another of these exoteric senses as primary, or fundamental, or ubiquitous without recognizing that they are all susceptible of carrying the same esoteric sense. It is that esoteric sense that I hope to articulate in the following pages.

Of course, we do not need to be reminded that in dealing with such a complex and exacting poem as *The Cantos*, one would be foolish to contend that any *one* reading should be privileged over all others. Michael Bernstein prudently asserts that Pound is ultimately unable to make his

---

The notes to Chapter IV are found on pp. 152-58.

poem "cohere" because he cannot bring the mythical and historical elements into harmony. He cautions that we cannot "aestheticize" the poem without misconstruing and misrepresenting its very nature: "History and politics are both present in *The Cantos* — indeed their presence is one of the poem's greatest strengths as well as a source of grievous weakness — and it is more damaging to Pound's intentions to deny their relevance than to confront openly their implications" (33). I argue that *The Cantos* are intended as the epic of the New Age, an argument that privileges the poem's *mythos* because it most clearly expresses the esoteric sense which provides the poem with such coherence as it has.

The Cantos appeal to a historical fantasy, current in Kensington theosophical and occult circles, according to which *gnosis* survived from antiquity in the minds of enlightened individuals and in certain secret societies. Most particularly, *The Cantos* reflect the occult belief in the imminence of a New Age prophesied by occultists at the turn of the century. Indeed, it would appear that the poem was to be the epic expression of the New Age, much as Virgil's *Aeneid* expressed the Augustan Empire.[1]

Beginning with a *nekuia*, an ancient equivalent of the modern séance, the poem moves through history in an arbitrary and seemingly haphazard manner. Like the souls summoned by Odysseus in the *nekuia*, Pound "calls up" the souls of enlightened individuals, both dead and alive, and it is these souls which populate his epic. His catalogue of enlightened souls includes Sigismundo Malatesta (who dominates *A Draft of XXX Cantos*), Thomas Jefferson, John Adams, Gemistus Plethon, Apollonius of Tyana, and even Benito Mussolini. Curiously and erroneously, Pound chose Mussolini as the Aeneas of the New Age. After the celebration of Jefferson and the account of the failure of the American Revolution in *Eleven New Cantos XXXI-XLI* (1934), Pound deals with the parallels between American and Italian history in *The Fifth Decad of Cantos XLII-LI* (1937). The increased attention to the Italian dictator and modern Italy is a consequence of Pound's admiration for Mussolini, declared unequivocally in *Jefferson and/or Mussolini* (1935), and reflects an apparent intention to celebrate modern Italy as the fulfillment, the new renaissance, of his historical fantasy.

The events of World War II did not shake Pound's faith in Mussolini but forced him, nonetheless, to alter his plan to celebrate Italy as the manifestation of his occult vision. *The Pisan Cantos* become a dirge for the demise of the New Age. Mussolini appears in the opening lines of this section of the poem not as a defeated leader but as a martyr, another misunderstood and repressed enlightened soul in the line of Manes, the founder of Manicheanism:

> The enormous tragedy of the dream in the peasant's bent
> shoulders
> Manes? Manes was tanned and stuffed,
> Thus Ben and la Clara *a Milano*
>   by the heels at Milano
> That maggots shd/ eat the dead bullock
> DIGONOS, δίγονος, but the twice crucified
>   where in history will you find it? (74/425).

Instead of building a real city, Pound is forced to return to the city of Dioce, the imagined place variously echoed in the first thirty cantos. With *The Pisan Cantos*, then, the poem's perspective shifts from historical survey to lyrical meditation. In the last two installments of the poem, *Rock Drill* (1955) and *Thrones* (1959), Pound returns to the Mediterranean and Chinese cultures while searching for analogues to the imagined New Age and its illuminated souls.

Although the events of history did not allow him to carry out his intended programme within his poem, Pound never abandoned it. When he could no longer claim the historical reality of modern Italy as a manifestation of his belief in a New Age, he internalized the paradigm and elaborated on it, creating a New Age of the mind. The esoteric sense displaces the exoteric vehicles. Pound shifts from history to historical fantasy; from the world to the mind; from the exoteric journey to an esoteric palingenetic *mythos*. The palingenetic paradigm is the esoteric sense of the historical and narrative patterns, but it, too, has an esoteric side: the palingenetic process of soul-making, the *poiesis* or "making" of enlightened souls.

This palingenetic paradigm has three stages: κατάβασις / δρόμενα / ἐποπτεία (*katabasis / dromena / epopteia*). This palingenetic pattern is elucidated in cantos which best illustrate Pound's use of initiation rituals. Though in this study I concentrate on individual cantos, I believe that the model works for *The Cantos* as a whole.

As stressed in Chapter I, the poem does not so much describe or report on an initiation rite as it enacts an initiation for the reader. The reader of *The Cantos* is intended to undergo the confusion, disorientation, and *catechesis* of the initiand; in doing so, it is hoped that he will arrive at a revelation and be transformed from a participant in the mysteries (*mystes*) to an *epoptes*, one who "has seen" or experienced the ineffable secret. The act of reading the poem is meant, then, to constitute the initiation. The "lyric" or "paradisal" moments in the poem embody the revelation that accompanies the initiation. Although the poem draws on the language, *dramatis personae*, symbols, and images of the mystery cults in its re-enactment, it is not to be expected that any particular rite—such as that of Eleusis—will be faithfully followed.

With few exceptions, scholars have failed to take notice of the poem's initiatory nature, and the cantos selected for examination here have not received adequate attention.[2] Canto 17 has received little, if any, attention—except for Libera's identification of the Porphyry source and Surette's discussion of it in terms of the Eleusinian Mysteries. Canto 23 has been largely ignored, even though I think that it is one of the focal cantos, bringing together, as it does, many of the strands of the first thirty cantos. Dekker and Pearlman among others have done painstaking analyses of canto 47, but no scholar has emphasized the importance of the *hieros gamos* or ritual copulation, which is at the very centre of this canto, as the particular exoteric form that the initiation rite takes in *The Cantos*. Cantos 90 and 91 have been described by Libera as "the most mystical of the *Cantos*" (117), and much has been done to elucidate the difficulties these cantos present for the reader.[3] But Terrell's clues concerning the mystical symbolism of these cantos have yet to be taken up (*Companion*, II.546-50)—and this is an aspect which my discussion seeks to correct.

I would like to turn now to a brief discussion of what I call the palingenetic structure of *The Cantos*. *Palingenesis* or rebirth is the process of soul-making. The term is also used to describe a tripartite ritual structure. *Katabasis* means descent and constitutes an initial stage of the initiation. Often represented as an actual descent, it takes the form of a sexual descent or *hieros gamos*—hence the proliferation of copulative imagery in *The Cantos*. *Dromena* signifies the stage of wandering and confusion suffered by every *mystes* before the *epopteia*, the final stage and the *telos* of the palingenetic process. *Epopteia* means the state of "having seen" and is a general term for revelation. It is exoterically represented by *metamorphosis* or theophany. Metamorphosis exoterically expresses the moment of sudden change, the moment of revelation, the *epopteia*. Metamorphosis is thus the outward expression of the completed palingenesis in *epopteia* whose sense is the *soteria*, the state of salvation reached by the *mystes* once he has achieved the *gnosis* or revelation—that is, once he has been transformed from *mystes* to *epoptes*.[4]

This tripartite structure of *katabasis / dromena / epopteia* fits well with Pound's outline of the "main scheme" of *The Cantos* which he sent to his father in 1927:

> ... Live man goes down into world of Dead [*katabasis*]
> ... The "repeat in history" [*dromena*]
> ... The "magic moment" or moment of metamorphosis, bust thru

from quotidien [*sic*] into "divine or permanent world." Gods, etc. [*epopteia*] (*L* 210).[5]

This "main scheme" explains Pound's choice of Book 11 of the *Odyssey*, the *Nekuia* or calling forth of the dead, as the starting point of his "tale of the tribe" — even though, as I will explain shortly, the tag "Live man goes down into the world of dead" is not an accurate description of what happens in the *Odyssey*. But Pound's "main scheme" is also useful because it clearly suggests *The Cantos'* palingenetic nature — that is, a *katabasis* or encounter with death within a transcendent or palingenetic framework with the ultimate purpose of achieving the *epopteia*, the all-encompassing term for the state of *gnosis*, a state whose outward sign is the *hieros gamos* and the "moment of metamorphosis."

Kay Davis, correctly I think, sees the Eleusinian rites implied in Pound's outline (17-28). Beginning with the *Homeric Hymn to Demeter* and by way of Leon Surette's discussion, in *A Light from Eleusis*, of Plutarch's disclosures about the Eleusinian rites, Davis outlines the major features of the Eleusinian myth, the story of Demeter and her daughter Koré or Persephone. I have already discussed the Eleusinian mysteries in some detail in Chapter II of this study. To summarize: the *mystes* or initiate takes part in a *pompe* or procession which brings him from Athens to a dark, underground chamber in Eleusis (*katabasis*). There he experiences the *dromena* or wandering and confusion before achieving the *epopteia*, exoterically represented as the illumination or sudden awareness of brilliant light and esoterically understood as the *arrheton*, an ineffable secret equated with an inexpressible awareness of, and union with, the *theos* or *nous*.

Pound's understanding of initiation rites was shaped on the models in Homer's *Odyssey*, the *Homeric Hymn to Demeter*, Virgil's *Aeneid*, Plutarch's *Lives*, the Egyptian *Book of the Dead*, Ovid's *Metamorphoses*, Dante's *Divine Comedy*, and various Gnostic, Hermetic, and Neoplatonic writings. We should add the commentaries Pound read — from Porphyry to Péladan and Mead. Pound read Homer, Ovid, and Dante in the Neoplatonic and occult manner as mystical allegories or stories of divine revelation clothed in a mythical framework.

One example of an influential occult allegorization of Odysseus's descent that Pound probably knew is found in the long footnote Thomas Taylor appends to his translation of Porphyry's "Cave of the Nymphs":

> ... the allegory, respecting the descent of Ulysses into the infernal regions, which, exclusive of its connection with Ulysses, contains ... some of the greatest arcana of the Grecian theology. As it respects Ulysses, it appears to me to insinuate his flying to the assistance of nec-

romancy, in order to know the result of the ills with which he is surrounded, through the anger of his natal daemon. Hence Tiresias is nothing more than a departed spirit evocated [sic] by magical art, for the purpose of disclosing the secrets of futurity, and informing Ulysses how he may return to the true empire of his mind (Taylor 327-28).

Mead also speaks eloquently of the need to decipher the myths of the ancient world, for he believed that it was the custom of the ancients to conceal the most profound truths under the guise of simple stories. Here follows one of several statements by Mead in which the technique of double-reading is used to discuss the nature of myths:

> The perfection of the highest virtue and the opening of the real spiritual senses constituted the highest degree of the Mysteries; another and most important part of the discipline was the training in the interpretation of myth, symbol, and allegory, the letters of the mystical language in which the secrets of nature and the soul were written, so plainly for the initiated, so obscurely for the general. Without this instruction the mythical recitals and legends were unintelligible. They were and are still unintelligible. . . .
> The symbols of the Mysteries and the mythical narrations summed up and explained the workings of occult nature and the powers, faculties and nature of the human soul (*Orpheus* 155-56).

That Pound shared Mead's opinion about the exoteric/esoteric nature of the myths is made clear in one of his statements, already mentioned in Chapter I, regarding Ovid's *Metamorphoses*: "I assert that a great treasure of verity exists for mankind in Ovid and in the subject matter of Ovid's long poem, and that only in this form could it be registered" (*GK* 299).

I want to suggest that, motivated by his familiarity with Hellenistic ritual, Pound read the ancient works as representations of initiation rituals having a common origin. While one can discover, as Peter Hamilton Laurie, Leon Surette, and Kay Davis have done, the Eleusinian rites of initiation in both Pound's "main scheme" and many of *The Cantos*, it is probable that "Eleusis" is metonymic for all of the mystery cults and that Pound's understanding of this mystery is syncretic.

Canto 1 begins with the *katabasis* or descent of ritual initiation: "And then went down . . ." (1/3). Pound is careful to note that the man descending into the world of the dead is "alive," and thus fully conscious. Odysseus, at the outset of the poem, is like the *mystes* of ritual initiations, an experience about which Mead writes the following:

the passing into the realms of the dead [in both the Eleusinian and Mithraic versions], while living, refers to the initiation of the soul of the candidate into the states of after-death consciousness, while his body was left in trance. The successful passing through these states of consciousness removed the fear of death, by giving the candidate an all sufficing proof of the immortality of the soul and of its consanguinity with the gods (Taylor 319).

Mead's emphatic "while living" is echoed in the first step of Pound's scheme. The aim or goal of ritual initiation is the expansion of the initiand's consciousness into a state where he awakes to his relationship with the gods, and participates in their world.

In "Eleusis / Repeat / Metamorphosis," Davis writes that the second element in Pound's scheme "suggests the rebirth basis" of the vegetation myth of the Eleusinian rites (19). This step I call *dromena*, since it is the soul-making or death and rebirth, the process leading to the *epopteia*. In *The Cantos*, as already mentioned, the *katabasis* has two exoteric forms: the descent and the *hieros gamos* or "divine marriage." *The Cantos*, then, begins with a *katabasis*. In the opening canto Odysseus descends to "the Kimmerian lands" and there performs a ritual sacrifice for the conjuring up of the dead who, by drinking blood ("and he strong with blood"), can answer his questions about the future. What Odysseus participates in is, in fact, a sort of spiritualistic séance or necromancy.[6] *Hieros gamos* or ritual copulation is another exoteric form that the initiation rite takes in *The Cantos*, most notably in canto 47. The twice repeated cryptic Latin chant "Sacrum, sacrum inluminatio coitu" (36/180) is not deciphered until canto 47 where, as we shall see, the sacred sexual union leading to illumination is explained more fully.

The third and final step of Pound's scheme involves the "'magic moment' or moment of metamorphosis," expressed as a sudden "break through" during which man is "transported" from the ephemeral to the permanent world of the gods. In *The Sacred and Profane*, Mircea Eliade characterizes initiation as a "Rupture of Planes." Pound's cruder phrase, "bust thru," shows that his understanding of initiation is similar to Eliade's.

The third step is one of radical transformation and constitutes the completion of the process of palingenesis. Man's entry into "the divine or permanent world" of the gods is the *epopteia* of initiation rites which Pound in *The Cantos* calls the "full Εἰδώς" ("nor was place for the full Εἰδώς," 81/520). The Greek word εἰδώς, probably paraphrased best in English as "seeing knowledge," illustrates Pound's understanding of the *epopteia* as sacred, eternal knowing which is, nonetheless, unmistakably connected with visible forms.⁷ Myths of metamorphosis are exoteric manifestations of such transformations, outward and visible signs of an inward and invisible transformation.

2. "The Cave of Nerea": Canto 17

Having begun *The Cantos* with the Odyssean *katabasis* motif, Pound maintains the Odyssean parallel faithfully until, in canto 15, he adopts the Dantesquean ἀνάβασις (*anabasis*) for his own ascent from the Hell of contemporary society to purgatory. The shift from one model to another is not at all inappropriate in light of Pound's understanding of the *Commedia Divina*, an understanding that explains his choice of models for *The Cantos*. Commenting on Dante's poem Pound writes that

> the *Commedia* is, in the literal sense, a description of Dante's vision of a journey through the realms inhabited by the spirits of men after death; in a further sense it is the journey of Dante's intelligence through the states of mind wherein dwell all sorts and conditions of men before death; beyond this, Dante or Dante's intelligence may come to mean "Everyman" or "Mankind," whereat his journey becomes a symbol of mankind's struggle upward out of ignorance into the clear light of philosophy. In the second sense I give here, the journey is Dante's own mental and spiritual development. In the fourth sense, the *Commedia* is an expression of the laws of eternal justice (SR 127).

Since an actual descent into the underworld does not take place in *The Cantos*, the literal sense of the *Commedia* is not imitated by Pound in his epic. The second sense in which Pound read Dante's poem corresponds to the historical perspective and content offered in *The Cantos*. As for the third sense, Odysseus, along with such personages as Malatesta, Mussolini, and Jefferson, assumes the role of the prototypical hero whose palingenetic experience represents everyman's "struggle upward out of ignorance into the clear light of philosophy." The fourth sense represents the desired *telos* of Pound's epic, regardless of whether or not the poem succeeds in expressing "the laws of eternal justice."⁸

Having repeated the descent motif twice in the first sixteen cantos, Pound opens canto 17 with a scene of metamorphosis. According to Plotinus, "the meaning of going down to Hell is to lose sight of (the soul's divine) form" (Libera 65). Accordingly, *The Cantos* begin in the dark, formless Kimmerian lands, "Covered with close-webbed mist, unpierced ever / With glitter of sun-rays" (1/3). Darkness and formlessness are associated, then, with the *dromena*; the taking on of form, which is a kind of metamorphosis, is a sign of the proximity of the world of the gods. The

Dionysian metamorphosis of canto 17's opening line ("So that the vines burst from my fingers" [17/76]) is the outward sign of *epopteia* and captures the exact moment of the "bust into the permanent world" of the gods. At least, this was Pound's intention in composing this canto; he called canto 17 "a sort of paradiso terrestre" (*BRLB*) following "hell in Canti XIV, XV" and "purgatorio in XVI" (*L* 210).

Canto 17 begins where canto 1 ends. It would appear that the psychopomp guiding the narrator from the world of the dead is Aphrodite, "Bearing the golden bough of Argicida" (1/5). Replacing Hermes, the traditional psychopomp, with his sister Aphrodite and altering Χρυσορράπις 'Αργειοφόντης ("the golden *wand* of the Argus Slayer") to the "Golden *bough* of Argicida" are Poundian techniques of using, transforming, and conflating traditional myths into his own syncretic *mythos*. Having participated in a sort of spiritualistic séance, the protagonist is ready to traverse a terrestrial hell. His guide here is Aphrodite, and she is holding the "golden bough," which, in the *Aeneid*, guarantees the hero's safe passage to and from the world of the dead. That Aphrodite, the goddess of eros, acts as guide here is appropriate for two reasons: first, Odysseus has come to "the Kimmerian lands" straight from Circe's bed (an account of this incident is related by Pound in cantos 39 and 47) and his sailing after knowledge has been his reward, in a sense, for having slept with the goddess; and, second, throughout *The Cantos*, Pound is searching for an *epopteia* which only Aphrodite may reveal.

Canto 17 presents some sort of ritual initiation and, like so many of the first thirty cantos, it includes elements from all three stages of the initiation: the *katabasis* ("And thence down to the creek's mouth"); the stillness and absolute lack of sound of the stone place ("in the stillness," "without sound"); the other-worldliness of the light ("The light now, not of the sun"); the presence of deities ("Zagreus," "*chorus nympharum*," "Hermes and Athena," "Zothar," "Koré," "Aletha"); and the mention of the mystical number three ("for three days").[9]

Though it is hard to pin down its exact nature, the character of this initiation can be better understood if we consider its source, Porphyry's commentary on a passage from Book 13 of the *Odyssey*. Book 13 focusses on Odysseus's return to Ithaca. Here we read how the Phaeacians, who were magnificent seafarers, brought Odysseus back to Ithaca in a deep sleep and, without waking him, left him on the shore together with the rich gifts bestowed upon him by Alcinous and Arete. In his commentary, Porphyry focusses on Homer's description of the landing place (13.102-12):

> High at the head a branching olive grows,
> And crowns the pointed cliffs with shady boughs.
> A cavern pleasant, though involv'd in night,
> Beneath it lies, the Naiades delight.
> Where bowls and urns, of workmanship divine,
> And massy beams in native marble shine;
> On which the Nymphs amazing webs display,
> Of purple hue, and exquisite array.
> The busy bees, within the urns secure
> Honey delicious, and like nectar pure.
> Perpetual waters thro' the grotto glide,
> A lofty gate unfolds on either side;
> That to the north is pervious by mankind:
> The sacred south t' immortals is consign'd (Taylor 297).

In the lines immediately preceding those just quoted, the place of Odysseus's landing is described as Φόρκυνος δέ τίς ἐστι λιμήν ἁλίοιο γέροντος (13.96), that is, "a cove named after Phorcys, the old man of the Sea." This "ἅλιος γέρων" is elsewhere called Nereus and is the father of the sea-nymphs, the Nereides — hence Pound's "Cave of Nerea," that is, the cave of one of Nereus's daughters.

Porphyry is mentioned by name in only two cantos, 91 and 101. That Pound knew of "Porphyry on 'The Cave of the Nymphs' in *The Odyssey*" is certain, as evidenced by the following line from canto 91: "Souls be the water-nymphs of Porphyrius" (616).

One notable discussion of Porphyry's commentary is found in volume 5 of Mead's *Echoes from the Gnosis*, entitled *The Mysteries of Mithra* (1908).[10] Mead stresses the importance of Porphyry's treatise in preserving some important scraps of information relating to the Mysteries of Mithra. Mead begins by noting that the "Cave of the Nymphs" is "an allegorical, philosophical and mystical interpretation of a famous passage in Homer" in which Porphyry "tells us that the Ancients very properly symbolized the world by a cave" (59-60). In his discussion of Porphyry's commentary, made up largely of Mead's own translations of the original text, Mead emphasizes Porphyry's allegorical reading of this mythical account of palingenesis or return of the soul as well as the "honey rites" of Mithraism, "gate" symbolism, and the importance of "generation." His conclusion would surely appeal to Pound both because of the theosophical emphasis on the common origins of ancient rites and also because of Mead's emphasis on "generation" which can also be found in canto 17:

One side of the Magian Mysteries, therefore, dealt with the descent of souls into generation, and the other with the ascent of souls and their freedom from the necessity of rebirth — that is, with their becoming gods. And this agrees with the nature of the Lesser and Greater Rites of all great Mystery-institutions (*The Mysteries of Mithra* 64).

Taylor is in general agreement with Mead and includes a translation of Porphyry's "admirable work" in his *Selected Works of Porphyry* (1817) because, as he explains, "it contains some deep arcana of the natural and symbolical theology of the ancients, together with some beautiful observations respecting the allegory of Ulysses" (297). Surely enough, Homer's portrayal in Porphyry's commentary is that of an authoritative witness to a revelation, belonging to a wisdom tradition supposedly shared by Pythagoras and Plato, and containing the key to the mysteries of spiritual hierarchies and the fate of souls. Robert Lamberton, in his introduction to a recent translation of Porphyry's commentary, explains that Porphyry read *The Odyssey* palingenetically, that is, as a series of adventures or exoteric manifestations of Odysseus's spiritual or esoteric rebirth or genesis:

> The text serves initially as a pretext for the elaboration of a vast amount of lore about the symbolism of stone, of caves, of bees, and so forth. But the important point is that Porphyry has a context of interpretation into which this use of the text fits, a context which is developed only in the closing pages of his essay. At that point he makes it clear that he and the tradition he taps read the *Odyssey* as an allegory in the broadest sense, that not only the details of the text but the poem as a whole constitutes a screen of poetic fiction masking a general truth about human experience. It is only at this point that we learn that all the episodes of Odysseus' wanderings, the stories told by narrator and protagonist as events in the world, are in fact events contained within the spiritual life of Odysseus, who is himself "the symbol of man passing through the successive stages of γένεσις" (6-7).

According to this reading, Homer is assigned the role of a visionary sage, and his work is seen as belonging to the wisdom tradition.

What encourages the search for a secondary, concealed meaning in Homer's passage, according to Porphyry, is the text's surface, with its apparent contradictions and lack of coherence. How, for example, is one to read the oxymoronic "ἀγχόθι δ' αὐτῆς ἄντρον ἐπήρατον ἠεροειδές" (13.103: "A cavern pleasant, though involv'd in night")? In his search for a meaning forced upon him by the text's ambiguities, Porphyry subjects Homer's symbols to an analysis by analogy. Drawing upon an imagination well equipped with the minutiae of cultic and religious tradition, Porphyry differentiates among several layers of symbolism and builds up the history of cave-shrines, surveys the ritual uses of honey, examines the significance of rock and water symbolism, and so forth.

Porphyry himself belongs to the tradition transmitted to the Latin West that views Homer as a visionary sage and his poem as a mystical rendition of his wisdom. This tradition was current even when Homer's poems were not read. Robert Lamberton notes that what survives the epics themselves during the Middle Ages is

> not so much a specific reading, a specific interpretation, as an idea of the scope of their meaning, one which must be understood if we are to perceive *how* Dante could feel he was working within an integral and continuous tradition of epic which connected him, by way of Virgil, to Homer. Although the tangible proofs are lacking, it seems inescapable that the Neoplatonic tradition of reading the epics as mystical allegories is the missing link: Dante belongs in the tradition of Virgil and Homer because *they all wrote about the same thing*, or so the surviving ancient traditions regarding Homer, and current at the beginning of the 14th century, would lead Dante and his contemporaries to believe (14).

This tradition survives to the time of Thomas Taylor and later — at least, from his introductory remarks it is clear that Taylor sees himself as belonging to this tradition.

Taylor begins his translation of Porphyry's commentary by interpolating his own summary of the Homeric passage's "occult signification" (Taylor 297-98). This "sacred cave," Porphyry says, "is filled with ancient wisdom" and he sees his task as the disclosure of "its symbolical consecration and obscure mysteries" (Taylor 300). The ancients, Porphyry argues, thought of caves as symbols of the cosmos generated out of matter. Because matter, symbolized by rocks and stones, is inert and resists the imposition of form, they thought matter to be infinite in the sense of formless — and thus flowing waters, darkness, and obscurity were also apt symbols for matter. On the other hand, matter is always in a state of flux and it is on account of its taking form and achieving order that the world is beautiful and pleasant (κόσμος, *cosmos*). The ancients thus took the cave to be a symbol of invisible powers as well as of the generated and perceptible cosmos.

Caves were used, Porphyry tells us, by Persian mystagogues who, "mystically signifying the descent of the soul into an inferior nature and its ascent into the intelligible world, initiate the priest or mystic in a place which they denominate a cave" (Taylor 301). Though temples became more important later, the earliest humans consecrated caves to their gods.

For example, the Couretes in Crete dedicated a cave to Zeus, as did the people of Arcadia to Lycaean Pan. Presiding over the caves, and in particular over the everflowing waters found in caves, are the Naiads, aquatic nymphs who represent "all souls passing into the humid and flowing condition of a generative nature" (Taylor 303) — hence Pound's cave of Nerea should probably be seen as a place sacred to souls.

On the connection between souls and water, Porphyry notes that souls were thought to settle upon the water which was nourished by the divine spirit; he adds, interestingly enough, that the Egyptians depicted all their gods as standing not on dry land but rather in a boat — the sun along with the rest of them — and that they are to be thought of, in this particular manifestation, as souls descending into *genesis* and hovering over the water.[11] Homer's cave is decorated with stony amphorae and mixing-bowls, the symbols of the aquatic nymphs. The Naiads are busy "weaving on stony beams purple garments wonderful to behold" (Taylor 305). This weaving signifies the making of bodies for the souls coming down into *genesis*, the stone representing the human bones and the purple cloth the flesh woven of blood, since "the body is a garment with which the soul is invested" (Taylor 305).

Besides his emphasis on the union of body and soul, Porphyry also emphasizes the soul's attraction to the flesh, understood here as sexual desire. The cave's urns are filled with "honey delicious," which theologians have used to symbolize, among other things, the "desire of coition." This explains the attraction felt by the divine essences and their descent into the fluctuating realm of generation. The nymphs are called by the ancients "bees," since "souls are, indeed, the authors of all the pleasure peculiar to our nature" (Taylor 307).[12]

Porphyry also pays particular attention to the symbolism of "gates." The cave of the nymphs in Ithaca is said by Homer to have had two gates, one looking toward the north and "said to be pervious to the descent of men" into generation, and the other facing southward and said to be "not the avenue of gods, but of souls ascending to the gods. On this account *the poet does not say it is the passage of the gods, but of immortals*" (Taylor 310-11). The sacredness of gates, recognized by Homer, is emphasized by Porphyry who adds that, since the gate is a holy thing, in ancient times it was not permissible to speak at any gate, and also for this reason, the "Pythagoreans, and the wise men among the Egyptians, forbade any person to speak while passing through gates or portals; for at that time the divinity who is the principle of the universe is to be worshipped in silence" (Taylor 314).

At the head of the harbour, in Homer's passage, an olive tree has been planted which, according to Porphyry, is a symbol of Athena, goddess of wisdom. The olive tree signifies that the universe was not spontaneously generated but resulted from the union of intelligible nature and wisdom. It is necessary for Odysseus to sit with Athena beneath the olive tree, take counsel with her, and "effectually [learn to] amputate and destroy that hostile rout of passions, which lurk [sic] in the secret recesses of the soul" (Taylor 321). Thus, according to Porphyry's reading, Homer uses Odysseus as a symbol of everyman passing through the successive stages of generation until, at length, he confronts and conquers his passions and "being stripped of the torn garments by which his true person was concealed, he may recover the ruined empire of his soul" (Taylor 322). The Leucothea episode in the *Odyssey*, to which Pound refers a number of times in the later cantos, represents the "cleansing" of Odysseus of human passion, a fact which the Nausicaa episode illustrates.

Porphyry ends his commentary on the Homeric passage, then, with pointed emphasis on the spiritual, esoteric sense of Odysseus's exoteric journey. Though the passage selected for analysis by Porphyry is closely connected to Odysseus's homecoming, at no point does Porphyry concern himself with Odysseus's return to Ithaca (the Homeric *nostos*) nor with his reunion with Penelope. Instead, he is interested in Homer's representation of "the images of divine things under the concealment of fable" and thinks that it is not at all "proper to believe that interpretations of this kind are forced" (Taylor 322). Taylor, taking this line of argument further, attaches to his translation a long footnote in which the esoteric and palingenetic sense of Odysseus's adventures are examined (Taylor 322-42).

Like Porhpyry, and unlike James Joyce, Pound does not seem at all interested in Odysseus's *nostos* and his reunion with Penelope. Pound's Odysseus is not interested in Helen of Troy, but in palingenesis: "Getting the feel of it, of his soul, / while they were making a fuss about Helen" (98/684).

Pound's reading of the *Odyssey* in *The Cantos* certainly belongs to this allegorical and occult tradition.[13] Interestingly, many of the symbols which Porphyry's allegorical reading emphasizes find their way into canto 17. While "Cave of Nerea," "gate-cliffs of amber," along with the whimsical "porphyry smooth," are the only obvious allusions, Pound's emphasis on stillness and silence, his use of water and stone imagery, and the presence of certain gods and goddesses point to Porphyry's work as a probable source.

The action of canto 17 consists of a *katabasis* which is nevertheless difficult to map out because Pound interweaves at least three different stories or exoteric occurrences, all of which can be related to Porphyry's allegorical commentary: (1) Odysseus's arrival in Ithaca and his initial confusion upon waking from a deep sleep provide the framework for (2) a ritual initiation taking place within the "Cave of Nerea" and later in an Egyptian landscape, and (3) this initiation is interrupted by Pound's own Venetian recollections. The typically sudden shifts from one story, and from one landscape, to another make it difficult to follow the course of the *katabasis*. Adding to the difficulty is the problem of identifying the participants, since it is not always clear whether we are following the actions of Odysseus, of a *mystes*, or of Pound himself. Yet this confusion or infolding should be attributed to Pound's conception of himself as both Odyssean hero and participant in a ritual syncretic initiation — a conception natural enough, since all *mystai* and every initiation are ultimately one and the same.

The opening passage of canto 17 begins with an allusion to Dionysus in his role as Δενδρίτης (Dendrites, tree spirit) and ends with a ritual shout or cry to Dionysus as Zagreus:

> So that the vines burst from my fingers
> And the bees weighted with pollen
> Move heavily in the vine-shoots:
>   chirr — chirr — chir-rikk — a purring sound,
> And the birds sleepily in the branches.
>   ZAGREUS! IO ZAGREUS! (17/76).

Although Dionysus ended his Hellenic career as a specialized or functional god of wine, intoxication, and ecstasy, he began as a divinity of vegetation in general.[14] Like Hermes, Dionysus appears in Hellenic iconographic art as a herm. The symbol of both gods of fertility is naturally the phallus. Pound's opening allusion is, I think, to Dionysus as god of fertility, possibly to the god as depicted in a beautiful hylix, reproduced by Jane Harrison in her *Prolegomena to the Study of Greek Religion* (427). This hylix, in which Dionysus is shown holding a branch from a vine-tree in his left hand, might give the illusion that the vine is growing through the god's fingers. In canto 17, this opening image of growth is accompanied by contending images of industry and lethargy or physical fatigue organized around sounds of feline contentment. The reference to the industrious bees is possibly an allusion to Porphyry's sexual interpretation of the "busy bees" in the Homeric passage. Since they are also symbolic of the souls coming into generation, the bees are appropriate to this passage which "represents" the metamorphosis of a god.

Interrupting the canto's narrative is a ritual shout, "ZAGREUS! IO ZAGREUS!" which signals the presence of the god of the mysteries. "Zagreus" is an Orphic name, the particular title given by Orpheus to Dionysus or Bacchus the Son. The Orphic interpretation of the palingenetic Dionysian myth is of considerable interest. The name Zagreus does not appear in Homer. He is essentially a ritual figure, the god of the mysteries. Both Taylor and Mead treat the anthropogonic Dionysus myth as an *hierotelestia*, that is, as a sacred story or arcane narration.[15]

The story of the Orphic Zagreus is a myth of regeneration which, at the same time, explains the creation of humankind out of the ashes of the Titans. Mead, providing his own occult commentary within square brackets, quotes from Taylor's "A Dissertation on the Eleusinian and Bacchic Mysteries" the following pertinent elements of the Orphic story:

> Dionysus, or Bacchus [Zagreus, the human Soul], while he was yet a boy, was engaged by the Titans, through the stratagems of Juno, in a variety of sports, with which that period of life is so vehemently allured; and among the rest, he was particularly captivated with beholding his image in a mirror [the Astral Light which allures the young soul]; during his admiration of which he was miserably torn in pieces by the Titans [cosmic and elemental powers, which absorb the energy of the soul through its desires for things of sense]; who, not content with this cruelty, first boiled his members [powers] in water [the psychic sphere], and after roasted them by the fire [the spiritual sphere]. But while they were tasting his flesh, thus dressed, Jupiter [the parent-soul], roused by the odour, and perceiving the cruelty of the deed, hurled his thunder at the Titans [the human soul as it grows in stature turns to its father-soul, and the divine fire (thunder) "converts the Titans to its own essence"] – but committed the members of Bacchus to Apollo, his brother [the solar part of the soul, or "Higher Ego"; Bacchus being the lunar part, or "Lower Ego"] that they might be properly interred [converted by the alchemy of spiritual nature]. And this being performed, Dionysus (whose "heart" during his laceration was snatched away by Pallas [Athena, Minerva]), by a new regeneration . . . again emerged, and being restored to his pristine life and integrity, he afterwards filled up the number of the Gods. . . . But in the meantime, from the exhalation arising from the ashes of the burning bodies of the Titans, mankind was produced (*Orpheus* 118-19).

In Mead's reading the Titans represent the desires of the soul for things of the senses, and the travails of Zagreus exoterically represent palingenesis or soul-making.[16]

The ritual shout is followed by a *katabasis* beginning at a landscape inhabited by Artemis as πόντια θήρων (*pontia theron*), that is, Artemis as mistress of the whole of wild nature.

> With the first pale-clear of the heaven
> And the cities set in their hills,
> And the goddess of the fair knees
> Moving there, with the oak-woods behind her,
> The green slope, with white hounds
>   leaping about her;
> And thence down to the creek's mouth, until evening,
> Flat water before me,
>   and the trees growing in water,
> Marble trunks out of stillness,
> On past the palazzi,
>   in the stillness,
> The light now, not of the sun.
>   Chrysophrase,
> And the water green clear, and blue clear;
> On, to the great cliffs of amber (17/76).

In her first appearance in *The Cantos* in canto 4, Artemis is situated among her attendant nymphs and is seen as ἁγνή (*agne*) in the very special sense of inviolate and inviolable virgin (with Actaeon paying with his life for his glimpse of her divine nakedness [4/14]). Here, however, Pound uses the goddess's presence simply to punctuate the direction of the *katabasis* from a pastoral setting to the city's artifice. The whole canto itself is arranged in terms of shifts from country to city, to cave, to city.

The pastoral morning vision with its resident goddess left behind, the *mystes* begins his descent. This descent takes him through a dreamscape of other-worldly calmness, a dreamscape unmistakably Venetian. The description of Venice as a stone forest emerging from the flat stillness of the waters recalls Porphyry's use of the water-stone motif. The petrifaction of the Phaeacian ship, together with its crew, upon entering the harbour of Scheria on its return from Ithaca (*Odyssey*, 13.146-64) might be another possible source of inspiration for the water-stone motif used here.

The shift from the northern Adriatic city to the harbour of Phorkys in Ithaca is announced by the hieratic phrase "The light now, not of the sun." Transported through the "great cliffs of amber" into the "Cave of

Nerea," the narrator is also making his *katabasis*, completing a movement from the Arcadian outdoors to the enclosed space of a cave. The "Cave of Nerea" passage is this canto's most significant and perhaps most memorable (references to the passage's rhetoric and "sensory modality" are included within square brackets to facilitate the discussion that follows):

	Between them
	Cave of Nerea,
[sight]	she like a great shell curved, [anastrophe]
[hearing]	And the boat drawn without sound,
[smell]	Without odour of ship-work,
[hearing]	Nor bird-cry, nor any noise of wave moving,
[hearing]	Nor splash of porpoise, nor any noise of wave moving,
	[epanaphora and antistrophe]
	Within her cave, Nerea,
[sight]	she like a great shell curved
	[epanalepsis]
[touch]	In the suavity of the rock,
	cliff green-gray in the far,
[sight]	In the near, the gate-cliffs of amber,
	And the wave
[sight]	green clear, and blue clear, [isocolon and
[sight]	And the cave salt-white, and glare-purple, polysyndeton]
[touch]	cool, porphyry smooth,
	the rock sea-worn.
[hearing]	No gull-cry, no sound of porpoise,
[touch]	Sand as of malachite, and no cold there,
[sight]	the light not of the sun. [ellipsis and anastrophe] (17/76-77)

Writing about this passage, Libera says that here, "As we have found so often [in *The Cantos*], Pound imitates the mood of his source — Homer's emphasis on the stillness of the cave — while miraculously inventing and mingling images to make poetry all his own" (83). Through his handling of sound patterns, metre, and syntax Pound conveys a sense of the *mysterion*. All of the reader's physical senses, except taste, are here engaged as he or she is drawn into contemplating a dreamscape where a mysterious silence reigns. While, on the one hand, the words themselves insist on the absence of sound, on the other, the poet's use of alliteration and assonance, shifting metres, and such rhetorical devices as anaphora, antistrophe, ellipsis, anastrophe, isocolon, and polysyndeton provides a powerful incantation, informing the silence with the dynamics of divine mystery.

The exact nature of the initiatory experience taking place within the cave is not represented. Pound does not profane the rites of initiation; he simply evokes their sanctity and magic. The poem does not describe or report on an initiation rite but, instead, enacts an initiation for the reader. Whatever revelation there is must be generated directly by the poem, itself the exoteric expression of a revelation apparent only to the initiate.

Although no attempt is made to describe the events within the cave, the speaker, as the directions linked with visual perspective that are included in the text show ("Between them," "Within her cave," "in the far," "in the near"), is familiar with the initiation ritual. What is described is the soundless *katabasis* of the *mystes*, a movement from the outside world into the cave of generation. Here the initiate experiences the *epopteia* or the "full Ειδώς." Presiding over the ritual is Nerea, a sea-nymph, who, considering the similarity between these two verses, "Nerea, / she like a great shell curved" and "with the great shell borne on the seawaves" (74/443), can be seen as an analogue of Aphrodite. The experience is visual and dominated by a proliferation of alchemical colours and semi-precious stones ("Chrysophrase," "green clear and blue clear," "amber," "green-gray," "salt-white, and glare purple," "cool, malachite") viewed under the other-worldly "light not of the sun." Expressed strictly in visual terms (remember that Pound saw the mysteries in terms of "immediate sight"), the *mystes's* experience is so intense that all other senses are suspended and the initiation is "sensed" exclusively in terms of sight. Sound in "splash of porpoise" and "noise of waves moving" and touch in "no cold there" are brought to our attention so that they can be rejected in favour of the dominance of the sense of sight.

Since the mystery cannot be shown or explained, Pound does not attempt to discuss any of the details of the initiatory experience ("The mysteries are *not* revealed, and no guide book to them has been or will be written" [L 327]). There are, nevertheless, a number of details he provides that go a certain distance toward suggesting the kinds of things he associates with the initiation. Remembering that the Egyptian depicted their gods as being transported on boats and Pound's use of this motif in the later cantos (e.g., "the golden sun boat" [96/652] and "The boat of Ra-Set moves with the sun" [94/641 and 98/684]), it could be conjectured that the vision involves the appearance of some god or goddess upon a boat. In addition, Pound probably intends us to visualize a scene where souls float upon the water of the cave, some of them coming into genesis and others ascending to the permanent world of the gods. The silence of the place, on the other hand, could be attributed to the occult belief in the sacredness of gates—a belief originating, as suggested above, with the Pythagoreans and their Egyptian followers who thought that speech was forbidden while passing through gates. Pound is certainly aware of the occult belief in the sacredness of gates and refers to it in the later cantos (e.g., "And that all gates are holy" [94/634 and 100/716]).

Considering the emphasis upon generation in Porphyry's commentary, it is also possible that Pound envisions the ritual of initiation taking place within the "Cave of Nerea" as an *hieros gamos*. I have already remarked that one exoteric form that the initiation rite takes in *The Cantos* is sexual copulation—and I intend to discuss this motif further in my analysis of canto 47 later on. As already suggested above, the simile used to describe Nerea, "she like a great shell curved," could be taken as an allusion to Aphrodite. Pound always thought that sex was sacred and remarked that "For certain people the *pecten cteis* [female genitals] is the gate of wisdom" (*SP* 56). On account of their resemblance to the vulva, sea-shells were used in ancient times in many religious rites in agrarian and initiatory ceremonies in which they usually symbolized regeneration.[17]

The exact nature of the initiatory experience is not revealed. Pound's practice in *The Cantos* of veiling the mystery is congruent with ancient occult practices. We know only that ancient initiatory ceremonies were founded on divine myths. The *mystes* did not learn anything new, since he already knew the myth, nor was he taught any really secret doctrine. He simply performed the rituals and had sacred objects revealed to him. The purpose of the initiation was palingenesis or spiritual regeneration. By virtue of his initiation, the *mystes* attained another mode of being, he became one with the gods. But he was sworn to secrecy!

In canto 17, the initiation is not completed until the canto's last verse paragraph. But immediately after describing the cave of initiation, the *mystes* is rewarded with a glimpse into the permanent world of the gods. This is a vision of a pastoral landscape populated by a chorus of nymphs, fauns, gods, and hieratic animals:

Zagreus, feeding his panthers,
        the turf clear as on hills under light.
And under the almond-trees, gods,
        with them, *choros nympharum*. Gods,
Hermes and Athene,
        As shaft of compass,
Between them, trembled—
To the left is the place of fauns,
        sylva nympharum;

> The low wood, moor-scrub,
>   the doe, the young spotted deer,
>   leap up through the broom-plants,
>   as dry leaf amid yellow.
> And by one cut of the hills,
>   the great alley of Memnons.
> Beyond, sea, crests seen over dune
> Night sea churning shingle,
> To the left, the alley of cypress (17/77).

It would seem that we are thus returned to the world of Artemis as described in the canto's opening lines. The ambiguity of such lines as "the turf clear *as* on hills under light" [italics mine], however, makes it difficult to decide whether the *mystes* has left the cave and is "under [natural] light" or whether this is a vision presented to him while he is still inside the cave.

The ritual shout ("ZAGREUS! IO ZAGREUS!") is answered with the appearance of Zagreus feeding his panthers. With him are Hermes and Athena. Guy Davenport explains the presence of these two gods within the pastoral boundaries of Arcadia in this way:

> Between Zagreus Dionysus and the chorus of nymphs Hermes and Athene tremble "as shaft of compass." By framing Hermes, god of commerce, and Athene, goddess of the intellect, within such pastoral boundaries, the canto suggests that Arcadia is their home.... Hermes and Athene both guided Odysseus and were in that sense his "compass," but the trembling compass needle in this ideogram suggests that the counsels of the two gods, acumen and wisdom, are man's advantage over and supplement to the world of Dionysus, panthers, and spotted deer (196).

This reading seems to me to be wide of the mark. I suggest, instead, that Hermes is here because of his similarity to Dionysus as a phallic god. Athene, born from Zeus's head is, of course, the goddess of Sophia or wisdom. The compass, taken by Davenport to represent balance, is probably a phallic symbol. The use of the dash ("Between them, trembled—") brings about a sudden pause. Here we have a grammatical mark, a sign of ellipsis, which renders incomplete the simile "As shaft of compass... trembled—." Keeping in mind Pound's emphasis upon generation in the canto, it is possible that it is the "phallus," the traditional symbol of fertility, that is missing here. To take this one step further, it is probably not too far-fetched to see Hermes and Athena, in light of Gnostic doctrine, as the male and female principles of the universe: Hermes as Power and

Potentiality and Athena as Sophia or Thought or Incarnation. Thus, within the pastoral world of Arcadia, we are presented with another θεογαμία (*theogamia* or *hieros gamos*).

The pastoral landscape ("The low wood, moor-scrub...") suddenly fades into a funereal seascape of tombs and cypresses (17/77). Here is Terrell's gloss on "Memnons": "Memnon, son of Tithonus and Eos. A large statue near Thebes, Egypt (supposed to be of Memnon), was reputed to produce a musical sound when struck by the light of dawn [Dawn = Eos]" (*Companion*, I.74).[18] Correct though it is, the mythological gloss is, in the present context, peripheral; here by "Memnon" we are to understand not a specific location but rather any graveyard lined with monumental statues and alleys of cypress trees. The composite landscape (Egyptian alley of Memnons and Mediterranean alley of cypress trees), with graves beneath it, is probably meant by Pound to describe another threshold through which souls descend into generation and ascend to the world of gods just described above.

The cypress trees provide the transition from the funereal seascape noted above to a seemingly autobiographical reminiscence of Venice metamorphosed into a petrified landscape:

>   A boat came,
> One man holding her sail,
> Guiding her with oar caught over gunwale, saying:
>   "There, in the forest of marble,
>   "the stone trees — out of water —
>   "the arbours of stone —
>   "marble leaf, over leaf,
>   "silver, steel over steel,
>   "silver beaks rising and crossing,
>   "prow set against prow,
>   "stone, ply over ply,
>   "the gilt beams flare of an evening"
> Borso, Carmagnola, the men of craft, *i vitrei*,
> Thither, at one time, time after time,
> And the waters richer than glass,
> Bronze gold, the blaze over the silver,
> Dye-pots in the torch-light,
> The flash of wave under prows,
> And the silver beaks rising and crossing.
>   Stone trees, white and rose-white in the darkness,
> Cypress there by the towers,
> Drift under hulls in the night (17/77-78).

Here we are presented with a glimpse of Pound sailing down the Grand Canal; the poet's biography enters his poem's mythology, and he is seen participating in a scene like the one already depicted in his description of the Cave of Nerea. Pound, then, places himself within the Venetian landscape and has himself deliver the above lines—quotation marks included. The hypnotic effect of these lines, achieved primarily through simple repetition of words, the use of the isocolon, and the use of anapests, signals the poet's participation in some kind of psychic experience.

The motif of "boat sailing" is important in joining some of this canto's strands. The *katabasis* motif begins with someone sailing "down to the creek's mouth," entering the Cave of Nerea on a boat, and, in the canto's penultimate passage, being "shipped thence / to the stone place," which can be variously taken as the Cave of Nerea—that is, the place of the transmigration of the souls, rather like Yeats's Byzantium—or Venice.

Libera argues for Pound's experience of Venice as a place of exquisite artifice and glory and as a place of alchemical transformation that occasions a radical change in the poet himself (which he records in this canto). The actual experience must have been undergone not at the time of this canto's composition but, probably, much earlier. As Libera writes,

> Venice opened him to a world of art that was both sensuous and well-crafted; the permanent effect upon him could only be described as a transformation, the kind once symbolically enacted in mystic rites. The Dionysian lines with which the Canto opens are a form of epigraph, indicating that in the experience to follow, Pound, like an ecstatic worshipper, becomes the very god of energy he worships.... Although the "plot" of Canto 17 brings Pound from Venice to the cave of initiation and back, as if there were two distinct realities, one senses that the stone cave with its amber cliffs is actually identical with the "stone place," Venice, and is perhaps the hidden heart and occult symbol of that city. The initiation is an initiation to art, leading to a further fertilization in Pound's own poetry (90-91).

Libera's point is well taken; but I disagree with her emphasis on the purely aesthetic impact of the initiation. Though the *mystes* might well become a hierophant of art (as Pound himself did), his initiation is first and foremost a religious act. In addition, the petrified landscape is at once a place of artistic permanence and a funereal image of chthonic inertia.

After the tag "In the gloom the gold / Gathers the light about it" (17/78), there is one more shift, this time to a landscape which is at once Mediterranean and Egyptian.

Now supine in burrow, half over-arched bramble,
One eye for the sea, through that peek-hole,
Gray light, with Athene.
Zothar and her elephants, the gold loin-cloth,
The sistrum, shaken, shaken,
              the cohorts of her dancers.
And Aletha, by bend of the shore,
         with her eyes seaward,
         and in her hands sea-wrack
Salt-bright with the foam.
Koré through the bright meadow,
         with green-gray dust in the grass:
"For this hour, brother of Circe."
Arm laid over my shoulder,
Saw the sun for three days, the sun fulvid,
As a lion lift over sand-plain;
              and that day,
And for three days, and none after,
Splendour, as the splendour of Hermes,
And shipped thence
         to the stone place,
Pale white, over water,
         known water,
And the white forest of marble, bent bough over bough,
The pleached arbour of stone,
Thither Borso, when they shot the barbed arrow at him,
And Carmagnola, between the two columns,
Sigismundo, after that wreck in Dalmatia.
    Sunset like the grasshopper flying (17/79).

An initiation is definitely taking place here, as the return to the "stone place," that is, Venice or the Cave of Nerea, is preceded by a return to a "place" that reminds the reader of the closing lines of canto 15, where the protagonist describes the exhaustion felt at the end of his journey through hell and his vision of the sun:

        Plotinus gone,
And the shield tied under me, woke;
The gate swung on its hinges;
Panting like a sick dog, staggered,
Bathed in alkali, and in acid.
'Ηέλιον τ' 'Ηέλιον

>   blind with the sunlight,
> Swollen-eyed, rested,
>   lids sinking, darkness unconscious (15/66-67).

Davenport claims that the lines referring to "Athene" contain an allusion to Odysseus's beaching on Scheria, the land of the Phaeacians (*Odyssey* 5.470-93). I think that it is more likely, and also more consistent with the "Cave of Nerea" passage, that Pound is here thinking of Odysseus' beaching on Ithaca (*Odyssey*, 13.117-19).

Here the protagonist, exhausted from his *katabasis*, looks toward the sea while he is being attended by Athena. Visions, inhabited by goddesses whose names in at least two cases are Pound's inventions, appear before him. First Zothar, possibly an Egyptian deity, appears naked, except for the gold-loin cloth covering her *pecten cteis*, in the midst of her hieratic elephants and the sounds of the sistrum to which her attendants dance. This vision is succeeded by another in which Aletha (an invented goddess of the sea) appears, standing on the Ithacan or Venetian shore "with her eyes seaward."[19] Then Persephone approaches, in her role as Koré, and places her arm on the protagonist's shoulders, reminding him of his experiences in Circe's palace (to be related in cantos 36, 39, and 47). Most commentators take the apostrophe ("For this hour, brother of Circe") as an allusion to Jason's ill-starred quest for the Golden fleece (*Odyssey*, 10.137ff.), since Circe's brother was Aeetes, the king of Colchis. But here it is clearly Koré speaking, addressing the protagonist or *mystes* in familiar terms, and standing beside him as he is going through his initiation. As Akiko Miyake explains, the title of "brother of Circe" must be given to those initiated in the mysteries. This is made clear in canto 106 where the goddess of initiation steps out of the stone house and reveals herself to the reader:

> between the two pine trees, not Circe
>   but Circe was like that
>   coming from the house of smoothe stone
> "not know which god" (106/754).

Miyake argues for a double-reading of these lines; she notes that this goddess is both Circe, the formidable goddess of the senses, as well as the Eleusinian goddess of initiation. How one sees her depends on whether he or she has or has not been initiated into the mysteries. To the uninstructed, the goddess appears in her exoteric guise, "exactly like Circe," while "the title 'Brother of Circe' ... must be given to the heroes properly initiated [the *mystai*], who have already mastered all the tricks of this goddess, Circe [that is, her esoteric nature], and who are now equal to her" (Miyake 90). Furthermore, the traditional mystical significance of "*three* days" and the vision of the sun indicate that an initiation is, indeed, taking place.

Though the penultimate passage of canto 17 begins with an image of a Mediterranean pastoral landscape and ends with a return to the urban "stone place" of Venice or the Ithacan cave, most of the images associated with the initiation at this point carry associations with Egypt. "Zothar" and her elephants, the orgiastic or frenetic sounds of the "sistrum," and the description of the equatorial sun at dawn ("the sun fulvid") rising "as a lion lift[s] over sand-plain" all suggest Egypt. As the *mystes* is slowly re-emerging from the "darkness unconscious" (15/67), he perceives Helios "as the splendour of Hermes." The Egyptian associations should lead us to see this Hermes not as the Hellenistic Hermes of the rest of *The Cantos* but rather as Hermes Trismegistus, the λόγος (*logos*, word) of the *Corpus Hermetica*, who appears in Trismegistic literature in the form of light. For example, Poimandres's vision involves the transformation of the world into light and out of this light the Logos appears:

> ... and straightway, in the twinkling of an eye, all things were opened to me, and I see a Vision limitless, all things turned into Light—sweet, joyous [Light]. And I became transported as I gazed....
>
> [Thereon] out of the Light... a Holy Word (Logos) descended on that Nature. And upwards to the height from the Moist Nature leaped forth pure Fire; light was it, swift and active too (Mead, *Thrice-Greatest Hermes* II.3-4).

The palingenetic character of *The Cantos* involves both a *katabasis* to the world of the dead as well as an ascension to the world of light. Porphyry's description of the cave's gates representing the thresholds through which the souls ascend or descend is probably conflated by Pound in *The Cantos* into one gate ("You who dare Persephone's *threshold*" (93/631; emphasis mine) leading to either the hylic world of the uninitiated or to the ethereal world of the gods. The *mystes* is the only one who can pass freely from one world to the other—and this is the basic function of the palingenetic initiation. Again, central to this rite of initiation, as Pound probably understood it, was an encounter with the dead. This is the reason for Pound's inclusion, in his description of what may be seen as a description of Venice or the "Cave of Nerea" or of the Underworld in the final lines of the canto, of the three dead men, Borso, Carmagnola, and Malatesta. The presence of these men emphasizes the landscape's chthonic character and, more importantly, points to the preoccupation of most initiation rites with the life after death.

The mystes's *katabasis* into the "Cave of Nerea" represents, then, the mystical descent of the soul into the underworld. The *katabasis* initiates palingenesis, since the *mystes* undergoes a radical process of self-transformation. Finally, the *mystes* is rewarded with a radiance, a palingenetic "full Ειδώς," which is probably seen by Pound in terms of the Trismegistic Logos.

3. "Never with this Religion / Will You Make Men of the Greeks": Canto 23

Canto 23 constitutes one of the many expressions in *The Cantos* of Pound's stand in favour of the "ecstatic-beneficent-and-benevolent" state and his opposition to the dogmatist (*GK* 223). Most of canto 23 is taken up with motifs associated with the ecstatic state; however, the state of religious "fanatics," "scarcity economists," and "repressors" is also well represented here. The canto opens with a reference to the potential of the individual human mind and ends with a theophany representing the fulfilment of that potential. Weaving together many of the elements of initiation rituals, Pound gathers earlier references to Odysseus's *katabasis*, to an *hieros gamos*, to Neoplatonism, and to the world of the troubadours and creates an initiatory experience. This experience includes at least two important focal points of occult history: the Albigenses and Georgius Gemistus Plethon.

As already noted earlier, Plethon (1360?-1452?), who "brought a brand of Platonism into Italy and is supposed to have set off a renaissance" (*GK* 45), is one of Pound's heroes or enlightened souls. As a member of the Greek delegation which came to Italy in 1438, Plethon took part in the Councils of Ferrara and Florence and, on that occasion, played a major role in the transmission of Greek philosophy to the awaiting minds in Italy. Pound considers Plethon to be a participant in and an expositor of the *nous*. Within his celebration of the *nous* in canto 23, Pound also introduces a troubadour story of ἔρως (*eros*) and θάνατος (*thanatos*). The anecdotal aside with which this story ends, "And they called us the Manicheans / Wotever the hellsarse that is" (23/109), should be seen in terms of Pound's persistent interest in the plight of the Albigenses, and sheds light, as I will show below, upon Pound's invective against all repressors.

Typographically canto 23 is divided into eight sections of varying lengths. The principal subject matters found in this canto are the following: (1) the Neoplatonic philosophers of light and their belief in human reason, which they regard as the active manifestation of divinity in the world; (2) Plethon's attempts to bring about a reform of the declining Byzantine state; (3) modern science and the rise of the new *polymetis* and *polytropos* hero: the example of Pierre Curie; (4) a poem by Stesichorus in the original which "rhymes" with Odysseus's *katabasis*; (5) the decline and destruction of Provençal culture; and (6) a reference to the first *Hymn of Aphrodite*. In terms of the *katabasis / dromena / epopteia* pattern, the fourth section belongs to the first phase, the first, second, and third to the second phase, and the sixth to the third phase.

These elements, ranging from ancient myth to modern science, seem unrelated and incoherent. However, through rigorous application and careful consideration of each fragment the sense or significance of the canto as a whole can be discovered in a structure which reflects Pound's understanding of initiation rites.

Since the movement of canto 23 is cyclical, I will start my analysis with its third verse paragraph, instead of its first:

>   With the sun in a golden cup
> and going toward the low fords of ocean
> Ἅλιος δ' Ὑπεριονίδας δέπας ἐσκατέβαινε χρύσεον
> Ὄφρα δι ὠκεανοῖο περάσας
>   ima vada noctis obscurae
> Seeking doubtless the sex in bread-moulds
> ἥλιος, ἅλιος, ἅλιος = μάταιος
> ("Derivation uncertain." The idiot
> Odysseus furrowed the sand.)
> alixantos, aliotrephès, eiskatebaine, down into,
> descended, to the end that, beyond ocean,
> pass through, traverse
>   ποτὶ βένθεα
> νυκτός ἐρεμνᾶς,
> ποτὶ ματέρα, κουριδίαν τ'ἄλοχον
> παῖδάς τε φίλους ... ἔβα δάφναισι κατάσκιον
> Precisely, the selv' oscura
> And in the morning, in the Phrygian head-sack
> Barefooted, dumping sand from their boat
> 'Yperionides! (23/107-108).

This passage introduces another *katabasis*. The Greek lines are adapted from Iohannes Schweighaeuser's bilingual (Greek and Latin) edition of Athenaeus's *Deipnosophistae* ("Learned Dining-Club"). This work belongs to the tradition of literary banquets that derives from Plato's *Symposium*. It is of interest because it preserves much out-of-the-way information and substantial fragments of otherwise lost works. The particular passage which Pound uses here is from a fragment of a lost poem by the seventh-century B.C. Greek choral-lyric-poet Stesichorus; its subject is the sun's daily journey. According to Stesichorus, Helios traverses the sky by day and, at the Western bounds of the ocean, exchanging his chariot for a golden cup, floats back to the East through darkness, and rests in a laurel grove. It was in Helios's cup that Herakles passed over the ocean on his way to get the cattle of Geryon, his tenth labour, which is said to be a conquest of death.[20]

Pound begins by rendering into English the first two lines of the Greek fragment which describes the Sun's night sea-journey (see Appendix I). Then, with Schweighaeuser's text still open in front of him, he transcribes the first two lines from the Greek which he has just translated. Pound presents himself in the act of translation and inscribes his difficulties with the original text in the verse of the canto. Using the Latin translation as an aid, he is reading the Greek and its Latin translation simultaneously. That he is using the Latin translation to aid himself with the Greek original is indicated when he jumps to the bottom of the page of the original text and transcribes half of the Latin version of the next Stesichorus verse: "ima vada noctis obscurae." Next, Pound adds a phrase which is utterly out of context here: "Seeking doubtless the sex in bread-moulds"—a phrase to which I will return later on in this discussion. In the next line, he produces an equation: ἥλιος, ἅλιος, ἅλιος = μάταιος. Many critics condemn this kind of "word-play"; but it seems to me that their disapproval springs from their failure to comprehend and appreciate Pound's ingenious methods of transcription, translation, and association.[21] Pound's equation is not a spontaneous play of words but rather the result of a carefully and ingeniously constructed sequence of associations. The stimulus for it is provided by a textual emendation found in the *Athenaeus* text. In emendation number three it is pointed out that ἀέλιος is a variant of ἥλιος. The translator's curiosity is thus naturally aroused and Pound opens his Liddell and Scott *Greek-English Lexicon* to look up the meaning of ἅλιος.[22] There he finds that ἅλιος is the Doric equivalent for the Attic poetic form ἥλιος (see Appendix II). He also finds two more entries for the same word: ἅλιος, "of the sea" and ἅλιος = μάταιος, "fruitless, unprofitable, idle...." Pound transcribes the lexicon's entries and he also records the lexicographer's note on the third ἅλιος which reads "Deriv.[ation] uncertain."

The lexicographical game does not end here since the lexical commentary on the third ἅλιος initiates a process of association in Pound's mind through which μάταιος, meaning idle, reminds him of Odysseus's unwillingness to join the Greek princes in their expedition to Troy; hence: "The Idiot / Odysseus furrowed the sand." The epithet "idle" then reminds Pound of Odysseus's feigning madness when Agamemnon's envoys came to enlist him for the Trojan war. He yoked an ox and an ass and plowed a field, sowing salt in the furrows.

Guy Davenport reports that Stesichorus is sensitive to "the tension of opposing meanings of ἅλιος, ... and symbolized in his poem the double nature of the word, growing and ungrowing, light and dark, order and confusion" (220). Pound seems to have recognized this tension, and chancing upon the happy accident by which the triply repeated ἅλιος is framed in the Greek lexicon by ἀλίξαντος, "worn by the sea," and ἁλιο-τρέφης, "sea-reared," he transliterates these two words. He also transliterates the word ἐσκατέβαινε from the first line of Stesichorus and translates it immediately into English (17/107).

Following this Pound transcribes the Stesichorus lines, describing Herakles's return to the grove overshadowed with baytrees. Not being one to hesitate in pursuing associations between what he encounters in his reading and the thesaurus of phrases and tags which he retains in his mind, Pound makes another connection: "Precisely, the selv' oscura." Here he equates the Greek phrase which means "laurel-shade grove" with the Italian phrase *selva oscura* ("dark forest"). The phrase *selva oscura* is used by Pound as a familiar point of reference to Dante — that is, the "dark forest," the "Dark World" before palingenesis found in canto 1 of Dante's *Commedia*. Therefore, we find ourselves back in the "dark world" of cantos 14-16.

Pound's lexicographical game charts his discovery of various ideas connected with the meaning of ἅλιος, including the sea's double nature. But even when he seems to be drifting aimlessly in his insistence on following the arbitrariness of the Greek Lexicon's word order, Pound's attention never deviates from his original subject, Herakles's *katabasis*.

The fragment which Pound adapts from Stesichorus maps out a *katabasis* from sunlight to dark to sunlight again, from Helios in his golden cup to δάφναισι κατάσκιον or the *"selv' oscura,"* to a morning scene depicting sailors dumping sand from their boats under the eye of "Yperionides!" When we remember that the labours of Herakles were undertaken for a prize and that this prize was immortality, this *katabasis* takes on new meaning. The subject of the Stesichorus passage, as Pound probably reads it, is the soul-freeing doctrine of palingenesis. In *The Doctrine of the Subtle Body*, Mead isolates the concept of the human soul and discusses at length Neoplatonic beliefs in the "radiant body" which envelops it.[23] Since the most detailed statement on this subject known to him is that by Synesius (A.D. 365-430?), Mead gives a full translation of it. In his discussion of the trials of the soul, Synesius explains that the soul is either striving upward to the "light-wrapped land" of bliss or is weighted down and descending into the "black-rayed gloom-wrapped land" of misery (105-107).[24] Synesius uses Herakles's ἄθλοι (*athloi*, contests or trials) as an example. Speaking about what is a gnostic concept, Synesius discusses the palingenetic nature of Herakles's *athloi*: "the so-called trials, which the sacred stories (*hieroi logoi*) say Hercules underwent and any other hero who valiantly strives for freedom, until they succeed in raising up their spirit to a height where the hands of nature cannot reach it" (*The Subtle Body* 104). It can be conjectured from this, then, that Pound's insistence in the Stesichorus passage on what we could call, borrowing the term from Mead, the "gloom-wrapped land" ("vada noctis obscurae," "poti venthea / nuctos eremnas," "daphnesi kataskion / Precisely, the selv' oscura"), points toward his occult understanding of Herakles's *athloi* as an allegory of palingenesis.[25]

I mentioned that the phrase "Seeking doubtless the sex in breadmoulds" seems utterly out of context. When we consider, however, that the Stesichorus passage follows directly the little pastiche on contemporary scientific inquiry, it becomes obvious that the phrase is intended to enforce the parallel between Herakles's *katabasis* and scientific research.

Critics are divided as to how this scientific inquiry should be read.[26] According to Pearlman, science is seen as a constructive force and the scientist as a new hero-*polumetis* or creative Odysseus who, in order to partake of the divine knowledge, involves himself in "repeated exposure of both mind and body to [dangerous] realities" (104). Angela Elliott, on the other hand, sees this scientific inquiry in the context of the Luciferian myth of dangerous pursuit of knowledge, since Pierre Curie burns himself with radium but persists, nevertheless, and continues his experiments ("Pound's Lucifer" 247-48). I think that the analogy between science and Herakles's successful *athlos* points to Pound's understanding of the scientist as an Odyssean hero.

There is another interesting aspect of scientific inquiry that Pound critics have not examined closely. Pound elsewhere alludes to Pierre and Marie Curie's discovery of radium and the phenomenon of radium's transformational properties (1898). In 1910 Pound wrote that "*La virtù* is the potency, the efficient property of a substance or person. Thus modern science shows us radium with a noble virtue of energy" (qtd. in Kenner, *The Pound Era* 154). In 1913 we find him writing that "the thing that matters in art is a sort of energy, something more or less like electricity or radio-activity, a force transfusing, welding, unifying" (qtd. in Bell 222).[27] And again, in 1912, he writes that "The Art of Poetry consists in combining these 'essential to thought,' these dynamic particles, *si licet*, this radium, with that melody of words..., and with that 'form' which shall most delight the intellect" (*SP* 360).

I think it is probable that behind these statements lies Pound's familiarity with the occult collapse of the distinctions between matter and spirit (*hyle* and *nous*) in favour of a cosmos thoroughly permeated by spirit as a creative, causative agent. It is as a hero of the cosmos of ordered dynamisms that Marie Curie's words about her husband Pierre are placed between the fragments involving the Neoplatonists and Herakles's palingenetic *katabasis*.

It is worth noting that Pound's concern with scientific discovery parallels that of some occultists. For example, Moina Bergson, in her "Preface" to the 1926 edition of her husband's (MacGregor Mathers) *The Kabbalah Unveiled*, writes that

> The gigantic strides made by science since the end of the last century, the staggering facts disclosed by its practical demonstrations, simultaneously with the development of the great occult movement, must strike all thoughtful people as the evidence of some imminent change in the evolution of this planet. Material science would appear to be spiritualizing itself and occult science to be materializing itself.... Matter and Spirit are only opposite poles of the same universal substance (vii-viii).

Mrs. Mathers goes on to discuss the indivisible unity of the cosmos under the ONE, a single god or a harmony of Supreme Forces. Interestingly enough, it is the idea of Radium as a medium that Mrs. Mathers chooses in demonstrating that there is little difference between monotheism, polytheism, and pantheism, since the indivisible unit may be one of many beings whose actions are unified or a unity whose action is pluralized: "... take Radium as being so very close in nature to the one element of the Ancients and note its triune manifestation, through the alpha, beta and gamma rays" (xi).

As Mrs. Mathers does here, occultists seized on radiation as a subtle essence which was not physical or "hylic," and discussed the ultra-material potentialities of radium as proof of the existence of a power that science could not explain. After all, one of the possible explanations offered by Marie Curie hinted at the substance's metaphysical attributes. As Robert Reid puts it,

> [Marie Curie] supposed that her radioactive substances were borrowing their energy from some external sources and releasing it. Was it possible that there were some still unknown radiation permeating the whole of space which her radium was capturing and then releasing? (Lord Kelvin

even went so far as to suggest that radium was getting its energy by absorbing mysterious "ethereal waves"!) (115).

Curie's, and even more pointedly Lord Kelvin's, conjecture regarding the origin of radiation was seized upon by various occultists as proof of the traditional occult notions of the "subtle body."[28]

Pound follows the Stesichorus fragment (in which the curious verse discussed above is inserted) with, in Peck's description, "a Homeric beaching of ships, as on some interlude on the return, and follows that with an idyllic, composite landscape — one more version of the Ithacan moment" (65-66). Peck's description of the fourth section of canto 23 is rather accurate, except that the moment described is not so much Ithacan as it is Circean or Calypsean. (Pound, we need to remember, is not really interested in Penelope.) The idyllic interlude is full of Homeric echoes (for example, "Where a man might carry his oar up") as well as echoes of an erotic drama of violence which has been developed in earlier cantos (including cantos 3 and 4). The interlude begins with an Odysseus figure awaking to behold a beaching of ships and a scene of satyrs dancing in the background of a Mediterranean landscape. The idyll is "composite" because the Odysseus figure seems to be beached in a Chinese landscape, and the lady who is remembered is Fa-Han:[29]

> Fa Han and I at the window,
> And her head bound with gold cords.
> Cloud over mountains; hill gap, in mist, like a sea coast (23/108).

The position of Fa-Han at the window serves to remind us of an earlier female figure placed in a similar setting: "Parisina — two doves from an altar — at the window" (20/90). The composite moment seems to exist in the mind of Niccolo d'Este who, as in earlier cantos, is in a "sort of delirium" (L 210).

For those who fail to see the connections between this idyll and Niccolo's delirium, Pound repeats "arras" twice in the same line ("Under the arras, or wall painted below like arras" [23/108]). This word alerts us to the recognition that the two lovers of this scene are Parisina Malatesta and Ugo Aldobrandino. Their story, which is the story of the Este family, is told by Pound in cantos 8, 20, 24 and is completed in canto 26.

The reference to the adulterous love and death of Parisina and Ugo in the idyllic passage of canto 23 serves to remind us, first, of all the tales of sexual violence and murder which we encounter in the early cantos (especially in canto 4), and, second, it reintroduces, by juxtaposition, the story of Peire de Maensac, of which Pound gives us two versions in *The Cantos*.

The first version appears in canto 5, condensed from the version in "Troubadours — Their Sorts and Conditions" (*LE* 96-97):

> And Pieire won the singing, Pieire de Maensac,
> Song or land on the throw, and was *dreitz hom*
> And had De Tierci's wife and with the war they made:
>   Troy in Auvergnat
> While Menelaus piled up the church at port
> He kept Tyndarida. Dauphin stood with de Maensac (5/18).

Though adultery is the cause of the war in both "Auvergnat" and "Troy," the parallel is not yet complete, since de Tierci, unlike Menelaus, does not get his wife back nor does the castle fall.

As retold in canto 23, the story of de Maensac is linked with the destruction of the Albigenses. Thus Pound manipulates the account of the story he gave in his essay so that both the cause of the wars (adultery) and the consequence (destruction of castle and of a culture) correspond to the story of Troy:

> And my brother De Maensac
> Bet with me for the castle,
> . . . .
> And Tierci came with a posse to Auvergnat,
> And went back for an army
> And came back to Auvergne with the army
> But never got Pierre nor the woman.
> And he went down past Chaise Dieu,
> And went after it all to Mount Segur,
> after the end of all things,
> And they hadn't left even the stair,
> And Simone was dead by that time,
> And they called us the Manicheans
> Wotever the hellarse that is.
>
> And that was when Troy was down, all right,
>   superbo Ilion . . . (23/108-109).

The narrator of this passage is clearly Austors de Maensac, Peire's brother. Tierci, we are told by Brooke-Rose, after failing to win back his unfaithful wife, "joined (a little late in the day) Simon de Montfort's Albigensian Crusade, which destroyed a whole civilization and its hard clear poetry of erotic love" (212). The last two lines of Austor's narrative ("And they called us the Manicheans / Wotever the hellsarse that is") depict the Catholic church's manipulative methods and the age's confusion whereby it was possible for people to be persecuted for being something they were not (wonderfully captured in Pound's colloquial language).[30] Pound regarded the Albigensian Crusade as "a sordid robbery cloaking itself in religious pretence, [which] had ended the *gai savoir* in southern France" (*SR* 101). Here Pound places Montségur (the symbolic last stronghold of the Provençal glory) and the ruins of the Provençal civilization beside the fallen city of Troy.[31]

Leon Surette first discussed the important part played by the French Rosicrucian Joséphin Péladan (1885-1918) in the shaping of Pound's belief in the existence of an underground mystery cult (*Eleusis* 34-39, 40-41, 57-60). Pound first regarded Péladan's ideas with skepticism which later became cautious agreement until finally, in the 1930s, he adopted the general outline of Péladan's hypothesis and identified Albigensianism with Eleusis. The following long quotation from "Terra Italica" provides a clear indication of Pound's position which, it should be added, conforms to the fantasy history of the occult outlined in Chapter II of the present study:

> For all its inclusiveness the new religion [Christianity] was for fifteen and more centuries troubled by heresies, mostly uninteresting and perhaps all of them traceable to some cult it had not included.
>
> One cult it had failed to include was that of Eleusis.
>
> It may be arguable that Eleusinian elements persisted in the very early Church, and are responsible for some of the scandals. It is quite certain that the Church later emerged riddled with tendencies to fanaticism, with sadistic and masochistic tendencies that are in no way Eleusinian.
>
> It is equally discernible upon study that some non-Christian and inextinguishable source of beauty persisted throughout the Middle Ages maintaining song in Provence, maintaining the grace of Kalenda Maya.
>
> And this force was the strongest counter force to the cult of Atys and asceticism [Mithraism].... The usual accusation against the Algigeois is that they were Manichaeans. This I believe after a long search to be pure bunkumb. The slanderers feared the truth. I mean they feared not only the force of a doctrine but they feared giving it even the publicity which a true bill against it would have required.
>
> The best scholars do not believe there were any Manichaeans left in Europe at the time of the Albigensian Crusade. If there were any in Provence they have at any rate left no trace in troubadour art.
>
> On the other hand the cult of Eleusis will explain not only general phenomena but particular beauties in Arnaut Daniel or in Guido Cavalcanti.

....
> I suggest that students trying to understand the poesy of southern Europe from 1050 to 1400 should try to open it with this key ... [that is, the survival of the cult of Eleusis] (*SP* 58-59).³²

But what drew Pound's mind back to the subject of de Maensac and the Albigenses whom he associates with the Provençal culture and the Eleusinian mysteries? The answer to this question must be sought, I believe, in Pound's concept of the celestial tradition in which Plethon, with whom the first section of this canto is concerned, is included. The Albigenses, the troubadours, and Plethon are all seen by Pound as inheritors of the pagan mysteries.

Since at the heart of the Eleusinian mysteries there was an encounter with the dead and some theophanic revelation, this point is important for our understanding of canto 23, where we have a *katabasis*, a theophanic revelation which seems linked with the revelation of the *epopteia*, and an *hieros gamos*, the enactment of a literal sexual union, performed in the mysteries by the Hierophant and the Priestess of Demeter.

The sixth part of canto 23 ends with the destruction of a temple (Montségur) as well as with the destruction of the Provençal culture. The seventh part then opens with the evocation of the end of another culture: "And that was when Troy was down, all right, / superbo Ilion..." (23/109). But Pound cuts short his account of the destruction of Troy and the use of the aposeiopesis signifies his expectation that the reader will fill in the gap. Then, the ending of one culture is succeeded by the beginning of another, and Pound picks up, *in medias res*, Ovid's account of the flight of Anchises and Aeneas from Troy to Rome:

> And they were sailing along
> Sitting in the stern-sheets,
> Under the lee of an island
> And the wind drifting off from the island
> "Tet, tet...
>   What is it?" said Anchises.
> "Tethnéké," said the helmsman, "I think they
> "Are howling because Adonis died virgin" (23/109).

Aeneas and Anchises, sailing through the Aegean, hear a foreign chant ("Tet, tet...") which they cannot make out. The helmsman, who has probably travelled to Greek ports and understands Greek, comes to their aid, identifies the words and interprets them: "the women," he says, "are wailing because Adonis died virgin." The muddled sounds reaching the ship are part of the rites associated with the worship of Adonis which involved ceremonial wailing and singing of dirges over the effigy of the dead youth. The reference to Adonis, the beloved of Aphrodite who was killed by a boar, introduces into the poem a variation of the myth of the *threnos* or lamentation of the Great Mother for her lover — a motif repeated in canto 47.

Still another variation of this myth is the story of Aphrodite and Anchises told in the *Homeric Hymn to Aphrodite*. Pound alludes to this next by paraphrasing Aphrodite's attempt to hide her identity from Anchises: "King Otreus, of Phrygia, / "That King is my father" (23/109). The allusion brings to mind the theogamy of Anchises and Aphrodite, of which Aeneas was the issue. Aphrodite tried to hide her identity from Anchises by pretending that she was the daughter of Otreus, king of Phrygia. In this the goddess succeeds since "ὁ δ' ἔπειτα θεῶν ἰότητι καὶ αἴσῃ / ἀθανάτῃ παρέλεκτο θεᾷ βροτός, οὐ σάφα εἰδώς" (66-67: "Then by the will of the gods and destiny he [Anchises] lay with her, / a mortal man with an immortal goddess, not clearly knowing what he did)" (*Hesiod: The Homeric Hymns and Homerica* [(416-17]).

Carol H. Cantrell has noted the use of the word εἰδώς ("knowing") in the second of the two lines quoted above and has observed that, because Anchises does not know the identity of the goddess, he comes to know her sexually but fails to achieve the "full Ειδὼς," the ultimate knowledge [or *gnosis*] which comes when the union between the knower and the known is reached (16-18).[33] That is, Aphrodite appears to Anchises not in her Eleusinian but in her Circean aspect. The "full Ειδὼς" is reserved here, then, for the narrator and reader/*mystes* who as initiates are meant to witness and experience the revelation of the goddess in the canto's final lines.

The reference to the theogamy of Aphrodite and Anchises is accompanied by a theophany, and so canto 23, like canto 1, ends with the birth of Aphrodite:

> and saw then, as the waves taking form,
> And the sea, hard, a glitter of crystal,
> And the waves rising but formed, holding their form.
> No light reaching through them (23/109).

This must be a description of Aphrodite emerging from the sea ('Αφροδίτη = "emerging from the foam"). The description is very important for a number of reasons: first, the theophany represents the *mystes's* ability to break through to a vision of the gods (it is "a burst thru from quotidien into divine"); second, the image of the crystal wave is a formula for the ecstatic moment — here the emergence of the visible form of the goddess from the sea-foam; and third, the last line of this canto links the present theophanic moment with the Eleusinian mysteries, since the crowning moment in these mysteries is preceded by a *katabasis* to a realm where natural light does not enter.

Canto 23's conclusion with a theophany brings us back to the beginning of the canto, which depicts a similar moment. The Neoplatonic light from "God's fire" invoked in the opening lines is a paradigm of the way divinity manifests itself and operates in human intelligences:

> "Et Omniformis," Psellos, "omnis
> "Intellectus est." God's fire. Gemisto:
> "Never with this religion
> "Will you make men of the greeks.
> "But built wall across Peloponesus
> "And organize, and . . .
>   damn these Eyetalian barbarians."
> And Novvy's ship went down in the tempest
> Or at least they chucked the books overboard (23/107).

Before discussing the importance of Plethon for canto 23, it is interesting to note how Pound manages to engage and include almost all the important Neoplatonic philosophers in the first few lines of this passage — and this role-call of Neoplatonic philosophers corresponds to the one we find in *Guide to Kulchur* (225). The passage opens with a quotation from Porphyry. These words are spoken, however, by Psellus, a later Neoplatonist (eleventh century). The first two words have already been quoted in canto 5 in relation to still another Neoplatonist of the fourth century, Iamblichus ("Iamblichus' light, . . . / 'Et omniformis': Air, fire the pale soft light" [5/17]). The next quotation is spoken by Plethon. In canto 15 it is Porphyry's teacher, Plotinus, the greatest Neoplatonist, who leads Odysseus-Pound out of the darkness of Dante's Hell to the earthly paradise. Pound manages, then, to present one of the central Neoplatonic dicta followed by a roll-call of the most important Neoplatonists.

The Latin phrase quoted at the beginning of canto 23 ("And every intellect is capable of assuming every shape") is central to the philosophy of the Neoplatonists, who believed in the ability of the human mind to participate in the *theos*, the *nous* or divine mind. This phrase, which signals the presence of several Neoplatonists at the beginning of canto 23, is also important because Gemistus Plethon can be seen, first, as the organizing centre of many of the Italian themes of the first thirty cantos and, second, as an essential link in Pound's conception of the chain of the "celestial tradition." Libera's "Casting His Gods Back into the NOUS: Two Neoplatonists and The Cantos of Ezra Pound," is the most complete study of the importance of Plethon for Pound. But even Libera misses, or rather fails to place enough emphasis upon, a very significant point: Marsilio Ficino's absorption of the idea of the Tradition of Wisdom as presented by Plethon. It is with this point in mind that I would like to rehearse some of the material which Libera includes in her excellent article.

There are seven references in all to Plethon in *The Cantos* and at least three more in the drafts which were not included by Pound in the final text.[34] The first three references (8/31, 23/107, and 26/123), together with the three references found in the Malatesta drafts, give us a rather complete sketch of the life of this Byzantine Neoplatonist—of course, the reader still needs to place these references in chronological order and to fill some of the gaps.

A Byzantine political reformer and Platonist philosopher, Plethon[35] was born in Constantinople but spent the later and better known part of his long life in the Peloponnesian capital of Mistra, near ancient Sparta, as a high official and political adviser of the princes of the Byzantine imperial house who resided there. It is in his role as political reformer that Pound presents Plethon in canto 23 (107).

From various extant testimonies from Plethon's time, it appears that he tried to bring about a reform of the declining Byzantine state, and to strengthen its resources and defences against the mounting Turkish threats and Western pressures. It is in this light that we should view Pound's elliptical lines which refer, first, to Plethon's attempt to establish a new pagan religion; second, to a letter he sent to Emperor Manuel II (ca. 1510) in which he outlined the urgent need for the erection of a wall across the Isthmus of Corinth designed to hold back the waves of Moslems; and, third, to his strong opposition to making an appeal to the Latins for military help.

Blaming the imminent danger faced by the empire upon the passivity of Christianity, Plethon proposed a radical reorganization for Byzantium. Attempting to reconstruct a new polytheistic system that would provide a new basis or culture, he created a new theogony in which Zeus is the highest god, followed by Poseidon, god of the sea, through whom all gods are governed and all things created—this is what we might call a hydrogenetic system or theogony.

Plethon was a prolific writer, producing a large number of learned tracts on such subjects as the Incarnation of Jesus Christ and the Procession of the Holy Spirit (hence Pound's flippant allusion: "And in February they all packed off / To Ferrara to decide on the holy ghost / And as to which begat the what in the Trinity.—" [26/123]), as well as numerous works on rhetoric, history, philosophy, politics, national defence, geography, mathematics, philosophy, astronomy, and music. The longest and most important of these works is the one entitled Νόμοι (*Nomoi* or *Laws*), of which many fragments are extant today. In this "frankly pagan" and "outspokenly polytheistic" work, "Plethon set forth a new system of philosophy, by which he hoped to replace the Christian religion and help restore Greece to her ancient glory" (Anastos 186).

Pound shows himself aware of the controversial nature of Plethon's work and, no doubt, is attracted to it for that reason. In both *Guide to Kulchur* and *The Cantos*, Pound refers to Plethon's hydrogenetic system and, especially in *Guide to Kulchur*, to his influence and extant writings. First, in canto 8 (31) and in the *Pisan Cantos*, Pound points to the relationship between Plethon's notions about Poseidon and the sculpted aquatic scenes in the Tempio: "ὕδωρ / HUDOR et Pax / Gemisto stemmed all from Neptune / hence the Rimini bas reliefs" (83/528). Then, in *Guide to Kulchur*, Pound provides many more details about his interest in Plethon and his writings:

> Gemistus Plethon brought over a species of Platonism to Italy in the 1430s. I take it he is more known by his sarcophagus in Rimini than by his writings. There is a ms. of his greek in the Laurenziana in Firenze, a German named Schulze [Fritz Schultze] (or something of that sort) included him in a study of philosophy, I think Gemisto gets a whole vol. whereof a copy lies in the Marciana (Venice). A bit of him was translated early into latin and printed in the back pages of an early edtn. of Xenophon, but left out of the reprints. I think it is the edtn. of 1496. And they say Gemisto found no one to talk to, or more generally he did the talking. He was not a proper polytheist, in this sense: His gods come from Neptune, so that there is a single source of being, aquatic (udor, Thales etc. as you like, or what is the difference). And Gemisto had distinct aims, regeneration of greek people so they wd. keep out the new wave of Barbarism (Turkish) etc.
>
> At any rate he had a nailed boot for Aristotle, and his conversation must have been lively. Hence (at a guess) Ficino's sinecure, at old Cosimo's expense, trained to translate the greek neoplatonists. Porphyry, Psellos, Iamblichus, Hermes Trismegistus. . . .
>
> Whence I suppose what's-his-name and the English mystics with reference to greek originals sometimes (John Heydon etc.) (GK 224-25).

As already mentioned earlier, it is clear that in Pound's syncretic tradition Plethon occupies a central position as the individual most responsible for the transmission of the "celestial tradition" to the West. In fact, Pound's inclusion of Plethon in his standard occult list of carriers of the "celestial tradition" is clear in both *The Cantos* and his prose writings.

Plethon was one of the delegates who, in 1438, followed the Byzantine emperor and Patriarch of Constantinople to Italy and participated in the famous Council of Ferrara-Florence (referred to by Pound in cantos 8/31 and 26/123-24). The purpose of the conference was to effect a reconciliation between the Greek and Latin churches and secure aid for Byzantium's fight against the Turks. Plethon himself did not endorse the proclamation of the reunion of the Churches. Later developments justified his unwillingness to join the other Byzantine champions of the proclamation. The Greek mission was a failure because the short-lived reunion of the churches was not accompanied by the military aid for which the Greeks had hoped. Nonetheless, Plethon's presence in Italy was instrumental in the reintroduction of Platonism to the West. In Florence Plethon was befriended by Cosimo de Medici. Cosimo's encounter with Plethon prompted him to found a Platonic school, establishing the study of Neoplatonism in the West.[36] Pound, as is made clear in the quotation from *Guide to Kulchur* (1938) as well as in the following passage from a 1914 article that appeared in *The New Age*, was aware of and interested in these developments:

> Ficino was seized in his youth by Cosimo dei Medici and set to work translating a Greek that was in spirit anything but "classic." That is to say, you had, ultimately, a "Platonic" academy messing up Christian and Pagan mysticism, allegory, occultism, demonology, Trismegistus, Psellus, Porphyry, into a most eloquent and exciting and exhilarating hotch-potch, which "did for" the mediaeval fear of the *dies irae* and for human abasement generally" (*GB* 112).

Despite their light-heartedness ("messing up"), Pound's comments are favourable — and it is clear that in the course of his comments on the syncretist character of Ficino's system Pound finds this "system" not only "eloquent" but also "exciting" and "exhilarating." After all, following Ficino's example, Pound is concocting here his own "celestial tradition"!

In addition to "old Cosimo," Plethon can also be related to Sigismundo Malatesta. The reference to Novvy, Malatesta's younger brother (23/107), alerts us to Malatesta's presence in Florence during the Council; he, too, was impressed by Plethon's conversation so that, according to Pound's theory, "the ideas of Plethon had a direct influence in the bas-reliefs that Sigismundo Malatesta commissioned Agostino di Duccio to execute at the Tempio: 'Gemisto stemmed all from Neptune / Hence the Rimini bas reliefs'" (Libera 273-74).[37] The associations between Plethon and

Malatesta extend even further since the latter, when he went to Peloponnesus in 1464, searched for Plethon's remains, found them, brought them back to Rimini, and placed them in one of the sarcophagi of his Tempio Malatestiano.[38]

Plethon's function with regard to the Tempio is catalytic; as well, the importance Pound attaches to his role in the transmission of the "celestial tradition" to the West is unquestionable. In canto 23 Plethon stands with those Neoplatonists who, throughout *The Cantos*, advance the dictum according to which each human being has the ability to achieve the state of divine *nous*. The canto ends fittingly, then, with an image depicting the theophany of Aphrodite, which represents the initiate's successful achievement of *gnosis*.

4. "Yet Must Thou Sail after Knowledge": The *Katabasis* after Gnosis in Canto 47

I have already remarked that an important exoteric form that the initiation rite takes in *The Cantos* is ritual copulation. Pound makes copulation conform to the traditional tripartite structure of mystery rites such as those of Eleusis; but since it has rarely been represented in literature, he has had to invent formulae and expressions for the *hieros gamos*. Pound restructures the traditional association of unrequited love and transcendence as the "unromantic" act of phallic penetration. The gynecological nature of his imagery has mitigated against any very candid discussion of it. This section is an examination of canto 47 that argues for a "schema of increasing enlightened consciousness" and the centrality of the *hieros gamos* in *The Cantos*, and views phallic penetration as a form of *katabasis* leading to *epopteia* or palingenetic illumination. The act of phallic penetration in canto 47 (already stated in more sexually explicit terms in canto 39) parallels the *mystes's* passing through the "hylic" cosmos of cantos 44-46 on his way to achieving the "order of the dimension of stillness" (Emery 41) of canto 49 and the state of *nous* of canto 51 – a state first grasped in *The Fifth Decad of Cantos* in terms of the enlightened pastoral economics outlined in the "Siena Cantos" (42-43). The state of *nous* is equivalent to the stage of *epopteia* when the *mystes* is metamorphosed inwardly and is readied for the attainment of *soteria* or salvation.[39]

In the 1930s Pound was trying to salvage, among other things, the two examples that exhibited the workings of the "Intellectual Light" in the world and which he considered absolutely necessary for intelligent communication: the American Constitution and the Leopoldine Reforms.[40] *Eleven New Cantos XXXI-XLI* (1934) deals mostly with the men who either were responsible for the *genesis* of the American Constitution or showed their enlightenment by trying to uphold it—that is, these cantos present the *dromena* of the American paradigm (cantos 31-35 and 37) and look forward to Mussolini (canto 41) as the one modern-day leader who exhibits the values exemplified in the actions of Pound's American political heroes. This sequence of cantos also contains two examples of the *epopteia*: canto 36 presents, by way of Cavalcanti, Pound's contemplation of "the creative power of emanating light" (Emery 113), a state of being that follows coitus, an act unequivocally expressed in the *mystes's* cry: "Sacrum, sacrum, inluminatio coitu" ("Sacred, sacred, the illumination in intercourse"); and canto 39, a restatement of the ecstatic cry, exoterically represents the *mystes's* / Odysseus's chthonic conquest of the goddess (Circe), corresponding thus to the rite of Eleusis, leading to restoration, and "look[ing] forward to 'the great healing'" (Oderman 100) of cantos 47, 49 and 90-91.

The "Siena Cantos" link the *Fifth Decad* (1937) with the earlier *Eleven New Cantos* (1934) by dealing with the founding of the Sienese bank, the "Monte dei Paschi," a paradigm of enlightened as well as successful economic paideuma corresponding to Pound's presentation of the American paideuma of Jefferson, Adams, John Quincy Adams, and Martin Van Buren—a paideuma *in potentia*. In fact, the *Fifth Decad* was intended as "preparation for the palate"; and the shift from American history to seventeenth-century Italy thus signals Pound's apparent intention to celebrate Mussolini as an enlightened ruler and modern Italy as the fulfillment of his historical fantasy.

Rooted in the will of the people ("there first was the fruit of nature / there was the whole will of the people" [43/218]) and based on the "abundance of nature" ("CREDIT rests *in ultimate* on the ABUNDANCE OF NATURE, on the growing grass that can nourish the living sheep" [*SP* 194]) rather than made "*ex nihil*" (46/233), the miracle of the Monte dei Paschi is the economic equivalent to the Eleusinian *epopteia* which includes the insight that copulation is good for the crops.

Depending as it does on communal credit, the abundance of nature, and "built for beneficence, for reconstruction," the *epopteic* ethos of the Sienese bank (which is viewed by Pound as an example of "enlightened consciousness" "bust[ing] thru") stands in stark opposition to the usurious principles of the "hell banks" that are "created [*ex nihil*] to prey on the people" (*SP* 270) and which cause the kind of artistic and ritual deprivation invoked in the "usura" cantos (45 and 50). The founding of the Sienese bank is an achievement comparable to Sigismundo's building of the Tempio, Mussolini's projected ushering in of the New Age, and the setting up of "the statue of Aphrodite again over Terracina" (*GK* 191). In fact, in canto 43 the "BANK," "the New Mount" is transformed into one of Pound's sacred temples, replacing the church cathedral as the goal of the modern religious procession which he, casting himself into the role of a Sienese notary, has witnessed and describes (43/216-17).[41]

Canto 44 traces the history of the bank and Siena into the eighteenth century, focussing on Pietro Leopoldo, Grand Duke of Tuscany (1765-90), who advocated many governmental reforms; and Pound celebrates him because he thinks that he possesses an "enlightened consciousness" issuing forth in economic and civil reform. The canto ends with a litany in which Petro Leopoldo's reforms are recorded:

> And before him [Napoleon] had been Pietro Leopoldo
> that wished state debt brought to an end;
> . . . .
> that said thou shalt not sell public offices;
> that suppressed so many *gabelle*;
> that freed printers of surveillance
>   and wiped out the crime of lèse majesty;
> that abolished death as a penalty and all tortures in prisons
> which he held were for segregation;
> that split common property among tillers;
> roads, trees, and the wool trade,
> the silk trade, and a set price, lower, for salt;
>   plus another full page of such actions . . . (44/227-28).

This litany of "enlightened" measures is punctuated by the use of the epanaphora, also the dominant rhetorical figure in canto 45; thus the first "usura" canto is anticipated rhetorically as well as by way of contrast: the founding of the Sienese bank "has been to keep bridle on usury" (43/228).

Canto 45 is "hylic" in the sense that it constitutes a diatribe against "usura."[42] Usury, which elsewhere is characterized as "a murrain and a marasmus" (*GK* 109), is seen here as a sin against nature and natural abundance—the subject of cantos 42 and 43. Usury, "age-old and age-thick," occupies a central place in Pound's cosmos and bears the burden of his critique of human failure. Pound's litany against usury achieves its purposes rhetorically (through the use of epanaphora, isocolon, and litotes, which predominate in this canto).[43] By using the epanaphora and the isocolon Pound places rhetorical emphasis upon usury's ubiquity. "Usura" is offered as the cause of failure in every imaginable human activity: architecture, music, painting, crafts, agriculture, economics, sex, and religion. Throughout canto 45, Pound uses litotes, suggesting man's potential for achieving the opposite of that which he criticizes. In other words, Pound's rhetoric compels the reader to contemplate not only the deprivation and devastation caused by "usura" but, even more significantly, the splendour of the *epopteic* creativity in the absence of "usura." For example, when Pound writes that, "with usura / hath no man a painted paradise on his church wall (45/229), he is implying that the vision of an earthly paradise is still within man's reach — but the practice of usury must first be eliminated.[44]

One form that Pound's critique takes in canto 45 is the pointing out of the debasement of coitus in an usurious age. In a poem that emphasizes the importance of ritual copulation as the surest way to the *epopteia*, "usura" is seen as the cause for sexual depravity. Thus usury is seen as degrading the value of eros, turning it into whoredom:

> Usura slayeth the child in the womb
> It stayeth the young man's courting
> It hath brought palsey to bed, lyeth
> between the young bride and her bridegroom
>   CONTRA NATURAM
> They have brought whores for Eleusis
> Corpses are set to banquet
> at behest of usura. (45/230)

It comes as no surprise that Pound chooses here not just any one rite but that of Eleusis. After all, it is the *hieros gamos* above everything else that Pound views as the central act of the Eleusinian mysteries — how seriously he takes the threat presented by the usurers is clear in the final image of canto 45, an image presenting the profanation of the Eleusinian temple.[45]

The images of abortion, abortive love, sterility, and the analogy between whores and corpses are thus succinct statements of Pound's belief that usury debauches what is sacred. According to his analogy, as whores are to sex (where sex should be a communal celebration and a means of illumination) so are corpses to a banquet (also a communal celebration). But what is the use of corpses brought to a banquet? Are corpses the guests or the meal? The analogy, especially its second part, is problematical. Perhaps Pound means that "at the behest of usura" the sacramental *hieros gamos* of the mysteries has been debased to the point that the communal banquet becomes a game for necrophiliacs. Usury thus causes the destruction of the central symbol of the mysteries: coitus and the attendant *epopteia*.

Pound commented on these lines in a 1938 letter to Carlo Izzo:

> "Eleusis" is *very* elliptical. It means that in place of the sacramental
> -_____ in the Mysteries, you 'ave the 4 and six-penny 'ore. As you
> see, the moral bearing is very high, and the degradation of the sacra-

ment (which is the coition and *not* the going to a fatbuttocked priest or registry office) has been completely debased *by* Xtianity, or misunderstanding of that Ersatz religion (*L* 303).

Pound argues here that while copulation itself is the sacrament, the marriage ritual is an empty form. He isolates the evils arising from a misunderstanding of the mysteries and from human greed, and, in his own "elliptical" way, he holds up the Eleusinian celebration of the natural cycle as a counterforce to usury—a celebration whose focus is the "sacramental [fucking]."[46]

The rhetorical fervour of canto 45 is succeeded by the more expository and discursive canto 46, where the attack against "usura" is made in terms of economics. Here Pound's attack against the international bankers, profiteers, munitions manufacturers and dealers, and all those interested in quick profits is balanced by a list of constructive men labouring in a "hylic" hell created by the worshippers of Geryon, the prosopopoeia of "usura." Pound's list of constructive men includes Orage, Douglas, Mussolini, Jefferson, and Van Buren. It is thanks to these men that the hope for the triumph of the Eleusinian ethos is never surrendered.

The polemic against "Geryon" and "hyperusura" (46/23) gives way, in the pivotal canto 47, to an explicitly depicted *hierogamy*, esoterically equivalent to Pound's economic insights in cantos 42 and 43. Canto 47, the fourth Odyssean canto so far (1, 20, 39, 47—one such canto per section), achieves the ritualization of both the *katabasis* and the *hieros gamos*. The effects of this "act," which is simultaneously both a *katabasis* as well as an *hierogamy*, have already been rehearsed, in less delicate terms, in canto 39: "Girls talked there of fucking, beasts talked there of eating, / All heavy with sleep, fucked girls and fat leopards. . . ." In that canto Odysseus's sexual *katabasis* ("His rod hath made god in my belly") presages and is equivalent to the Odyssean *nekuia* ("Been to hell in a boat yet?") of canto 1. It would seem, then, that Pound conflates into one the *katabasis* ("Live man goes down into the world of Dead") with the *hieros gamos*—in either case the result is a "bust thru" to the *theos*. The two *hierogamies* of cantos 39 and 47 differ insofar as the first represents the *mystes's* union with the goddess Circe in her chthonic or exoteric aspect while the second one is a union between the *mystes* and the goddess in her esoteric aspect—in other words, the *gnosis* or insight, embodied in the ecstatic shouts of canto 47, has to be delayed until the *mystes* has conquered the chthonic aspect of the goddess through his *katabasis* into the hylic world of *dromena*.

The coarseness of the language used to describe the sexual *katabasis* in canto 39 is replaced in canto 47 with a lyricism that is perhaps unparalleled for its beauty in *The Cantos*. Interweaving images adapted from the vegetation rites of Adonis, contemporary Catholic rites, the story of Circe and Odysseus as narrated in the *Odyssey*, and the rites of sowing and plowing as explained in Hesiod's *Works and Days*, Pound creates a composite rite which is, in fact, his own version of ancient cults. The various strands are brought together by the idea of the *hieros gamos* as seen within Gnostic allegory. The *hieros gamos* is allegorized as the union of the active, procreative, masculine principle (Odysseus, light, sky, ploughman, phallus, *nous*, order) with the passive, creative, female principle (Circe, Aphrodite, Sophia, Tellus or earth or *hyle*, cunnus or *pecten cteis*, confusion).[47] The *katabasis* is both the *Nekuia* and the sexual act. Both are seen as a fall of the male principle (*nous*, soul) into the female principle (matter), leading to a new state, allowing the *mystes* to come into communion with an "unchangeable force within and beyond all the seeming change and impermanence of the universe" (Emery 11). In other words, canto 47 re-enacts a rite that allows the *mystes* access to the "full Ειδώς."[48]

Leon Surette has already established Pound's familiarity with Mead's Gnostic interpretation of the Simon Magus legend, concluding that by "linking a divine manifestation of beauty . . . [Helen of Tyre] with the raw commercial sexuality of a brothel, the legend provides a bridge between Aphrodite and Circe, a bridge that Pound most certainly uses in cantos 39 and 47" (*Light* 64).[49] The legend of Simon Magus and Helen of Tyre is a particular example of the Gnostic myth which deals with the fall of the female Pistis Sophia or Wisdom (archetype of the ψυχή, the soul) into matter where she remains imprisoned until she can be liberated through the agency of the salvific male (archetype of νοῦς, the mind or spirit). In the Simon Magus legend, the fallen Sophia, sometimes provocatively called *Sophia Prunikos*, "Wisdom the Whore" (Jonas 187), is imprisoned within a human body. Sophia or Helen has had to wander throughout the centuries from vessel to vessel in ever-changing bodies (the body of Helen of Troy has been one of them) until she ends up in a brothel (the soul as a fallen woman) from which Simon, the unrecognized Σωτήρ (*Soter*, Saviour) who has descended from above, delivers her. In Mead's words,

> The main symbolism, which the evolvers of the Simon-legend parodied into the myth of Simon and Helen, appears to have been sidereal; thus the Logos and his Thought, the World-Soul, were symbolized as the Sun (Simon) and the Moon (Selene, Helen); so with the microcosm, Helen was the human soul fallen into matter and Simon the mind which brings about her redemption. Moreover one of the systems appears to have attempted to interpret the Trojan legend and myth of Helen in a spiritual and psychological fashion (*Fragments of a Faith Forgotten* 167-68).

As to the theogony of this Gnostic system, Simon Magus' *The Great Announcement* includes this passage:

> Of the universal Aeons there are two growths, without beginning or end, springing from one Root, which is the Power Silence invisible, inapprehensible. Of these one appears from above, which is the Great Power, the Universal Mind, ordering all things, male; and the other from below, the Great Thought (or Conception), female, producing all things (*Fragments of a Faith Forgotten* 173).

Mead himself insisted upon the symbolical nature of the legend's language and warned against taking "these allegories of the Soul as literal histories, for nothing but sorrow will follow such materialization of divine mysteries" (*Simon Magus* 75). But Pound, for whom sexual orgasm and the state of divine illumination often become fused (that is, the exoteric and esoteric phases of the initiation, respectively), pays no attention to Mead's warning.[50] The *hieros gamos* of canto 47 may be seen, then, as a ritual analogue of the penetration of the Great Thought by the Universal Mind, of matter by spirit, and this leads to *palingenesis*, revelation, and rebirth.

At the start of canto 47, the Circean catechism concerning the necessity for sailing to Hell "after knowledge" (47/236) is interwoven with references to ancient Near East rites celebrating the death and resurrection of Tamuz, the Babylonian fertility god who is the equivalent of Adonis, the beloved of Aphrodite. Both the death and resurrection of the god are symbolized here: his death by the "red flame" and "the small lamps float[ing] seaward" and "the sea ... streaked red with Adonis";[51] and his rebirth by the "Wheat shoots ris[ing] new by the altar, / flower from swift seed" (47/236). The following lines, adapted from Bion's *Lament for Adonis*, allude to a classic paradigm of θρῆνος (*threnos* or lamentation) which is part of the sacred drama of Adonis's death and rebirth and which parallels the imitation by the Eleusinian *mystai* of Demeter's mourning for Koré. The *threnos* is re-enacted here:

> Τυ Διώνα ["You Dione"]
> TU DIONA
> Και Μοῖραι' ᾿Αδονιν ["And the Fates (weep) for Adonis"]
> Kai MOIRAI' ADONIN (47/236)

The *katabasis* of death is equivalent to the sexual *katabasis* of male into female and thus the twice-repeated verse, "By this gate art thou measured" (47/236, 237), can be taken to refer to both the estuary of a river as well as the female vagina, seen here as a gate of death and rebirth. Intensifying the sexual symbolism, Pound describes female sexuality as an undirected life force which has an irresistible effect upon the male, including the cautious Odysseus (47/237-38). We know from Porphyry, among others, that in ancient times mysteries took place in caves; it is to a cave, then, both as a place of initiation and as symbolic female anatomy, that Odysseus, like other male creatures, is drawn:

> Moth is called over mountain
> The bull runs blind on the sword, *naturans*
> To the cave art thou called, Odysseus,
> By Molü hast thou respite for a little,
> By Molü art thou freed from the one bed
>   that thou may'st return to another
> The stars are not in her counting,
>   To her they are but wandering holes.
> Begin thy plowing
> When the Pleiades go down to their rest,
> Begin thy plowing
> 40 days are they under seabord,
> Thus do in fields by seabord
> And in valleys winding down toward the sea.
> When the cranes fly high
>   think of plowing (47/237).

Unlike the woman, who gives no care to the signs of seasonal propriety, the man pays close attention to the natural cycle. Pound is uncompromising about the active and passive roles played by male and female in the sexual rite which results in the coordination of human acts (e.g., plowing) with the natural cycle.

Besides the ritual celebration of the natural cycle, Pound is also thinking here of Odysseus's encounter with Circe. Protected by the sympathetic magic of Hermes's μῶλυ (moly), Odysseus gives in to Circe's invitation and to his own appetite. According to Thomas Taylor, Circe is "the goddess of sense." Odysseus or the soul must come to the cave or body where he must meet with, and overcome the power of, Circe—a power which is corruptive but necessary for the completion of the initiatory *katabasis*. This is how Taylor presents the matter:

> "Homer calls Circe, the daughter of the sun, the period and revolution of regeneration [παλιγγενεσία] in a circle, who ever connects and combines all corruption with generation, and generation again with corruption" [Porphyry in Stobaeus 141]. Hence, we may observe that the Aeean isle, or this region of sense, is with great propriety called the

abode of trouble and lamentation. In this region, then, the companions of Ulysses, that is, the thoughts and natural powers of his soul, are changed by the incantations of the goddess; and his opinions and natural motions, rashly wandering from the authority of ruling intellect, are converted through the allurements of delight, into an unworthy and irrational habit. Ulysses, however, or the rational soul, is by the assistance of Mercury [Hermes], or reason, prevented from destruction. Hence, intellect, roused by its impassive power, and recollecting the ills which its natural faculties endure; at the same time, being armed with prudent anger, and the plant moly, or virtue, which is able to repel the allurements of pleasure, wars on the goddess of sense, and prevents the effects of her fascinating charms ... (Taylor 326).

As already explained in the discussion of cantos 17 and 39, the union with Circe corresponds to the *katabasis*, a preliminary phase of the initiation. In her exoteric guise the goddess is Circe, and the act of phallic penetration disguises in gross physicality the spiritual, esoteric sense of the *mystes's* union with the *nous*. It is for this reason that the sexual *katabasis* is followed by the exhilarating cry of the mystes: "The light has entered the cave. Io! Io!" (47/238). This line signals the *mystes's* experience of orgasm (exoteric) and revelation or illumination (esoteric); the revelation, nonetheless, remains occult for the reader because it is a secret (*arrheton*) that cannot be explained or disclosed—the effects of the revelation are nevertheless proclaimed in the *mystes's* ecstatic cry: "Io! Io!"

Having answered the call by entering the gate which leads into the cave (mountain, *pecten cteis*), the male is subjected to the female's teasing rhetorical questions:

> So light is thy weight on Tellus
> Thy notch no deeper indented
> Thy weight less than the shadow
> Yet hast thou gnawed through the mountain,
>   Scylla's white teeth less sharp.
> Hast thou found a nest softer than cunnus
> Or hast thou found better rest
> Hast'ou a deeper planting, doth thy death year
> Bring swifter shoots?
> Hast thou entered more deeply the mountain? (47/238)

The antithesis between the phallic teeth gnawing their way through the mountain and the softness of the female "nest" is most telling—Pound is unmistakably explicit in his description of phallic penetration here. Indeed, the planting of the male seed in the female place of initiation brings forth swift "shoot." The *katabasis* is thus followed by the *epopteia* or illumination, as the twice-repeated cryptic "Sacrum, sacrum, inluminatio coitu" of canto 36 is here given full play:

> The light has entered the cave. Io! Io!
> The light has gone down into the cave,
> Splendour on splendour!
> By prong have I entered these hills:
> That the grass grow from my body,
> That I hear the roots speaking together,
> The air is new on my leaf,
> The forked boughs shake with the wind (47/238).

The "light" (Universal Mind, spiritual consciousness, *nous*, active intelligence, male, *mystes*, Odysseus, Anchises, Simon) enters the dark cave (Great Thought, material unconsciousness, *hyle* or matter, passive creativity, female, goddess, Circe, Aphrodite, Sophia, Selene) and the result is both "splendour" (Great Thought or soul, sexual rapture, mystical illumination, transformation of consciousness) and sprouting of plants in the spring. The god himself is pictured as taking part in the natural cycle. The sexual union of Odysseus and Circe, of Anchises and Aphrodite, of male and female becomes a sacred ritual act which may lead man to an understanding of the mystery of being. The act of entering through the "door" into "the hill" exoterically represents sexual penetration and esoterically represents a symbolic "bust thru" into a state of palingenetic awareness. This double sense is underlined in the reference to the rites of Adonis, described in such a way that the ritual fall or *katabasis* is seen both in terms of *coitus* and nature's impregnation:

> By this door have I entered the hill.
> Falleth,
> Adonis falleth.
> Fruit cometh after (47/238).

Gathering together some images from fertility rituals and the natural rhythms of life, canto 47 ends with a reference to the powers the *mystes* may expect to have acquired as a result of the *epopteia* or change in consciousness he has undergone:

> When the almond bough puts forth its flame,
> When the new shoots are brought to the altar,
> Τυ Διώνα, και Μοῖραι
> TU DIONA, KAI MOIRAI
> Και Μοῖραι ῎Αδονιν

KAI MOIRAI' ADONIN
    that hath the gift of healing,
that hath the power over wild beasts (47/239).

In placing the springtime act of ritual worship (the almond tree is the first plant to flower in Italy and Greece) beside the autumnal *threnos* of the Fates for the death of Adonis, Pound emphasizes once more the correspondence between human and natural palingenesis. The initiate understands the mysterious relation between the natural process and *coitus*. Pound implies that, like the god Dionysus (2/8) and Apollonius of Tyana (91/616; 93/623), the *mystes*, having now become an *epoptes*, "hath the [magical] gift of healing" and "the [magical] power over wild beasts."[52]

The *hieros gamos* of canto 47 results in the union with the "Permanent," the state of the *nous*, during which the *mystes* experiences "moments of awareness, moments of... clarity of vision" (Emery 17), moments which we may call *epopteic*. The mystes's Odyssean "sail[ing] after knowledge" or *gnosis* is depicted, then, as a *katabasis* to the *dromena* of the everyday world; but the mystes does not remain in the dark world of the *dromena* – as with the Eleusinian initiate, his is a palingenetic descent, a way down and out into a "dimention of stillness" (canto 49) which makes it possible to co-exist on the physical plane while, at the same time, he can commune with the *theos* of the "permanent world."

Notes

1. For the following brief summary of *The Cantos* I am indebted to Surette's work-in-progress, "The Birth of Modernism," and to his remarks during our conversations.
2. For exceptions see the work of Emery, Terrell, Libera, Miyake, Laurie, Elliott, Surette, Materer, and Oderman.
3. See Surette (*Light*), Neault, Boris de Rachewiltz, Flory, Brooke-Rose, Bacigalupo, and Wilhelm, *The Later Cantos of Ezra Pound*.
4. The terminology here is derived from my readings on the Mysteries of Eleusis and Gnosticism, and most particularly from Richard Reitzenstein's *Hellenistic Mystery-Religions*, Mead's numerous studies, and the books on Eleusis by Mylonas and Kerényi. It is Reitzenstein who points out that in the *Poimandres* Hermes, in his discourse dealing with the nature of the deity, had said that "no one could attain salvation, σωτηρία, without rebirth" (παλιγγενεσία) (47); and Mead, in *The Hymns of Hermes*, points out that "Rebirth or Regeneration was, and is, the mystery of the Spiritual Birth or Birth from Above,... the essential birth or *palingenesis*, the means of rebecoming a pure spiritual being" (50-51). The reader is also reminded that Pound himself was familiar with the terminology used here (see my discussion of the Eleusinian mysteries in Chapter II and Laughlin, *Pound as Wuz* [6, 85]). So far as I know, Boris de Rachewiltz was the first to use the term "palingenesis" in a discussion of Pound (177).

5. For similar attempts at defining the structure of Pound's "main scheme" and thus of *The Cantos* see Laurie's "The Poet and the Mysteries: Pound's Eleusis" and Kay Davis (esp. 17-28). Laurie defines Pound's schema as follows: *kathodos / palingenesis / metamorphosis* (40). Despite being rather "lyrical" (Oderman's term for Laurie's scholarship and style [148]), Laurie's study is fully informed, penetrating, and a delightful "read." Based on some of the same primary sources used here, it complements Surette's *A Light from Eleusis* and should be better known. Davis gives the same schema variously as "Eleusis: Descent / Repeat / Metamorphosis" and "dromena / repeat / epopte." As already pointed out in Chapter II as well as in note 4, Pound was familiar with many of these terms and equated *dromena* with sexual orgasm and the state of illumination with *epopteia*.
6. James Longenbach also makes this point ("The Order of the Brothers Minor: Pound and Yeats At Stone Cottage 1913-1916" 401).
7. In *The Religion of the Greeks and Romans*, C. Kerényi writes about the concept of εἰδώς: "for the Greeks seeing was included in knowing.... The inseparable connection of knowing and seeing... had the consequence that the Greeks at once 'saw' as 'form' everything that they 'knew'.... Greek 'knowing' means a viewing which, directed at the visible world, encounters something which is timeless and to that extent also eternal, forms which are invisible and can yet become objects of a vision" (145-46).
8. For a more detailed discussion of the similarities between Dante's and Pound's epics see Wilhelm, *Dante and Pound* (passim), Elliott, "Light as Image" (passim), and Surette, *Light* (55-56).
9. See also Libera's insightful discussion of the initiatory character of canto 17 ("Ezra Pound's Paradise" 81-91).
10. Libera argues that it was Yeats who called Pound's attention to Porphyry's work, since the Irish poet certainly knew of Porphyry's commentary in Thomas Taylor's translation ("Ezra Pound's Paradise" 86). Surely Pound himself knew of this translation and, most likely, was familiar with either the 1895 reprint of it in *Theosophical Siftings* entitled *Porphyry, On the Cave of the Nymphs in the Thirteenth Book of Odyssey* or in J.M. Watkins's 1917 reprint of it. As I suggest here, however, Pound's attention to Taylor's translation was more likely drawn by *The Mysteries of Mithra*, volume 5 of Mead's *Echoes from the Gnosis*. For Yeats's interest in Porphyry see Wilson, *Yeats and Tradition* (201-17).
11. The boat motif, we should note, is repeated often in *The Cantos* (e.g., cantos 90/605; 92/612; and 92/620).
12. Then again, "honey" is also the symbol of death; the ancients used to pour libations of honey to the chthonic deities, including Persephone or Koré whom they called μελίχρους, or "honey-like." For the meaning of "honey" in initiation rituals see also Mead, *The Mysteries of Mithra*, volume 5 of *Echoes from the Gnosis* 60-63.
13. Surette first identified the spiritual nature of Odysseus' adventures in *The Cantos* (*Light* 55). Akiko Miyake has also discussed Pound's palingenetic understanding of Odysseus's voyage and mentions specifically Taylor as a possible source. For example, she writes, following Taylor: "The descent of Odysseus into the underworld means the soul's descent into the darkness of body in order to meet the radiance of the transcendent which is hidden inherent within his soul and which is symbolized by Isis..." (86). Miyake consults Taylor's "A Dissertation on the Eleusinian

and Bacchic Mysteries" rather than "Concerning the Cave of the Nymphs." Of course, the two works have much in common.

14. See Harrison, *Prolegomena* (363-453) for details.

15. "ἱερότελεστία (*hierotelestia*, from ἱερός and τελετή, to discuss sacred things). "IO" is also probably a form of the incantation "AOI" which, as explained in Chapter III, was used in connection with Dionysus in his function as an Eleusinian god.

16. In his "A Dissertation on the Eleusinian and Bacchic Mysteries," Taylor concludes his discussion with a clear statement of the palingenetic function of the mysteries: "the design of the mysteries is to lead us back to the perfection from which, as a principle, we first made our descent" (413).

17. For more detailed discussions of the *pecten cteis* see Laurie, "The Poet and the Mysteries: Pound's Eleusis" (5-6) and Oderman (passim).

18. Terrell's gloss is more appropriate for the reference to Memnon in canto 94: "'Ηῳῳ Μέμνονι Memnon of the Dawn" (640).

19. That she is a sea-goddess we can assume from the fact that Aphrodite, who was born of the sea, is often pictured in *The Cantos* (though not identified) in a position similar to Aletha's here. For example, in Canto 39 Aphrodite is described in this way: "with the Goddess' eyes to seaward" (39/195).

20. To get the cup Heracles threatened Helios with his bow and arrows. There were several ancient accounts of the cup and many explanations of how Helios traveled from West to East. A number of these are quoted by the second-century author Athenaeus in Book 11, chaps. 38-39, of his *Deipnosophistae* from which the present Stesichorus fragment is taken.

    This passage, beginning with the Sun's nightly journey and Heracles's conquest of death, "rhymes" with the earlier descents to the underworld of Homer (in canto 1), Dante (in the Hell cantos), and the *mystes* of canto 17. In addition, we are reminded that the Sun often appears in *The Cantos* in connection with the *katabasis* to the underworld (e.g., cantos 15/67 and 17/79).

21. For a complaint along these lines see, for example, Dudley Fitts's early essay "Music Fit for the Odes," in *Ezra Pound: The Critical Heritage* (254).

22. That Pound consulted this dictionary frequently is evident from the references to it in canto 96: "(which is not in Liddell D.D.)" (96/656) and "vocabulary not in Dr. Liddell's" (96/658). What Pound cannot find in this lexicon of classical Greek is the Byzantine Greek of *Eparch's Book*.

23. "The soul," writes Mead quoting Damascius, "has a certain radiant vehicle (*augoeides ochema*), as it is called, starlike (*astroeides*) and eternal" (80-81). This concept will be discussed in more detail later. Mead returns to both Synesius and the concept of the *augoeides* often in his work (for example, see *Echoes from the Gnosis*, vol. 11, *The Chaldaean Oracles* passim).

24. Characteristically, Mead writes that "these two allotments—the 'light-wrapped' and the 'gloom-wrapped'—are the extremes, having as their portions the heights [and depths] of bliss and misery" (107). Elliott was the first to note Pound's possible debt to Synesius ("Light as Image" 138). For Yeats's familiarity with Synesius's writings see Wilson, *W.B. Yeats and Tradition* (144-45).

25. Akiko Miyake also treats Herakles's *katabasis* and the double nature of the sea in terms of palingenesis (88-89). Regarding Herakles's *katabasis*, Miyake, using Taylor, sees it as the soul's descent into body in man's attempt to find the pristine state of his soul. Miyake quotes from Taylor the following pertinent passage: "The soul . . .

descends Corically [or after the manner of Proserpine], into generation, but is distributed into generation Dionysiacally; and she is bound in body Promethiacally and Titanically: she frees herself therefore from its bonds by exercising the strength of Hercules..." (qtd. in Miyake 88-89). Taylor thus explains the Heraclean *katabasis* and *athloi* esoterically as the process through which the soul is delivered from the grip of matter and is freed for the resurrection. This process is seen, then, by Taylor as well as by Pound, as a palingenetic act.

26. McDowell and Materer also seem to concur with this reading: "Those who 'have passed the pillars and outward from Herakles's' (LXXIV/425) are the initiates of occult lore" (360). For discussions of the Luciferian context in which the reference to Herakles appears see Terrell, *Companion* II (363).

27. This quotation is from Pound's "The Serious Artist, III: Emotion and Poesy," *The New Freewoman* 1 (1913): 194.

28. In his *Edwardian Turn of Mind*, Samuel Hynes discusses the new discoveries of science during the 1890s which were perceived by many as a possible way out of the mechanistic world of positivism: "One way out of that world seemed to lie, paradoxically, through science. In the 'nineties the discovery of the X ray, of radioactivity, and of the electron had made the Victorian version of matter as obsolete as Genesis; and it seemed that further investigations might reveal new forces and new freedoms, by which the universe might be made teleological again" (136). For an account of this new conception of existence which shares much with occultist perception at the turn of the century, Hynes quotes from Edward Carpenter's *The Drama of Love and Death* (1912): "... the existence of the X and N rays of light, and of countless other vibrations of which our ordinary senses render no account, the phenomena of radium and radiant matter, the marvels of wireless telegraphy, the mysterious facts connected with hypnotism and the subliminal consciousness, and the certainty now that telepathic communication can take place between human beings thousand of miles apart — all these things have convinced us that the subtlest forces and energies, totally unmeasurable by our instruments, and saturated or at least suffused with intelligence, are at work all around us" (qtd. in Hynes 137).

29. Fa-Han is given by Peck as "bound-hair" which corresponds to εὐπλόκαμος, the epithet of Circe, meaning "fair-tressed": "ἔνθα δ' ἔναιε / Κίρκη εὐπλόκαμος..." (Homer, *Odyssey* 10.135-36). Wendy Flory reads the Fa-Han scene as autobiographical, with Pound and Olga Rudge or possibly Bride Scratton looking out of Rudge's apartment on the hill above Rapallo at the sea (136-38).

30. In his essay on "Cavalcanti, Medievalism," Pound explains this aside. He says that "For centuries if you disliked a man you called him a Manichaean, as in some circles to-day you call him a Bolshevic to damage his earning capacity" (*LE* 176).

31. In addition, in canto 20 the story of Niccolo d'Este is closely related to the fall of Troy: "And that was when Troy was down" (90). This line is also the opening line of the last section of canto 23 (109). The repetition is probably Pound's way of drawing our attention to the hypothesis that the Estes are the descendants of the Trojans.

32. The same hypothesis is put forward by Pound in his essay "Psychology and Troubadours" (*SR* 9), although not as clearly as here.

33. For a detailed discussion of the meaning of εἰδώς see Kerényi (*The Religion of the Greeks and Romans*, esp. 143-46).

34. References to Plethon in *The Cantos*: 8/31; 23/107; 26/123; 83/528; 98/685, 688, and 690. In his study of the Malatesta drafts D'Epiro has discovered two significant

details regarding Plethon which Pound omitted from the final text. The first deals with how Malatesta "finds Gemisthus' ashes" in Morea (#49, 16) (20). D'Epiro rightly claims that the inclusion of this incident would have balanced the rather developed account of Plethon's visit to Florence in 1493 (canto 8) and would also "have added a sense of closure to the incident: the man who might have inspired the Tempio ends up reposing therein" (20). The second detail deals with another reference to Plethon, also excluded from the final text, where "Plethon's catalytic function with regard to the Tempio is made more explicit than in the final text: '... Gemisthus, an old man talking the gods.// Came later/ Later Alberti that the painter should/ set hunger in men for building./ And thus grew, thus sprang to flower,/ sea poppy, luteumve papaver./ By the sea gate,/&/the sun's gate./ caught in the stone./ a song caught in the stone' (#53 36)" (28). In addition to the two references mentioned above, there is also the following reference in the Malatesta drafts:

> And Gemisthus ...
> who had talked the gods, gone back to Morea,
> but the word burning and hot ... (D'Epiro, #53, 43).

35. Plethon seems to have made a conscious effort, throughout his life, to copy Plato's example. The very name Plethon (Πλήθων), which Georgios Gemistos (Γεώργιος Γέμιστος) added to his own name after 1439, was chosen because of its resemblance to that of Plato (Πλάτων).

36. For detailed discussions of this point see Kristeller and Yates, *Giordano Bruno and the Hermetic Tradition*.

37. Libera also mentions Andrian Stokes's *Stone of Rimini*, which was in part inspired by Pound's Malatesta Cantos, and says that "If Pound had not already felt this 'water' theme himself, in his wilfully cryptic way, he offers a possibility unmentioned by Stokes—that a knowledge of Plethon's theory of the gods was behind Agostino's work" (375).

38. In *Guide to Kulchur*, Pound notes the importance of Malatesta in preserving something of Plethon: "And the Malatesta had his high sense of justice, for I think Gemisto wd. be even more forgotten without Sigismundo's piety" (160).

39. Though he uses none of the terminology employed here, Clark Emery has, to a certain degree, anticipated the present discussion. His comments on the structure of these cantos is illuminating. For example, he notes that "Canto 47 restates the nekuia-regeneration theme as the condition of escaping the degradation of 45-46" (126). And following a remark about how carefully Pound's transition from the Occident (cantos 1-51) to the Orient (cantos 52-61) has been made, Emery traces the outline of the movement from "usura" to Eleusinian energy to "the dimention of stillness" to the state of *nous*: "... how carefully is most clearly understood by a study of 45, 47, 49, and 51, each a passage of great lyrical intensity.... 45 reveals the sin, usura; 47 sets against it the active intelligence, Eleusinian energy; 49 complements 47 by stressing the value of order, the dimension of stillness. The teaching of 47 is not enough: the 'splendour on splendour' of the light that 'has gone down into the cave' needs to be qualified by the light that 'moves on the north sky line/ where the young boys prod stones from shrimp.' In the two teachings exists the potential of the culture which usury, social irresponsibility, distraction from fact, and loss of faith have rendered null..." (39-41). For a detailed and persuasive discussion dealing with the initiatory sequence found in the *Fifth Decad of Cantos* see Elliott's "Light of Image" (esp. 91-100). Elliott's study is excellent on the medieval background of

PALINGENESIS: *KATABASIS / DROMENA / EPOPTEIA* 157

"virtú" and its correspondence in *The Cantos* to the light of initiation. In a chapter entitled "Illumination: Keystone Canto 51" (13-71), Elliott finds that in canto 51 the poet achieves initiatory or occult awareness; she also speculates about the meaning of the canto's number, pointing out that Pound possibly was thinking of the Cabalistic concept of the Fifty Gates through which the intellect traverses before achieving complete awareness (66).

40. In a letter to Olivia Rossetti Agresti written sometime early in April 1950, Pound complains about how difficult it is to carry on his "kulchural" programme in an indifferent and ignorant world: "[it is] very difficult to be intelligible in a milieu that hasn't the GOGGGdamniEST idea of the American Constitution, and that has never heard of the Leopoldine Reforms" (BRBL). Of course, one of the functions Pound saw himself as performing in *The Cantos* involved the salvaging from the blackout of time and memory of historical events and texts he considered important for "kulchur."

41. Furia observes that "after being 'arse-wiped,' the oxen and the parade 'set off toward the Duomo' (43/217), but Pound makes the real cathedral in Siena the bank itself, describing its chartering as 'the Incarnation' (43/219)" (71).

42. I use "hylic" here in the Gnostic, dualist sense according to which the material world is set in sharp contrast to spirit, soul, and divinity. Pound's perspective, however, is not dualistic. In his view, the fall into matter is not necessarily a bad thing, and he would agree with Mead that there is nothing wrong with Sophia's *katabasis* into matter in the Simon Magus legend. Pound dismisses the "idiotic asceticism and [the] belief that the body is evil." He favours, instead, the "conception of the body as perfect instrument of ... intelligence" (*LE* 150 and 152).

43. Epanaphora, that is, intensive anaphora (the repetition of the same word at the beginning of successive clauses or verses), is used in lines 10, 14, 16-18, etc.; isocolon (the repetition of phrases of equal length and usually corresponding structure) is used in lines 35-36; and litotes (the denial of the contrary or understatement that intensifies) is used throughout the canto.

44. In a recent article entitled "Art and the Spirit of Capitalism: Iconography and History in the Usura Canto," Jeffrey Twitchell makes some rather pertinent remarks about Pound's aims in canto 45: "The Canto presents the achievements and heritage of the Quattrocento as cut short — not only recalling what has been but what would have been if the Renaissance flower had been allowed to continue blossoming. Pound puts before us what has been lost with the triumph of usura in the early 16th century, not so much the specific achievements as the very mode of seeing or being which these works objectify" (17).

45. This is what James Laughlin reports about Pound's understanding of the Eleusinian *hieros gamos*: "The burst of 'marvellous light' is the *dromena*, which Pound suggested to me was an orgasm. Yet I think the spiritual significance of the ritual was more important to him. In the *Usura* canto (45) he has the famous line, 'They have brought whores for Eleusis,' meaning that the usurers have profaned a shrine" (*Pound as Wuz* 85). The Eleusinian paradigm implied in Mr. Laughlin's recollection is slightly different from the one presented here. I have been arguing that the Eleusinian paradigm as it appears in canto 47 and elsewhere follows the pattern: *katabasis / dromena / epopteia*. That is, the "marvellous light" corresponds to the *epopteia* and thus follows *dromena*; thus the *dromena* corresponds to the coitus, followed by

the orgasm or *epopteia*. (See also my discussion of Mr. Laughlin's comments in Chapter II.)

46. Pound uses the term "fucking" in his letter (BRBL #1603). D.D. Paige, the editor of *The Letters of Ezra Pound*, has substituted the term with "_ _ _ _" – so as not to offend the sensibilities of the readers, I suppose. The only other instance of Pound's use of the word of which I am aware is in canto 39 (193). Mr. James Laughlin has told me that Pound was not foul-mouthed and that he was surprised at his use of this term in canto 39. Of course, by "sacramental fucking" Pound means the *epopteia* that follows the *hieros gamos* in his version of the Eleusinian mysteries.

47. For a discussion of Pound's celebrations of sexuality and Remy de Gourmont's influence upon him in this area, see Richard Sieburth (esp. 129-58). For brief but insightful discussions of the sexual union issuing forth in mystical or spiritual illumination in canto 47 see Laurie, "The Poet and the Mysteries" (14-15), Elliott, "Light as Image" (91), Surette (*Light* 64-65) and McDowell and Materer (esp. 356-57). The first to notice the gnostic aspects of the *hieros gamos* in *The Cantos* was Surette in "Helen of Tyre."

48. Clark Emery discusses the mysteries in terms of an awakening to the reality of the permanent realm of the *theos*. He explains that it is not "that the undivided Light does not continually pour (i.e. that there is not permanent essential Good); it is that we do not open our eyes to it" (21). The *katabasis* of canto 47 opens the *mystes's* eyes to this Light, and he can therefore enter, or participate in, the world of the "Intellectual Light" (canto 36).

49. My discussion of canto 47 incorporates many of the points already found in Surette (esp. *Light* 60-66); it differs from his insofar as it emphasizes the Gnostic character of the *katabasis*.

50. As already mentioned above, James Laughlin took pains to explain to me that in one of their private conversations Pound did indeed make the connection between sexual intercourse and the experience of the divine.

51. The ritualistic act described here by Pound is actually fashioned after the custom of setting candles afloat in Tigullio Bay on the night of July 3; the custom of the Italian women is associated in Pound's mind with Aphrodite's grief over the death of Adonis. For more details see Massimo Bacigalupo (71 and 271).

52. See also cantos 49/244 and 52/258.

V

"THE SUBTLE BODY": CANTOS 90 AND 91

1. "OUT OF EREBUS": CANTO 90

This chapter presents an analysis of cantos 90 and 91 in terms of the palingenetic pattern, especially the *epopteic* or metamorphic phase of the triple schema developed earlier (*katabasis / dromena / epopteia*). Canto 90 illustrates the rebirth of the *mystes* to a higher plane of existence (not a higher realm like the traditional paradise or heaven), and canto 91 illustrates the nature of that higher plane as understood through Mead's doctrine of the "subtle body." Thus, what is proposed here is an esoteric reading of these two cantos illustrating the spiritual drama enacted by the illuminated soul of the *mystes*.

A number of other cantos could have been chosen to illustrate this palingenetic stage. For example, the pattern is found in the *Pisan Cantos*, where the palingenetic drama is acted out—but there, because of the special circumstances, the stages which are emphasized are the *katabasis* and *dromena*, especially in the chthonic cantos 82 to 84. The later cantos also contain numerous examples of the palingenetic movement. But cantos 90 and 91 are the best brief and accessible illustration of palingenesis in *The Cantos*.

With but a few exceptions, the critical consensus about these cantos has changed little since Clark Emery's account of them as "paradisal" (1958). Emery wrote that in canto 90 "Paradise is regained—by the reader who has followed on the heels of the poet, and by the poet himself, who has been elevated 'from under the rubble heap.'... Canto 91 continues the ascent, from the circle of light to the circle of crystal..." (156). This "paradise regained" is either seen as an earthly or celestial paradise.[1] Although

---

The notes to Chapter V are found on pp. 184-88.

Emery's reading has not been challenged or fundamentally altered by later critics who have merely elaborated on and fleshed out his observations, exceptions to it are found in the work of Noel Stock, Angela Elliott, Leon Surette, and Colin McDowell and Timothy Materer.[2] For example, in *A Light from Eleusis*, Surette reads the later cantos as "palingenetic," even though he does not use this term and does not identify the occult provenance of his sources (see *Light*, esp. 235-39).

Like Surette's, the present discussion differs fundamentally from earlier ones in that it reads the paradisal imagery as the exoteric sign for an esoteric meaning or *gnosis*. In *The Cantos* the nature of paradise is a state of mind and not a place, since the *mystes* enters not a higher realm like that of the traditional paradise, but rather a higher plane of existence.[3] Thus, the palingenetic model explains the general character of the initiation as a state of mind and, even more significantly, as a state of being. In other words, what is proposed here is that cantos 90 and 91 represent the *mystes*'s rebirth into a higher plane of existence so that he exists simultaneously in the normal human plane while at the same time he is participating in a higher state of being.

This chapter begins with a forward-looking digression which precedes the discussion of the palingenetic aspects of cantos 90 and 91. This digression is undertaken in order to suggest the palingenetic character of the later cantos and to demonstrate that Pound is constantly thinking in terms of the "celestial tradition."

In the last section of "Notes for CXVII et seq.," whose last line was intended to be the poem's last line,[4] the palingenetic action of *The Cantos* is rehearsed for the last time:

> La faillite de François Bernouard, Paris
> or a field of larks at Allègre,
>   "es laissa cader" [and let himself fall]
> so high toward the sun and then falling,
>   "de joi sas alas" [his wings with joy]
> to set here the roads of France.
>
> Two mice and a moth my guides—
> To have heard the farfalla gasping
>   as toward a bridge over worlds.
> That the kings meet in their island,
>   where no food is after flight from the pole.
> Milkweed the sustenance
>   as to enter arcanum.
>
> To be men not destroyers (117/802).

This section includes "one last ideogrammic tribute to the troubadours" (Wilhelm, *The Later Cantos* 45), a metaphor of the psyche's preparation for its migratory flight into the empyrean, and a final aside, in the optative mood, in which Pound's programme is expressed.

The first verse paragraph places the Icarian failure of François Bernouard ("so high toward the sun and then falling") side by side with a natural image of the arch made by the flight of larks. The natural scene which is celebrated in the lines Pound quotes from Bernart de Ventadour's poem[5] is analogous to the "flight" of Bernouard, the artisan-visionary whose plan to print handsome editions of important books (like *XXX Cantos*) ended in bankruptcy. Bernouard's "failure" is another example of the destructive power of Usura which "has made printing a midden, a filth, a mere smear, bolted down by the bank racket which impedes the use of skills and implements for the making of proper books or of healthy populations" (*GK* 184).[6] Along with the lark's failure to reach the sun and Bernouard's failure to continue printing worthwhile books is implied Pound's own anxiety about the success of his epic.

Though real, the intimations of *katabasis* in the first verse paragraph are only momentary and are quickly succeeded, in the next verse paragraph, by the palingenetic soul-in-flight motif leading to the metamorphic "arcanum" which bestows upon those who enter it the power of healing and whose transformational power is such that destroyers may be turned into men. For Pound "the natural object is always the *adequate* symbol" (*LE* 5) and here, again, the gesture toward the "arcanum" has its genesis in the recollection of a particular, natural, auditory image: the "gasping" sound made by a butterfly.[7] The butterfly, the traditional symbol of the psyche, is also the palingenetic symbol par excellence, for it dies to a lower life and is reborn to a higher one. Here, Pound's company of psychopompoi ("two mice and a moth my guide") preside over the psyche's ascent which leads to "a bridge over worlds," a soul-bridge leading to the empyrean.

The paradisal image of souls in flight is continued in the next few lines where, as Richard Sieburth remarks, "the Odyssean moths of Canto XLIX [and the kingwings of migration of canto 106], called over mountain ... at last reach shore" at the end of *The Cantos* (158). Emphasis is placed here on the resting place of the butterflies ("the kings meet in their islands") and on the poisonous milkweed by which, paradoxically, the butterflies are sustained. Milkweed is probably the equivalent of μῶλυ (*molu*, Odysseus' protection against Circe's malign magic in the *Odyssey*). The partaking of *molu*/milkweed is, perhaps, the necessary condition for the great migratory flight which takes the psyche to the entrance of the "arcanum." Here, as elsewhere, the "penetration" into the "mysterium" remains esoteric, and Pound leaves us, at the very end of his epic, at the gathering place of souls and at the very point when the entry into the arcanum is about to take place. But we are permitted no glimpse of the actual entry. As already emphasized in Chapters I and IV, Pound is unwilling to describe or explain his syncretic rite because he believes that the "mysteries are *not* revealed, and no guide book to them has been or will be written" — though we could argue, as I do here, that *The Cantos* is designed to be such a guide book, but directed only to the elect, "those who have ears." *The Cantos* do take us a certain distance along Pound's palingenetic ritual; but they stop short of the *epopteia* or full revelation, an experience which can be attained by the reader/*mystes* but cannot be penetrated by the reader who sees only the exoteric manifestation of the mysterium.

How close to the arcanum Pound believes he has taken the attentive and willing reader/*mystes* is revealed in canto 116 where, in an apostrophe to the reader, he follows a statement about his poem's objective ("To make Cosmos — / To achieve the possible / . . . a little light / in great darkness") with a double question:

> I have brought the great ball of crystal;
>   who can lift it?
> Can you enter the great acorn of light? (116/795)[8]

Coming just before his self-interrogation concerning the coherence of his long poem — an issue not resolved within the poem itself — the emphatic first line followed by two questions shifts the burden of the responsibility from poet to reader. I intend to return to the symbolism of "the great ball of crystal" in my discussion of canto 91; for now let it suffice to say that these are not merely paradisal images but also pointed questions directed at the reader as *mystes*. The ordinary reader will take notice of these lines for their "lyric sentiment"; but the reader/*mystes* will understand them, Pound hopes, as forming part of the initiatory drama which, despite being incomplete on the page, is nevertheless occluded and is meant to be performed through an enlightened reading of the text. As stressed in Chapter I, *The Cantos* resemble in this the Hermetic writings which were designed with a similar purpose in mind.

Pound addresses the reader/*mystes* in a number of other places in *The Cantos*. The most pointed example is found in canto 90 where the poet's attempt to write the "paradise" he had planned in 1940 begins in earnest:[9]

> "From the colour the nature
>   & by the nature the sign!"
> Beatific spirits welding together
>   as in one ash-tree in Ygdrasail.

>   Baucis, Philemon.
> Castalia is the name of that fount in the hill's fold,
>   the sea below,
>   narrow beach.
> Templum aedificans, not yet marble,
>   "Amphion!"
> And from the San Ku 三
>   孤
>   to the room in Poitiers where one can stand
>   casting no shadow,
> That is Sagetrieb,
>   that is tradition.
> Builders had kept the proportion,
>   did Jacques de Molay
>   know these proportions?
> and was Erigena ours? (90/605)

Beginning with an allusion to John Heydon, Pound searches for paths leading to the third subject of his epic, the *epopteia* or "bust through into the divine." To this end he brings together a number of images, many of which have already been introduced earlier in the poem. Thus we encounter the union of "beatific spirits" in the context of the principle of universal correspondence as exemplified by "Ygdrasail," the ash tree of Norse mythology, whose roots and branches join heaven, earth, and hell. In an earlier canto, Pound encouraged his reader thus: "That you lean 'gainst the tree of heaven, / and know Ygdrasail" (85/545). The point here is that for Pound—for whom it is always this world that matters most—even though the roots of things might be in heaven, we arrive to a "full Ειδὼς" by understanding their particular manifestations on earth—this is the concept of correspondence, an idea which is universal in the occult and fundamental to it.

The idea of the divine tree is continued in the fifth line where the Ovidian characters, "Baucis, [and] Philemon," are presented as physical manifestations of the divine world of the gods of which they have been allowed to partake as a result of their natural kindness to Zeus and Hermes—a theme expressed early in "The Tree," the poem Pound placed at the beginning of his *Personae*. Before their final reward (their metamorphosis into two entwined trees), the couple served as keepers of the divine temple which was, in fact, their old cottage transformed by the gods into a *topos* of worship. This *topos* provides the link with the next cluster of images. From the temple suggested by the mention of Baucis and

Philemon we move to the temple of Delphi, near the brook of Castalia; next comes an image of "metamorphosis in action": we watch Amphion building the temple ("Templum aedificans") in Thebes with his music. The reader witnesses this marvellous event as it is taking place, while the building is being raised and is "not yet marble." It is precisely within this framework of activities, that of the building of temples, that Pound's next two references occur (90/605). These references, the first to a Chinese "secret society" and the second to the Knights Templar, are drawn from the beliefs and practices of Freemasonry. I think that Stock was the first one to point out this connection:

> But when we examine it [the passage quoted above] in detail we find it is based upon the idea of an ageless "secret society." The San Ku was a sort of masonic council in ancient China in connection with which we find a grade of initiation called the "Widow's Son" which is also to be found in some of the Romance literature of the Middle Ages and in the Masonic ritual of the present day. The town of Poitiers, which also crops up in the same Romance literature, is not only famous for its romanesque architecture but for its connection with the Order of Templars of which Jacques de Molay was grand master. And ceremonies remembering de Molay are also preserved today in some Masonic rituals (*Poet in Exile* 24).[10]

The idea of a secret community of *mystai* who have preserved a celestial tradition passed on by direct descent takes here the shape of a masonic brotherhood. This point is especially true since these *mystai* are viewed as "builders" who "had kept the proportions." Boris de Rachewiltz has convincingly shown that the science of keeping the right proportions is closely connected in Pound's mind with the erection of the temple and altar and the building of the city (188-91).

The references to esoteric architecture are central to Pound's concept of reconstruction and reconstitution. These lines from canto 90 have already made their appearance, in more or less the same form, in an earlier canto where the train of Pound's associations is perhaps even clearer than in canto 90:

> Only sequoias are slow enough.
>   BinBin is "beauty."
> "Slowness is beauty.":
>   from the

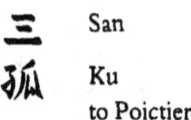
   San
   Ku
to Poictiers.

> The tower wherein, at one point, is no shadow,
>   and Jacques de Molay, is where?
> and the "Section," the proportions,
>   lending, perhaps, not at interest, but resisting.
> Then false fronts, barocco.
>   "We have," said Mencius, "but phenomena."
> monumenta. In nature are signatures
>   needing no verbal tradition,
> oak leaf never plane leaf. John Heydon.
>   Σελλοί sleep there on the ground
> And old Jarge held there was a tradition,
>   that was not mere epistemology (87/572-73).

The wisdom of Laurence Binyon, orientalist and translator of Dante, gives way first to San Ku, the Chinese Council of three instituted by Cheng Wang of the Chou dynasty (eleventh century B.C.) to "display brightly the powers of heaven and earth" and then to the tower of Poictiers, built by the Knight Templar Jacque de Molay (Grieve 418). Looking forward to canto 90 and backward to cantos 76 and 85, we find that a number of images ranging from "the tree of heaven" (85/545) to the golden "Section" of Pythagoras (87/573) have their source in the ancient Chinese tradition of *chien-mu*, a mythological tree situated at the "centre of the universe" (Rachewiltz 189-90).

The most interesting feature of this Chinese conception is that "the gnomon standing on the exact meridian does not cast any shadow on the day of the summer solstice" (Rachewiltz 190). This principle helps explain the following cryptic line: "a gnomon / Our science is from the watching of shadows" (85/543). On one level, the science described here is that of the astronomers who in the *Chou King* watch their gnomons or sundials and fix the seasons; on a more mystical level, this is a "science" used to discover the cosmic centre, since on the day of the summer solstice the sun and the shaft form a cosmic axis and no shadow is cast. Like the astronomers in *Chou King* who learned about their universe by observing "the shadows," Mencius's and John Heydon's "nature gospels" are also derived from observing the workings of nature—although the observer of nature does not need verbal instruction: "In nature are signatures / needing no verbal tradition, / oak leaf never plane leaf" (87/573).

The reference to John Heydon's "doctrine of signatures" explains Pound's allusion in the following line: "Σελλοί sleep there on the ground." The Selloi are the ancient inhabitants of Dodona, mantic priests and guardians of the oracle of Zeus (*Iliad* 16.234-35), where the god "was revered in the oracular oak" (Frazer 358). The association between Heydon's oak and Zeus's oracular oak reminds us of Pound's translation of Sophocles's *Women of Trachis* (1956), where Herakles can be heard saying: "The dead beast kills the living me / And that fits another odd forecast / breathed out at the Selloi's oak— / Those fellows rough it, / *sleep on the ground*, up in the hills there" (66; italics mine). The ancient San Ku, who were appointed to "display brightly the powers of the heaven and earth," are seen as equivalent to the Selloi who observed and listened to Zeus's oak tree oracle, another "tree of heaven."[11]

The idea of a science which springs "from the watching of shadows" functions as an organizing principle and links several associated images. The tower of the Hall of Justice in Poictiers, "the tower wherein, at one point, is no shadow," was built by the Knights Templar who were said to be in possession of the secret knowledge of this science of proportions (both architectural and seasonal). The Golden "Section" of Pythagoras, "a numerical process which seemed to involve mystical relationships representing proportions in nature," is a Western equivalent to the Chinese "science" and is supposedly part of the tradition in the possession of the Knights Templar (Terrell, *Companion*, II.495).[12] Associated with the tower of Poictiers in Pound's mind is the fortress-temple of Montségur, whose peculiar shape was designed to ensure that the light of the rising sun should fall on the altar at a certain time (*The Pound Era* 335); however, as in Poictiers, "in Mt Segur there is wind space and rain space / no more an altar to Mithras" (76/452).

Pound associates the destruction of the Knights Templar with contemporary economics, and conjectures that the Templar money dealers were distributors of credit ("lending, perhaps, not at interest, but resisting" [87/573]). The consequence of the suppression of the religio-economic vision of the Knights Templar produces bad architecture: "Then false fronts, barocco" (87/573).[13]

Out of all these associations emerging from an analysis of canto 87 and canto 90, the outline of a "tradition" can be discerned. This is Pound's rediscovered, fictional "tradition" according to which there is a continuity from the ancient rites of Delphi, Dodona, and Mithras to the medieval manifestations of the tradition in the Albigenses, the Knights Templar, and Erigena, and to its later appearances in John Heydon and others. It is a "tradition" which "Old Jarge," that is George Santayana, accepts; he, too, "held [that] there was a tradition, / that was not mere epistemology" (87/573).

The rhetorical questions regarding the brotherhood of the "celestial tradition" in the opening lines of canto 90 point to Pound's certainty that, indeed, such a tradition exists, and they initiate a meditation composed of visions of ascent and peopled by some of those who belong to the tradition. That is, the rhetorical questions, quite pointedly (lest we have missed it), emphasize the occult source of Pound's tradition, bring to our attention the fact that his *paradiso terrestre* is peopled by a galaxy of occult heroes or illuminated souls, and prepare us for the realization that his paradise is ultimately not a place but rather a state of being. It turns out, then, that the soul of the *mystes* does not depart from the ephemeral world but merely enters a higher plane of existence, and the individual becomes a Magus!

Following a meditation (90/605-606) upon the ephemeral world of man as seen against the background of the rise and the fall of the waves and also against man's capacity for love (this love corresponds to the "divine in man"), we encounter a lyric passage in which we hear the *mystes*'s voice announcing a personal ascent from the dark place of the soul:

> from under the rubble heap
>
>   m'elevasti
>
> from the dulled edge beyond pain,
>
>   m'elevasti
>
> out of Erebus, the deep-lying
>
>   from the wind under the earth,
>
>   m'elevasti . . .
>
> the viper stirs in the dust,
>
>   the blue serpent
>
> glides from the rock pool
>
>   And they take lights now down to the water
>
> the lamps float from the rowers
>
>   the sea's claw drawing them outward (90/606-607).

In describing the palingenetic ascent of the soul, Pound alludes to Greek, Egyptian, and Christian Easter rites. The re-emergence is "out of Erebus" (that is, out of the darkness of the Underworld[14]) and through "the crystal funnel of air" (90/608) into a world highlighted by the presence of light and water, images mediated by divine feminine presences like those of Aphrodite, Isis, the Muses of Castalia, Sibylla, or a "lone nymph":

> but the light perpendicular, upward
> and to Castalia,
>
>   water jets from the rock
>
> . . . .
>
> Grove hath its altar
>
>   under elms, in that temple, in silence
>
> a lone nymph by the pool (90/607).

While Zeus is busy erecting the stone altar out of the air ("the stone taking form in the air"), and while our attention is drawn to the performance of communal ceremonies ("And they take lights now down to the water..."; /"For the procession of Corpus / come now banners..."), the stage is set for the ascension of souls. A pastoral dreamscape appears before us ("the trees rise"; a "new forest" manifests itself) and into it emerge, magically, Dionysus's hieratic animals ("the great cats approaching"; "and where was nothing / now is furry assemblage"), voices are heard ("and in the boughs now are voices"), and scents fill the air ("myrrh and olibanum on the altar stone / giving perfume"). This is a composite rite, a paradisal version of the rite performed by Odysseus in canto 1. But this is no *nekyomanteia*. Here χθόνιοι (*oi chthonioi*, the earthly ones) are not mere shades emerging momentarily to satisfy the sacrificer's thirst for knowledge regarding his future. Here the ascension "out of Erebus" is real enough:

> out of Erebus, the delivered,
>   Tyro, Alcmene, free now, ascending
> e i cavalieri,
>   ascending,
> no shades more,
>   lights among them, enkindled,
> and the dark shade of courage
>   Ἠλέκτρα
> bowed still with the wrongs of Aegisthus.
> Trees die & the dream remains (90/608-609).

Unlike the "souls out of Erebus" of canto 1, described by Pound there as "cadaverous,... impetuous impotent dead" (1/3-4), the souls in canto 90 are "no shades more" but truly "delivered" and "free." Though the direction of their movement is heavenward and though they are escaping from the world of the dead, these souls, nonetheless, do not ascend into a celestial paradise. This is clearly indicated by the inclusion among them of "'Ἠλέκτρα" who is "bowed *still* with the wrongs of Aegisthus" [emphasis mine].[15]

The rite of the initiation is performed in canto 90 for the benefit of the *mystes* who descends into Erebus (*katabasis*), wanders in that dark region for a time (*dromena*), and then re-ascends to the same old world but now in possession of the *gnosis* (*epopteia*). In the words of Leon Surette, "The ascension is more like the return to the daylight world of the Eleusinian initiate, who, according to Plutarch, 'lives with pure and holy men,' and 'sees on earth the crowd' of the uninitiated 'crush and jostle themselves in the mud and darkness'" (238-39). Surette speaks of "the motif of resurrection" in canto 90 and, as I argue in this study, Pound viewed the initiatory experience as a sort of resurrection or palingenesis. The palingenesis is experienced by the initiates while the rest remain "mere shades."

The theme of resurrection is discussed at length by Mead in *The Subtle Body*. Mead writes that the Christian doctrine of a fleshly resurrection was repudiated by all Gnostic schools and, instead, in these schools "the resurrection is equated with the new birth or birth from above [palingenesis], the spiritual birth out of or through the pure virgin substance into the consciousness of immortality" (130). Mead goes on to point out that following his "resurrection" a man was thought to become a god. Though the ultimate purpose of the exercise was to enter paradise, the experience was not something which had to be postponed to a time after the *mystes*'s death: "The mystery of 'divinising' (*apotheosis*) or 'transcending death' (*athanasia*) was not ... to be deferred to *post-mortem* existence, though it had to be preceded by a mystical death. It was a mystery wrought in the living body of a man" (131).

Canto 90 represents a palingenetic experience such as the one described by Mead. There is no movement to an earthly paradise, nor is there a "transportation" taking place to a celestial paradise. The *mystes* remains on earth. But as a result of his *myesis* or initiation, he is now in the possession of gnosis and thus exists on earth while at the same time he enters another level of existence, a paradisal state of mind or being. The paradisal images of the canto should be seen, then, as a representation of this "state of being" entered by the *mystes* following his initiation.

2. "The Subtle Body": Canto 91

The motif of the *mystes*'s palingenesis is continued in canto 91. While canto 90 illustrates the motif of the *mystes*'s rebirth and rise "out of Erebus" into a higher plane of existence, canto 91 illustrates the nature of this higher plane as understood through the doctrine of "the subtle body"; and by introducing into the world of *The Cantos* such personages as Apollonius of Tyana, this canto points toward the nature of the illuminated soul of the *mystes* who does not depart from the world but rather enters a higher plane of existence.

In my discussion of palingenesis I have quoted from Mead's *The Doctrine of the Subtle Body*. In glossing the opening verses of canto 91, Carroll F. Terrell notes that with "the word 'body' Pound brings into *The Cantos* more specific allusions to the mystical symbolism of the alchemists as set forth in the summary work of G.R.S. Mead, *The Doctrine of the Subtle Body*" (*Companion*, II.546).[16] Terrell goes on to use a number of passages from Mead's work to gloss several of the verses of canto 91. Before tackling canto 91, I would like to examine Mead's discussion of the history and use of the term "subtle body."[17]

Pound indubitably knew enough of Mead's work on the "subtle body" theory to include the term *augeides* (which is a misspelling of *augoeides*) in his notes for canto 25:[18]

> languid move[ment] of the inner body.
>   preceding the meat move[ment]
> ....
> moving from wihot [without] the othr [other]
>   arms of siva
> ....
> augeides — the gods —

Augoeides is a term meaning approximately "luminous being" or "form of splendour." Mead insisted that the *augoeides* was a spiritual body joined to the physical body by a light-spark at a point near the head. Whatever his understanding of Mead's explication of the "subtle body," Pound's notes attest to his familiarity with an ethereal body associated with the world of the gods, attached to the hylic or "meat" body.

Like many of his other books and essays, Mead's *Subtle Body* is, to a large extent, an anthology of quotations from Neoplatonic, Gnostic, and Christian sources. The volume deals with the "spirit-body" and "radiant-body" concepts of Neoplatonic thinkers and with Christian and Gnostic notions regarding the "resurrected body." In the "Proem," Mead explains that his studies of the subtle-body concept "might perhaps be called studies in Alexandrian psycho-physiology" (8), since Alexandria was the chief centre of the philosophic culture which comes under his scrutiny here. Mead claims that man's subtle body "is of the material order, but of a more dynamic nature than his physically sensible frame" (4-5). In characteristically theosophical manner, he observes that even though the subtle body "pertains to the normally invisible," the latest concepts of modern physics come to the support of this ancient notion and also that the advance of science will ultimately prove this ancient hypothesis of the subtle body true.[19] Mead sees the subtle body notion as being at the core of astrology and alchemy. Alchemy, in its best forms, deals with things subtle, since the central secret of the alchemists was the deeper knowledge of palingenesis: "The prime secret of alchemical transmutation was an inner mystery — the purgation and perfecting of this subtle embodiment" (18).

Palingenesis was central to alchemy, and this is reflected in various ancient treatises, two of which Mead mentions. The first is a Hellenistic poem whose contents were thought by such notables as Porphyry and Proclus to enshrine the wisdom of Chaldaea. This poem is said to present, among other things, "a highly mystical doctrine concerning the nature of the subtle body, and of the soul and mind of man, and purports to reveal the mystery of the divine paternal fire and the secret of the life of the great mother" (30). The second treatise is the chief document of the Gnostic School of Simon Magus, the so-called *Great Announcement*. This, Mead says, "presents us with a highly developed doctrine of the divine fire and of the tree of life, and with psycho-physiological speculations which are entirely in keeping with the subtle body theory of psychical alchemy" (32).

In "The Augoeides or Radiant Body," repeated virtually unchanged in *The Subtle Body* as "The Radiant Body," it is explained that "In classical Greek, *augoeides* is an adjective meaning 'possessed of a form of *auge*' — that is, of a form of splendour, brightness, brilliance, radiance; hence brilliant, shining, radiant, ray-like, luciform, glorious, etc." (76). This etymological exegesis is followed by an investigation of Neoplatonic and Gnostic sources for the purpose of finding out what they have to tell us about "the *augoeides* as the radiant body, or glorious vehicle or vesture of the soul" (77). Quoting Damascius, the last occupant of the Platonic Chair in Athens, Mead says that the soul's radiant vehicle (*augoeides ochema*) is star-like (*astroeides*) and eternal. This brings Mead to the relation of *augoeides* to the physical body and, here, looking back to his essay on "The Spirit-Body," he makes the following distinction:

> The *augoeides* was ... thought more usually to be centred, as it were a light-spark, in the head — that is, its only point of contact with the physical body was imagined to be in the head — whereas the spirituous body ... was thought of as pervading the whole gross body and surrounding it (82).

Mead distinguishes between the *augoeides*, a corporeal but usually invisible body joined to the hylic body by a light-spark at a point in or near the head, and the "spirituous body," a sort of aura around the hylic or "gross" body. We have, then, three levels of being: the purely physical or hylic or "gross" body; the "spirituous body," the subtle soul-vehicle in its inferior aspect which envelops the hylic body; and the *augoeides*, the perfected subtle body.[20] Finally, the *augoeides*, a stage achieved through palingenesis, is an awareness of the "aethereal," the subtle nature of the universe. While providing as unambiguous a definition of the three levels of being as his polyvalent and polysemous sources will allow, Mead clearly perceives the process of palingenesis as dynamic and bidirectional; and it is this interest in palingenesis as a "medium" through which souls pass back and forth that Pound picks from Mead.

The substance of the *augoeides* is subtle, translucent, almost immaterial:

> Speaking of this heavenly 'body' [*augoeides*] from the macrocosmic standpoint, Philoponus tells us that, according to the Platonici, "the matter of celestial [bodies]" is not of the four elements, but "there is another kind of body—the fifth," element, or quintessence, and its form (*eidos*) is spherical.... "The everlasting, the sublime (*áno*) body, partakes of transparency; and he [Aristotle] calls it the out-flow [*chûma*] of the spheres, for all [of them] are transparent."... It pertains to the 'crystalline' (89-90).

All of this hangs on the central occult notion of, in Mead's words, "an intimate correspondence between man's psychical and sensible apparatus, or his inner embodiment, and the subtle nature of the universe" (12). This "theory of correspondence" between a subtle *organon* of the great nature, or world soul, and humanity grounds the doctrine of palingenesis. Mead explains that palingenesis was "the chief end not only of the higher mystery-institutions but of many an open philosophic school and saving cult of later antiquity," and that it can be imagined as an ascent from earth to the light-world (20), that is, as revelation or *gnosis* rather than as salvation or *soteria*.

Considering the various strands Mead brings together in his essays on the "subtle body," one is impressed with the number of the similarities between them and many of the images scattered in *The Cantos*, especially the later cantos, and the prose pieces. It might be useful to list the most important of these images as they appear in Mead: the subtle body is like (1) a light-spark, centred in the head, whose source is often said to be a divine fire; (2) it is the glorious vehicle or vesture of the soul; (3) it is transparent; (4) it flows like a crystal; (5) its form is spherical; (6) it is corporeal but more fine in its composition than the four elements; and, finally, (7) it is radiant, luminescent, and pellucid. In addition, Mead's palingenetic line of progression seems to involve a movement from the hylic to the spirituous and then to the *augoeides*—in other words, Mead's is a tripartite schema that corresponds to the following standard occult pattern: hylic, spiritual, celestial.

It can be argued that Pound draws on Mead's discussion of the "subtle body" to elaborate upon moments of metamorphosis, which we have seen is an exoteric form of the *epopteia* or revelation. The ultimate moment is represented by Pound in *The Cantos* as a "transportation" of the hylic into the subtle body.[21]

Canto 91 opens with two lines of a melody in medieval notations over Pound's adaptation of several lines of Bernart de Ventadorn's and Guillaume de Poitier's troubadour songs. As Leon Surette has shown, the poetry and music of Provence belong to a putative cult of *Amor*, reaching from Eleusis through Provence to Yeats, Mead, and Pound himself. Thus the canto's subsequent lines need to be located within Pound's understanding of the mystical cult of *amor*.

The ascension motif which I read as part of the palingenetic structure of *The Cantos* begins in canto 90 and is completed in canto 91, where the figure of the beloved becomes the focus of the lover's/*mystes*'s intentness:

> that the body of light come forth
> > from the body of fire
> And that your eyes come to the surface
> > from the deep wherein they were sunken,
> Reina — for 300 years,
> > and now sunken
> That your eyes come forth from their caves
> > & light then
> > > as the holly leaf (91/610).

It is tempting to gloss these lines with Mead so that the "body of fire" corresponds to the hylic world while the "body of light" represents the "spirituous," purified aura surrounding the "gross" body. Remembering the references to "crystal" later on in this canto ("& from fire to crystal / via the body of light" [615]), it would be more correct to say that Pound focusses here not so much on the stages of palingenetic purification but rather on the dynamic moment of the fluid and bidirectional transcendence and subsidence; in other words, Pound's imagery is an exoteric representation of the movement from *dromena* to *epopteia* and back to *dromena*. And, in what proves to be one of many images of ascent that culminate with that of "Queen Cytherea" (91/617), the reader witnesses the expression of a wish for the *anadysis* or rise out of the water of "Reina" ("Prob. the goddess Aphrodite, ... as well as a generalized epithet for 'Isis-Persephone-Demeter-Kuanon'" [*Companion*, II.547]), the "queen" or ideal woman, the "donna" of Provençal verse. (This is an *anadysis* and not an *anodos* because the ascent is from the sea and not from the underworld.)

In his use of the optative mood Pound signals that the movement from the hylic to the visionary world, represented here by Reina's ascent (she is represented synecdochally by her eyes) from the sea caves to the world of light above the water, is a forbidding and arduous task, and one not to be undertaken lightly. Since palingenesis involves a rebirth, it is preceded by death. The palingenetic experience is hence dreadful and perilous; this insight is crucial to our reading of Odysseus's refusal of transcendence later on in this canto contrasted with Apollonius's effortless ascension (Philostratus 7.283). Here the *anadysis* is not so much an actual experience, but an expression of the speaker's wish for the *anadysis* of Reina from the *dromena* of the hylic world.

The lines quoted above can be read palingenetically, then, as an escape from the watery realm of visionless imprisonment in the flesh to the "radiant" world sought by the *mystes*. But still the "eyes" are sunken "for 300 years, / and now sunken." The submergence of the visionary eyes may be seen as the *katabasis* or descent of the soul into the human body which, as in the *dromena* of the initiation, results in the beclouding of vision. As Mead explains:

> We learn, . . . from the myth of the imprisonment of the souls in fleshly bodies as a punishment, that when thus incarnate they lose the direct vision they previously enjoyed, and their sense becomes dim. They can no longer see heaven and their starry brethren in their true forms. They complain that their bodies are now "watery spheres," and their organs of vision "windows not eyes." (54)

Reina's anticipated or wished-for emergence from the sea is paralleled by a sequence of similar movements involving both goddesses and mortal women:

>   Thus Undine came to the rock,
>   by Circeo
>   and the stone eyes again looking seaward
>   Thus Apollonius
>   (if it was Apollonius)
>   Helen of Tyre
>   by Pithagoras
>   by Ocellus
>   (pilot-fish, et libidinis expers, of Tyre;
>   Justinian, Theodora
>   from brown leaf and twig
>   The GREAT CRYSTAL
>   doubling the pine, and to cloud.
>   pensar di lieis m'es ripaus
>   Miss Tudor moved them with galleons
>   from deep eye, versus armada

> from the green deep
> > he saw it,
> in the green deep of an eye: (91/610-11).

Undine is a "mythical sea creature with siren like attraction for men" (*Companion*, II.547); she usually represents the feminine or perilous nature of the waters and, in this case, the dangers of transcendence — like the Sirens in the *Odyssey*, where Odysseus experiences the seduction of transcendence but avoids it by having himself bound to his ship's mast. The figure of Undine also rhymes with that of Ino or Leucothea, Κάδμου θυγάτηρ (daughter of Cadmus), once mortal and now a sea-goddess, who emerges from the sea later on in this canto to save Odysseus from Poseidon's wrath (91/615-16).

Undine's *anadysis* may be viewed, in the present context, as representing the *mystes*'s vision of an ascent from the troubling world of the *dromena* toward a state of being that transcends the "TLEMOUSUNE" (91/615) or misery of everyday life. The rock to which Undine comes is "by Circeo," that is, near Circeo, a mountain near Terracina, a "seaport in C[entral] Latium, . . . where the ruins of a temple to Jupiter still stand" (*Companion*, I.162). The naming of Circeo and the allusion to Aphrodite in the following line remind us of Pound's remark in "Terra Italica": "Given the material means I would replace the statue of Venus on the cliffs of Terracina" (*SP* 53).[22]

Undine also corresponds to Ino / Leucothea / Leucochoe, a complex subject-rhyme with Reina and Elizabeth I, achieved by the double signs of *anadysis* and the "eyes." The other two females that appear in these lines are Helen of Tyre and Theodora (whose husband built the Ἁγία Σοφία or Divine Wisdom and codified Roman Law), the Byzantine Empress who had been an actress and thus is a Helen of Tyre type. Though Helen of Tyre and Theodora are not chaste (unlike Queen Elizabeth, a Diana or Athena type), their sexual practices are seen by Pound as sacred acts (*hieros gamos*): "et libidinis expers" ("and having no part in lust"). The restoring power of the *hieros gamos* is evident in the restoration to life ("the pine"), through the agency of the "GREAT CRYSTAL," of the "brown [dead] leaf and twig."

The "guides" or "pilot fish" in this palingenetic movement are Apollonius of Tyana and Ocellus. Apollonius is the first-century Pythagorean philosopher, wandering mystic, man of wisdom, and miracle-worker who is presented in Philostratus's *Life of Apollonius of Tyana* as a rival of Christ. He is one of the sages who belong to Pound's "celestial tradition," several of whom are listed in canto 91. (Apollonius's exploits are given in more detail later on in canto 91 and in even more detail in canto 94.) Terrell suggests that Appolonius's presence here can be explained by the fact that his transformation at the end of his trial in Rome rhymes with Helen's transformation in Gnostic tradition (*Companion*, II.547). Since Apollonius, like Undine, Aphrodite, and Helen of Troy, "came to the rock" ("Thus Undine . . . Thus Apollonius"), he is seen as partaking in the movement into paradise.²³ I think, however, that Apollonius is found here because as a Magus, or beatified one, he belongs to Pound's *paradiso terrestre*; this is a timeless state, a higher level of existence which the soul of the *mystes* enters not by departing from the ordinary world but rather by merely entering a higher plane of existence. The *paradiso terrestre* corresponds to the *augoeides* and may be equated to palingenesis or birth from above. Like Odysseus, Apollonius speaks to the dead (94/638) and, like Leucothea, he calms the seas. He is Pound's best example of the illuminated soul, and he is the individual most likely to be encountered by the *mystes* in this "paradise."²⁴

Because of his chastity Apollonius is the prototypical hero and probably the best representative of the illuminated soul; but there is also a galaxy of occult heroes populating *The Cantos*. A list would include all those who belong to what Pound calls the "celestial tradition" in *Guide to Kulchur* (for the list see Chapter I). These heroes are viewed by Pound in *The Cantos* as enjoying the paradisal state described in canto 91. If, as I believe, Pound read the *Odyssey* as an occult text, then, Odysseus, too, is a Magus. His voyages from one island to the next are, esoterically understood, interior voyages; and his adventures with the dead, with Circe, and with Leucothea, are also revelations.

The women appearing in canto 91, whether mortal or divine, seem to be analogues of Aphrodite and are united in that they, like Princess Ra-Set, seem in their ascension to enter "the protection" of the *augoeides*, Pound's "great crystal."²⁵ "The GREAT CRYSTAL" is an exoteric symbol of the "subtle-body" which unites the *mystes* with the primal creative fire in paradisal clarity. The importance of the subtle body concept for Pound is captured, I think, in the following lines – here "crystal" is presented as the medium through which move not only the gods but also those "who have some part of divine vision":

>   Crystal waves weaving together toward the gt/
>   healing
> Light *compenetrans* of the spirits
> The Princess Ra-Set has climbed
>   to the great knees of stone,
> She enters protection,
>   the great cloud is about her,

> She has entered the protection of crystal
> > convien che si mova
> > la mente, amando
> > > > XXVI, 34
>
> (91/611-12)

The rising and falling waves of canto 90 ("and the waves rise and fall" [606]), become here "Crystal waves weaving together toward the gt/healing." The motif of the transformation of the waves into crystal which Pound underscores with alliteration and assonance, recurs throughout *The Cantos* in association with theophanic moments.[26] The status of this transformational moment is dynamic (something like Pound's "vortex") and soteriological. Thus the "movement" from hylic to spirituous to *augoeides* is neither one directional nor static, but transitional. It is a dynamic movement esoterically understood as a bidirectional and fluid activity in the direction of transcendence but also subsidence back into the hylic world.

References to crystal formation from waves are signs of the presence of gods (and as I have been suggesting here a signal of the *mystes*'s entry into a higher plane of existence); but in the first two lines of the above passage the formed crystal is an exoteric representation of palingenesis, whose soteriological effect Pound calls the "gt/healing."[27] Here, again, we need to point out that the images which appeal to "εἰδώς" as "seeing" belong to the exoteric dimension of the *epopteia*, while those images which appeal to "εἰδώς" as "knowing" belong to the esoteric dimension of the initiation and have no equivalent in the hylic world. The reader of *The Cantos* is allowed a glimpse of the exoteric manifestation of palingenesis; the esoteric meaning, however, although intelligible and "entered into" by the *mystes*/reader, cannot be manifested.

It is the space or plane of the "gt/healing," the ultimate moment of palingenetic transformation, that "Princess Ra-Set" enters in canto 91. Ra-Set is an invented Egyptian goddess. Her name is made up of Ra, the Egyptian sun-god, and Set, the moon god, who is also the evil male deity whose association with moisture and passivity may be taken as feminine qualities. Boris de Rachewiltz explains that the transformation of the two ancient Egyptian male divinities into a single female entity "suggests that the poet's esotericism may... have a microcosmic as well as a macrocosmic significance" (181). This significance, he continues, is prefigured in *The Spirit of Romance* where Pound discusses "an ancient hypothesis [according to which] the little cosmos 'corresponds' to the greater, [and] man has in him both 'sun' [Ra] and 'moon' [Set]" (*SR* 94).

Pound's esotericism carries sexual connotations as well — which is to be expected considering his understanding of the *trobar clus* and his attitude toward the sexual act in general. Not only do we have an androgynous synthesis in the transformation of Ra-Set, but the interpenetration of spirit through the medium of light and Ra-Set's climbing to the "great knees of stone" (the knees were taken as the seat of virility) are all images that carry sexual implications. Thus, the union of Ra with Set, which represents the "essential cosmic equilibrium of good and evil," corresponds to the "*in coitu inluminatio*" (74/435), the *mystes*'s exoteric "seeing" of the *hieros gamos*, imaged here as Ra-Set's "entering" into the crystalline "subtle body." The whole passage carries both "spiritual" and "sensual" significance. Like Ra-Set and the other females of canto 91, in his vision the *mystes* enters the "GREAT CRYSTAL"—that is, he enters the plane of existence or state of mind populated by such personalities as Apollonius. But because the present *mystes* finds himself moving in this bi-directional process, the spirits illuminated here by light ("Light *compenetrans* of the spirit") appear in a "great cloud." Therefore, the "subtle body" appears to the reader as a "great cloud . . . about her [Ra-Set]" since, as Porphyry explains, "according to the Stoics, souls who love the body attract a moist spirit to them, and condense it like a cloud (for the moist being condensed in air constitutes a cloud). That when the spirit in souls is condensed by a superabundance of the moist element, they become visible" (*Subtle Body* 64-65).[28]

The manifestation of the goddess entering the substance of the "GREAT CRYSTAL" represents the culmination of the palingenetic process. In becoming aware at this stage of his initiation, the *mystes* himself enters this "substance." The purpose of the palingenetic experience is the rebirth or reconstitution of the *mystes*'s soul—this reconstitution is accomplished here, since the "protection" of the crystalline substance is also the "gt/healing," an exoteric metaphor for spiritual regeneration. Ultimately, the "gr/healing" is the goal of palingenesis in *The Cantos*!

The quotation from Dante ("convien che si mova / la mente, amando": "it is right that the mind should move by loving") returns us to Sir Francis Drake's vision of Miss Tudor:

Light & the flowing crystal
    never gin in cut glass had such clarity
That Drake saw the splendour and wreckage
    in that clarity
Gods moving in crystal
        ichor, amor (90/611).

In this remarkable image Drake looks into Elizabeth's eyes, sees the spirits illuminated by the light of "gr/healing" ("Light *compenetrans* of the spirits"), and is inspired by what he sees to great deeds: the defeat of the

Spanish armada.[29] But these lines are equally remarkable in their depiction of a world Pound elsewhere laments as lost to us:

> We appear to have lost the radiant world where one thought cuts through another with clean edge, a world of moving energies *"mezzo oscuro rade,"* *"risplende in sè perpetuale effecto,"* magnetisms that take form, that are seen, or that border the visible, the matter of Dante's *paradiso*, the glass under water, the form that seems a form seen in a mirror... (*LE* 154).

"These realities [which are] perceptible to the sense" (*LE* 154) seem to be recaptured here. The "subtle body" flows and pours and in its splendour and clarity the *mystes* sees "Gods moving." De Rachewiltz notes that "in hermetic philosophy, 'to know' or be aware of a god means to break through to and reunite with the creative state" (186). The perception of "Gods moving in crystal" represents such a reunification of the *mystes* and the "divine or permanent world" — a world elsewhere described as "The liquid and rushing crystal / beneath the knees of the gods" (4/15).

In the passage from the "Cavalcanti" essay quoted above, Pound attributes the loss of the "radiant world" to the lack of *"intelletto* [understanding]." This "radiant world" belongs to those numbered with the "celestial tradition." Pound proceeds to enumerate some of them before undertaking to describe another *katabasis*:

> Secretary of Nature, J. Heydon.
>   Here Apollonius, Heydon
>   hither Ocellus
>   "to this khan"
> The golden sun boat
>   by oar, not by sail
> Love moving the stars παρὰ βώμιον
> by the altar slope
>   "Tamuz! Tamuz!"
> They set lights now in the sea
>   and the sea's claw gathers them outward.
> The peasant wives hide cocoons now
>   under their aprons
>   for Tamuz
> That the sun's silk
>   hsien 顯   tensile
>   be clear
> Ἑλέναυς That Drake was the armada
>   & sea caves

>   Ra-Set over crystal
>   ⌣⌣ moving
>   in the Queen's eye the reflection
>   & sea-wrack—
>   green deep of the sea-cave
>   ne quaesaris.
>   He asked not
>   nor wavered, seeing, nor had fear of the wood-queen, Artemis
>   that is Diana
>   nor had killed save by the hunting rite,
>   sanctus.
>   (91/611-12)

Coming after the *epopteia* or revelation, these lines, whose world is populated by three members of Pound's "celestial" company (Apollonius, Heydon, and Ocellus), describe a composite, ritual miming made up of fragments taken from Oriental, Egyptian, Greek, Babylonian, Ligurian, Chinese, and English sources. Central to this rite is the motif of *katabasis*. Ra-Set, Pound's androgynous deity, descends to the underworld on the barge of the Sun, Helios ("In the barge of Ra-Set" [91/613]), which Pound depicts in the text by drawing an hieroglyph borrowed from de Rachewiltz's *Egizio degli Inferi* (Rome, 1959). De Rachewiltz tells us that Pound has excerpted the drawing along with the central concept of the ancient Egyptian Book of the Underworld. In this sacred text, de Rachewiltz explains, "we find a description of the nightly progress of the sun through the underworld, along with various magic formulae by which humans may attain immortality.... The symbolic oar signifies that the voyage is a carefully charted one that will not rely upon the fortuity of the winds" (184).[30]

The composite rite echoes the Adonis myth, another exoteric representation of the palingenetic ritual. The present *mystes* is aware of the dangers of transcendence but, unlike Anchises in canto 23, asks no questions about *katabasis* or death ("ne quaesaris. / He asked not") — nor does he show any "fear" of "Artemis / that is Diana," here an analogue of Reina and Miss Tudor. In this version of the ritual, the "peasant wives hide cocoons.../ under their aprons / for Tamuz" or Adonis; the "cocoons," symbols of metamorphosis and fertility, imply the potential for spiritual regeneration or palingenesis.

Borrowing from the final line of the *Paradiso*, Pound writes about "Love moving the stars." This love is metamorphosed into flowing light that pervades everything:

"The Subtle Body": Cantos 90 and 91

> Over harm
> Over hate
>   overflooding, light over light
> ....
> the light flowing, whelming the stars (91/613).

The alchemical process which underlies the "subtle body" concept is also described in this canto:

> & from fire to crystal
>   via the body of light,
>   the gold wings assemble (91/615).

These lines represent an advance on canto 91's opening lines in that the "crystal[line]" phase is added to those of the "body of fire" and the "body of light." This composite image of fire / light / crystal represents the "medium" of palingenesis.

Following a long passage whose source is Layamon's *Brut* and some personal reminiscences, Pound initiates another sequence of associations which begins with a mythological image of the "dawn" (Rhea, the mother of Zeus is pictured as a dawn goddess) and ends with a reference to Odysseus's encounter with Leucothea:

> That Rhea's lions protect her
> ....
> Rose, azure,
>   the lights slow moving round her,
> Zephyrus, turning,
>   the petals light on the air.
> Bright hawk whom no hood shall chain,
> They who are skilled in fire
>   shall read tan, the dawn.
> Waiving no jot of the arcanum
>   (having his own mind to stand by him)
> As the sea gull Κάδμου θυγάτηρ said to Odysseus
> KADMOU THUGATER
>   "get rid of parapernalia"
>   TLEMOUSUNE (91/615).

The "arcanum" of the passage turns out to be both an image suggested "by the dawn character *tan* (sun over horizon) which only a few may read" (Bacigalupo 298) as well as the magic veil which Leucothea, appearing in the form of a seabird, gives to Odysseus the *mystes*. Athough on the hylic level he is in real danger, and though Leucothea's instructions are clear ("'get rid of parapernalia,'" that is, get rid of the clothes given to you by Calypso), Odysseus, already an initiate into the mysteries and thus "having his own mind to stand by him," is not completely persuaded by the goddess's advice to get rid of his clothes and abandon his raft. Instead, he does the sensible thing and stays on his raft until it is destroyed by Poseidon. Odysseus's ability to think for himself and his ability to transcend the misery ("TLEMOUSUNE") of the hylic world are clear signs of his achievement of *gnosis*.[31]

Leucothea's instruction to Odysseus to get rid of his clothes provides the link to the next segment which begins with an amusing bath-house anecdote about Apollonius (91/616) and continues with Heydon's description of the state of the "subtle body" as a world full of light and populated by nymphs.

> to ascend those high places
>   wrote Heydon
> stirring and changeable
>   "light fighting for speed"
> and if honour and pleasure will not be ruled
>   yet the mind come to that High City . . .
>   who with Pythagoras at Taormina
> Souls be the water-nymphs of Porhyrius
> Νυκτὸς δ'αὖτ'αἰθήρ τε καὶ ἡμέρα Ζηνὸς πυρός (91/616).

Though not as reputable as Apollonius with whom he is unfavourably contrasted here, Heydon, too, is a Magus, one of the illuminated souls. Heydon was one of the major characters in Pound's abandoned Ur-canto III, where his vision of the goddess, as it is given in *The Holy Guide*, is described. The lines quoted above and those immediately following them are largely lifted from Heydon's *The Holy Guide*. However, as Leon Surette has noted, Pound does not revive Heydon's vision of the goddess. Instead, he takes "Heydon's statement that men desire heaven, and turns it into an assertion that the mind can attain heaven" (*Light* 265). Though he is unfaithful to Heydon, Pound uses phrases from Heydon's text to point out that the *mystes*, or rather his "mind," is able to "ascend those high places" and "come to that High City. . . ." Thus, Magi such as Apollonius, Odysseus, and Heydon himself can inhabit the hylic world of "TLEMOUSUNE" or *dromena* and at the same time enter a higher level of existence where "light [is] fighting for speed."

The canto ends with an affirmation of the validity of the visionary experience:

"Ghosts dip in the crystal,
                    adorned"
That the tone change from elegy
                    "Et Jehanne"
            (the Lorraine girl)
A lost kind of experience?
                    scarcely,
O Queen Cytherea,
            che 'l terzo ciel movete.
            ("which moves the third heaven" *Paradiso*,
                    Canto VIII, 37) (91/616-17).

The "crystal" into which "ghosts dip" is the palingenetic medium through which souls pass back and forth as in Porphyry's cave ("Souls be the water-nymphs of Porhyrius") or Yeats's "gong-tormented sea" (*Collected Poems* 281). Only the visionary (or the superior soul or Magus) can "see" this crystal, but everyone can see its product—the sensible world—and everyone can "feel" or "divine" the spiritual ("spirituous") and celestial (*augoeides*) realms it manifests. Once more, there are three levels here: the hylic; the intellectual, visionary, or "spirituous"; and the celestial or *augoeides* or "aethereal." The lover, poet, and philosopher have access to the first two levels. Only the Magus (Upward's "Divine Man") has access to the third. "Ghosts dip in crystal" in that they come back for visits (Joan of Arc heard voices) to sensitive souls or mediums. The request "That the tone change from elegy" is necessary because it is not death but rather palingenesis that is the subject here. The allusion to the visionary experiences of Joan of Arc (Villon's "Lorraine girl": a virgin, warrior, and mystic) serves as a rhyme to the experiences of Reina and Elizabeth. The answer to the rhetorical question "A lost kind of experience?" is, of course, a resounding "NO!" ("scarcely"). Picking up the optative mood of the canto's opening lines (*"That* the body of light come forth. . . . *That* the tone change from elegy"), Pound finally names Aphrodite as the goddess of his initiatory syncretic rite. He has already suggested her presence by naming a host of mortal women and goddesses whose characteristics she encompasses (Reina, Persephone, Diana, Helen of Troy, Miss Tudor, Tyro, Alcmene, Princess Ra-Set, NUTT, Pinella, Undine, Theodora, Leucothea, Merlin's mother, and "Et Jehanne"). The theophany of Queen Cytherea, Aphrodite reformulated in the aspect of a new and "strange" woman, represents the culmination of the process of initiation, since her appearance signals the movement from the ephemeral "into 'divine or permanent world'" of the gods. It is in this "permanent world" of the gods, the world of the *augoeides* and the "aethereal," the world inhabited by

Dante's angelic powers who by their "intellect" and "love" move the "third heaven," "the vision of coherence" (McDowell and Materer 359) with which canto 91 ends. And it is Mead who has provided Pound with the model or "ladder of ascent from the earth to the light-world" (*Subtle Body* 13).

NOTES

1. See, for example, Wilhelm's discussion which is still the standard one (*The Later Cantos of Ezra Pound*, esp. 29-63, 79-87, 167-78).
2. In "Gyre and Vortex: W.B. Yeats and Ezra Pound," McDowell and Materer deal with canto 90 in terms of the spiral and the vortex, images which they situate within the same occult tradition outlined in this study. I think, however, that the palingenetic paradigm, though it is not the sole analogy to be found in *The Cantos*, works better in the two cantos discussed here as well as in the poem as a whole. It works better because, unlike the vortex which is a specific and limited image, *palingenesis* is a sort of drama or story with actors and events that can be used to explain the multiple layers of the poem.
3. In "Religio," his mock-catechism, Pound refers to the *mystes*'s entry into the permanent world of the gods in this way:
    > When is a god manifest?
    > When the states of mind take form.
    > When does a man become a god?
    > When he enters one of these states of mind (*SP* 47).

    During the mysteries, the hierophant is the one who introduces the *mystes* into these states of mind, since he is the one who "manifests" to him the *theos*.
4. William Cookson reports that "Pound told Olga Rudge that he intended this to be the last line of the *Cantos*" (165).
5. For Pound's translation of this poem, which he calls the "best known of Ventadorn's songs," see *The Spirit of Romance* (41-42).
6. For additional examples of such "failures" in the Pound canon see Sieburth (156-57).
7. Cookson reports that line 34 refers to the "gasping" sound made by "a butterfly [which] was heard by Pound and Marcella Spann during a walk in the Tyrolese mountains" (164-65).
8. When we think of the exoteric/esoteric nature of the poem, we become aware that this passage can be read in at least two substantially different ways. For the reader who knows nothing about the poem's esoteric meaning, these are simply rhetorical questions; but for the *mystes* these become specific questions to which he can respond according to his or her progress along the palingenetic path — in other words, the *mystes* who can respond in the affirmative has, indeed, succeeded in participating in the poem's palingenetic rite.
9. Pound's original plan "to write Paradise" (120/803) was to begin after the completion of canto 71; "from 72 on we will enter the empyrean" (Stock, *Life* 376) he said in 1940. But because of historical circumstances, the original programme did not materialize. In fact, Pound wrote two cantos in Italian (72-73) which were not included in the text of *The Cantos* until the 1986 printing of the poem (New Directions). These two cantos, full of Italian patriotism (the first deals with the death of

Marinetti and the second is about an Italian girl's ambush of a Canadian platoon), point to the direction Pound envisioned his epic was about to take. The lacuna in the text reminds us that Pound was forced to shift to a new mode. His intentions having been carried adrift by the titanic waves of World War II, Pound wrote instead the *Pisan Cantos* which were not part of the programme he had envisioned upon the completion of the *Adams Cantos*.

10. Pound would probably quibble with Stock's claim about modern Masonry — at least with whether or not modern Masons are aware of the meaning of their rituals. This is suggested in a letter to Olivia Rossetti Agresti in which he discriminates between "real masonry" and its modern forms: "Real masonry, as from China etc. pure down to Mozart. and since flooded with mutts who have NOT the faintest inkling of the mysteries once guarded in an order..." (letter dated 7 December [1956], BRBL).

11. Terrell goes a step further. He points out that in *From Ritual to Romance* Jessie L. Weston connects the Knights Templar with pagan priests known as "Salloi," and conjectures that "Pound prob. rhymes the 'secret society' ambience of the Selli with other secret societies, such as the San Ku" (*Companion*, II.495).

12. See also Forrest Read, "The Mathematical Symbolism of Ezra Pound's Revolutionary Mind" (29ff.).

13. In a letter to Olivia Rossetti Agresti, dated 7 December [1956], Pound makes the same point about the degradation of Renaissance art into "barocco" (BRBL): "Large gap between Pitagoro and the year 1300. Section d'Or got lost, etc. and renaissance architecture went on... pot an' barocco.... Latter term derived from what? baro?" This is the same letter in which Pound reveals his interest in Masonry and Swedenborg.

14. According to Hesiod's genealogy in *Theogony*, Erebus and his sister *Nyx* (Night) were born of Chaos. Erebus later fathered *Aether* (Upper Air) and *Hemera* (Day) on *Nyx*. He is generally identified with Hades, god of the Underworld.

15. Of course, Aegisthus's "wrongs" refers to his murder of Agamemnon, Electra's father. According to Sophocles, Electra persuaded Orestes, her brother, to murder Aegisthus; but Pound seems to think that she is still saddened ("bowed") by Aegisthus's sullying of the parental marriage bed.

16. Though Mead's book did not appear until 1919, Pound was probably familiar with the concepts delineated therein from as early as 1910. The book's three essays had already appeared in *The Quest* I (1909-10): "The Resurrection of the Body," 271-87; "The Spirit-Body: An Excursion into Alexandrian Psycho-Physiology," 472-88; and "The Augoeides or Radiant Body," 705-24. It is of interest that W.B. Yeats refers to these essays in "Swedenborg, Mediums, and the Desolate Places" (1914), largely written during his first winter with Pound at Stone Cottage (1913-14).

17. That Pound was familiar with the doctrine of the "subtle body" is certain. Schneidau (in *The Image and the Real*) was the first to call attention to Pound's awareness of a long occult tradition behind the idea of mind as it is employed in "Psychology and Troubadours," a "tradition [which] was probably outlined for him by Mead, who was gathering material that was to appear in his *Doctrine of the Subtle Body in Western Tradition*" (126). More recently, Elliott, Bell, and Oderman have also dealt with Mead's "subtle body" theory.

18. The following verses are from the holograph notes for canto 25 (BRBL) as reproduced by Kevin Oderman. (I myself have also examined the holographs.) Though I

disagree with some of his conclusions, Oderman's careful and astute discussion of Mead's *Subtle Body* and its importance for Pound has been valuable in helping me understand this rather recondite subject — and though much more detailed than his, my discussion in this section follows, to a certain extent, Oderman's. See Oderman's discussion of the *augoeides* (esp. 70-75).

19. The claim for affinities between occult theories and modern scientific discoveries is a constant theme in occult writings. Occultists viewed scientific discoveries such as radiation as proof for their claims for a monistic cosmos. Though these claims need not be taken seriously, literary studies ought to pay attention to them because much of what passes for scientific materialism in Pound is a consequence of his understanding of occultism.

20. Mead discusses the notion of palingenesis on a number of occasions as "the bringing to birth of man's perfected subtle body" (esp. 41, 130-31, and 134).

21. Here are three examples, taken from Pound's prose, whose source is likely Mead's essays on the subtle body. In "Psychology and Troubadours" (1912), he discusses sex in terms of "a possibly *'subtler form of energy'*" and says that "Sex is . . . of a double function and purpose, . . . or as we see it in the realms of *fluid force*, one sort of vibration produces at different intensities heat and light" (SR 94). In his "Translator's Postscript" to Remy de Gourmont's *The Natural Philosophy of Love* (1922), Pound discusses light in these terms: "Let us say quite simply that light is a projection of the *luminous fluid, from the energy that is in the brain* . . ." (154). Finally, in *Guide to Kulchur* (1938), he speaks of the *nous* as a "*sea crystalline and enduring,* . . . *bright as it were molten glass that envelops us, full of light*" (44). The italics are mine; the emphasis is placed on concepts and/or phrases that approximate those in Mead's essays. Numerous other examples exist in the Pound canon.

22. See also SP (320) and cantos 17/78; 39/195; 74/341 and 344-45; and 106/779 and 754.

23. After having been delivered from a brothel in Tyre to be made Simon Magus's mystical spouse, Helen became a symbol of the female Great Thought "which descended into the world for the salvation of man." Helen, in her soteriological role, is "hav[ing] no part in lust" ("et libidinis expers"), at least not in the ordinary sense. We know that while Pound adopted the concept of the mystical union of Simon Magus and Helen of Tyre from Mead, he rejected Mead's reading of it as an allegory of the soul, accepting instead a more literal reading according to which coitus is central to the wisdom tradition of Eleusis, the Simon Magus myth, and the *trobar clus*. That Pound is thinking about this tradition is suggested by his veiled reference to Eleanor of Aquitaine, the queen of the troubadours, in the line from Arnaut Daniel's eleventh canzo: "Pensar de lieis m'es repaus" ("to think of her is my rest") (*T* 170-71).

24. As already suggested in Chapter II, Pound also knew Mead's *Apollonius of Tyana*, a commentary on Philostratus's *Life*. For a detailed discussion of Apollonius's role in *The Cantos* and Pound's sources see Surette (*Light*, esp. 239-49).

25. Clark Emery was the first to talk about the presence of many passages in which "'the bright as it were molten glass' envelops Pound or other figures in the *Cantos* 'full of light'" (10). The first to discuss the Eleusinian *mystes's*/Pound's entry into the *nous* or "great crystal" was Stock: "The remaining six cantos (90-96) are devoted to love and Eleusis. . . . It is love which has lifted him out of Erebus: 'You have stirred my mind out of dust.' The universe is alive to the initiate, who, permeated

by, or transformed perhaps into, the spirit of Eleusis, finds entrance into the 'great crystal of paradise'" (*Reading the Cantos* 98). See also Elliott ("Light as Image" 236-38) who elaborates on Stock's statement by showing how the *mystes* "enters," in canto 91, into the protection of love.

26. For example, in canto 23 Aphrodite's appearance is "staged" amid a scene in which waves are formed into crystal:

> and saw then, as of waves taking form,
> As the sea, hard, a glitter of crystal,
> And the waves rising but formed, holding their form (23/109).

27. There are a number of additional occurrences of this palingenetic motif in *The Cantos*, including the following: "Thus the light rains, thus pours, . . . / The liquid and rushing crystal / beneath the knees of the gods" (4/15); "the NOUS, the ineffable crystal" (40/201); "no cloud, but the crystal body" (76/457); "the sphere moving crystal, fluid" (76/457); "the crystal can be weighed in the hand / formal and passing within the sphere: Thetis, / Maya, 'Ἀφροδίτη" (76/459); "The light there almost solid" and "That the crystal wave mount to flood surge" (95/644); "That great acorn of light bulging outward" and "foam on the wave-swirl / Out of gold light flooding the peristyle (106/755); "the crystal body of air" (107/762); "the ball of fire / as brightness / clear emerald" (108/764). The best example is, of course, the one in canto 116: "I have brought the great ball of crystal; / who can lift it? / Can you enter the great acorn of light?" (795). For detailed discussions of the "crystal motif" in *The Cantos* see Elliott ("Light as Image" passim), McDowell's and Materer's essay (esp. 352-65), and Oderman (passim). McDowell and Materer also make the interesting and apt observation that "healing" is used by Pound "with reference to its meaning 'to make whole,' that is, to join the solar and lunar parts of mankind" (358).

28. Interestingly, Yeats misquotes this passage in "Swedenborg, Mediums, and the Desolate Places" (22), which, as already noted, was largely written during the winter of 1913-14 at Stone Cottage.

29. The Miss Tudor/Drake interlude corresponds to a number of similar episodes in *The Cantos* where a "hero" is inspired to great deeds by a woman (i.e., Helen of Troy, Eleanor of Aquitaine, Isotta, etc.). The Miss Tudor/Drake link is also an inverted analogue of Troy. Drake's victory saves Protestant England from Catholic Spain, the animosity between the two nations having arisen as a result of Henry VIII's, Elizabeth's father, divorcing Catherine of Aragon. Therefore, England/Troy rejects Helen/Catherine and defeats Achaea/Achilles.

30. De Rachewiltz also notes the thematic rhyme of the Egyptian sun-boat, the "golden cup" of the *Stesichorus* passage (canto 23), and the "moon barge" (80/510: "Cythera, in the moon's barge wither?"; 80/511: "in the moon barge βροδοδάκτυλος 'Ηώς"; 90/605: "Moon's barge over milk-blue water"). The lunar motif is developed in the *Pisan* and *Rock-Drill Cantos* until, eventually, it assumes the attributes of Isis-Luna (canto 93), a conflation of Isis (the Egyptian fertility goddess, who was also queen of the dead and whose mysteries are akin to those of Demeter and Persephone) and Artemis/Diana (the moon goddess). The lunar motif is further developed in cantos 96 and 97. In "all under the Moon is under Fortuna" (96/656), Pound seems to be referring "to the esoteric doctrine of the moon as the mediatrix of changes of fortune that are related to its various phases" (185). Finally, the lines "above the Moon there is order, / beneath the Moon, forsitan" (97/677) recall *De*

facie in orbe lunae, a little-known text attributed to Plutarch, according to which humans experience two deaths: "the first when his body is returned to the earth as a corpse and separated from the soul and the mind (νοῦς), the second when the soul is separated from the mind, an event which occurs on the moon when man's individual existence is reabsorbed into the cosmic cycle. Only initiates ascend beyond the lunar sphere to become what Plutarch calls 'conquerors'" (qtd. in de Rachewiltz 186).

31. For a thorough account of the Leucothea theme in *The Cantos* see Surette (*Light*, esp. 239-59).

APPENDIX I

On pages 190-91 two pages are reproduced from Iahannes Schweighaeuser's bilingual (Greek and Latin) edition of Athenaeus's *Deipnosophistae*.

By comparing the text on pages 190-91 with the Stesichorus passage in canto 23 (ll. 19-23) we can see how Pound's rehearsal of the *Deipnosophistae* works. First, Pound transcribes lines 1 and 2 of the Stesichorus fragment—found in lines 21 and 22 of canto 23 (1). Next, Pound jumps to the bottom of page 237 of Schweighaeuser and transcribes half of line 3 of the Latin version of the fragment (2). Noticing emendation number 3 on page 237 (3) he then goes off to his Greek Dictionary in an attempt to make sense of the variation (see Appendix II). ἐσκατέβαινε is then used again in line 28 of canto 23, but transliterated into Roman letters (4). Following this Pound transcribes part of line 3, part of line 4, and the whole of line 5 of the fragment—ll. 31-33 of canto 23—manipulating in the process the verse length for emphasis.

p. 469.   LIBER XI.   237

ἩΡΆΚΛΕΙΟΝ. Πείσανδρος, ἐν δευτέρῳ Ἡρα- XXXVIII.
d κλείας, τὸ δέπας ἐν ᾧ διέπλευσεν ὁ Ἡρακλῆς τὸν   Herculis
ὠκεανὸν, εἶναι μέν φησιν ἡλίου, λαβεῖν δ' αὐτὸ¹ παρ'   poculum.
ὠκεανοῦ Ἡρακλέα. Μήποτε δὲ, ἐπεὶ μεγάλοις ἔχαι-
ρε ποτηρίοις ὁ ἥρως, διὰ τὸ μέγεθος παίζοντες οἱ ποιη-
ταὶ καὶ συγγραφεῖς,² πλεῖν αὐτὸν ἐν ποτηρίῳ ἐμυθολό-
γησαν; Πανύασις δὲ, ἐν πρώτῳ Ἡρακλείας, παρὰ
Νηρέως, φησὶ, τὴν τοῦ ἡλίου φιάλην κομίσασθαι τὸν
Ἡρακλέα, καὶ διαπλεῦσαι εἰς Ἐρύθειαν. ὅτι δὲ εἷς
ἦν ὁ Ἡρακλῆς τῶν πλεῖστον πινόντων, προείπομεν.
e Ὅτι δὲ καὶ ὁ ἥλιος ἐπὶ ποτηρίου διεκομίζετο ἐπὶ τὴν
δύσιν, Στησίχορος μὲν οὕτως φησίν·

Ἀέλιος ³ δ' ὑπεριονίδας δέπας ἐσκατέβαινε
χρύσεον, ὄφρα δι' ὠκεανοῖο περάσας
ἀφίκηθ' ἱερᾶς ποτὶ βένθεα νυκτὸς ἐρεμνᾶς
ποτὶ ματέρα, κουριδίαν τ' ἄλοχον,

1 δ' αὐτὸν edd.   2 καὶ οἱ γραφεῖς corr. Caſ.   3 Ἅλιος vulgo.

38. *Heracleum:* id eſt, *Herculis poculum.* Piſander, libro ſecundo Heracleae, poculum in quo oceanum transvectus eſt Hercules, Solis fuiſſe poculum ait, accepiſſeque illud a Sole Herculem. Fortaſſe vero, quoniam magnis delectabatur poculis ille heros, propter illorum magnitudinem ludentes poëtae & hiſtorici, *navigaſſe in poculo* finxerunt. Panyaſis vero, primo libro Heracleae ait, a Nereo accepiſſe Herculem Solis phialam, eáque transnavigaſſe in Erytheam. Fuiſſe autem Herculem unum ex eis qui plurimum biberent, in ſuperioribus dictum eſt. Solem vero etiam ad occaſum transvehi poculo, Steſichorus ait his verbis:

Sol vero Hyperionis filius in poculum inſcendebat
aureum, ut per oceanum traiiciens
perveniret ſacrae ad ima vada noctis obſcurae,
ad matrem, & virginalem uxorem,

238 ATHENAEI DEIPNOSOPH.   C. 5.

παῖδας τε φίλους. ὁ δ᾽ ἐς ἄλσος ἔβα
δάφναισι κατάσκιον
ποσσὶ παῖς Διός.
καὶ Ἀντίμαχος οὑτωσὶ λέγει·
— Τότε δὴ εὔχρεῳ ἐν δέπαϊ [1]
Ἥλιον πέμπεσκεν [2] ἀγακλυμένη Ἐρύθεια.
καὶ Αἰσχύλος ἐν Ἡλιάσιν·
,,Ἔνθ᾽ ἐπὶ δυσμαῖς ἴσου [3] πατρὸς Ἡφαιστοτευ-
χὲς δέπας, ἐν τῷ διαβάλλων [4] πολὺν οἰδμα-
τόεντα φέρει δρόμου πόρον. [5] οὐδ᾽ εἰς [6] μελανίπ-
που προφυγὼν ἱερᾶς [7] νυκτὸς ἀμολγόν.‟

XXXIX. Μίμνερμος δ᾽ ἐν Ναννοῖ, ἐν εὐνῇ φησι χρυσῇ κατε- a
Mimnermus σκευασμένῃ πρὸς τὴν χρείαν ταύτην ὑπὸ Ἡφαίστου
de lecto
Solis. τὸν ἥλιον καθεύδοντα περαιοῦσθαι πρὸς τὰς ἀνατολάς·
αἰνισσόμενος τὸ κοῖλον τοῦ ποτηρίου. λέγει δ᾽ οὕτως·

1 χρυσείῳ εἰνὶ ὑπάστρῳ corr. Caf. cum Dalec.   2 πομπεῖ Ms.
Forf. πέμπευιν, aut πομπεῖ ἢ ἀγακλ.   3 δυσμαῖσι σοῦ
corr. Caf.   4 διαβάλλει Ms.   5 Forf. φερέδρομον.   6 ὅτ᾽
εἰσι coni. Cafaub.   7 ἰμερτᾶς edd.

liberosque caros. Ipse autem in lucum se contulit
lauris obumbratum
pedibus filius Iovis.

Et Antimachus ita scribit:
Tunc vero commodo in poculo
Solem in pompa ostendit illustris Erythea.

Et Aeschylus in Heliadibus:
Ibi in occidente est poculum patris tui, Vulcani
opus: in quo traiiciens, longum & aestuosum cur-
riculum conficit; cum abit fugiens nigris - equis-
vectam sacram noctem.

39. *Mimnermus* vero, in Nanno, ait: aureo in lecto, in hunc ipsum usum a Vulcano constructo, dormientem solem transvehi ad Orientem, obscure sic indicans poculi cavitatem. En eius verba:

APPENDIX II

The excerpt reproduced below is from *A Greek-English Lexicon*, by Liddell and Scott.

Motivated by his desire to understand emendation number 3 in Schweighaeuser's text (see Appendix I) which gives ἅλιος as a variation of ἥλιος (Sun), Pound opens his Greek lexicon and discovers that ἅλιος (1) is the Doric form for ἥλιος (the Attic form of the poetic ἠέλιος). Furthermore, he also notices that there are two more entries for ἅλιος, "of the sea" (2), and ἅλιος = μάταιος, "fruitless, unprofitable, idle . . ." (3). This process of looking up words in the dictionary is then reproduced by Pound in line 25 of canto 23. Having observed that ἅλιος = μάταιος, Pound also transcribes this and the lexicographer's remark "(Deriv. uncertain)" [not shown in excerpt] in line 26 of canto 23 (4). In addition, Pound notices that the triple ἅλιος is "enclosed" in the lexicon by the following two words: ἁλίξαντος, "worn by the sea," and ἁλιο-τρέφης, "sea-reared" (5). Since these two words are consistent with the double meaning of the nature of the sea, he transliterates and transcribes them in line 28 of canto 23.

ἁλί-ξαντος, ον, *worn by the sea*, χοιράδες Anth. P. 6. 89; ἁλ. μόρος *death by being dashed on the beach*, Ib. 7. 404.
ἅλιος, ὁ, Dor. for ἥλιος.
ἅλιος (A), α, ον, also ος, ον Soph. Aj. 357, Eur. Heracl. 82: (ἅλς):— *of the sea*, Lat. *marinus*, epith. of sea-gods, nymphs, etc., Hom. etc.; θυγάτηρ ἁλίοιο γέροντος, i. e. of Nereus, Il. 1. 556, Hes. Th. 1003, cf. Od. 4. 365, al.; θεαὶ ἅλιαι *sea-goddesses*, Nereids, 18. 432; of Apollo, Arist. Mirab. 107, cf. ἁλιπλαγκτος; ἁλ. ψάμαθοι the *sea-sand*, Od. 3. 38; ἁλ. πρών Aesch. (lyr.) Pers. 131, 879; κῦμα Id. Supp. 15; ναῦς, πλάτα, πρύμνη, etc., Pind. O. 9. 111, Soph. O. C. 716, etc.; ἁλία δρῦς, perh. the same as ἁλίφλοιος, Eupol. Αἶγ. 1. 4; v. Meineke ad l.
ἅλιος (B), α, ον: (ἄλη, ἀλίθιος):—like μάταιος, of things, *fruitless, unprofitable, idle, erring*, ἔπος, μῦθος, τόξος, βέλος, ὅρκιον, etc., Il.; in Od. only with ὁδός, 2. 273, 318; of a person, Il. 10. 324: neut. ἅλιον as Adv., *in vain*, 13. 505: and so best taken in 4. 179; so also Soph. O. C. 1469; but regul. Adv. -ίως, Id. Ph. 840.—Ep. word, used by Soph. in lyric passages.
ἁλιο-τρέφης, ές, *feeding in the sea, sea-reared*. φῶκαι Od. 4. 442.

WORKS CITED AND CONSULTED

Ackroyd, Peter. *T.S. Eliot: A Life*. New York: Simon and Schuster, 1984.
Adams, Stephen S. "Ezra Pound and Music." Diss., University of Toronto, 1974.
―――. "Books on Pound from University Microfilm International." *Canadian Review of American Studies* 17 (1986): 367-73.
Aldington, Richard. *Life for Life's Sake*. New York: Viking, 1941.
Alexander, Michael. *The Poetic Achievement of Ezra Pound*. London: Faber, 1979.
Anastos, Milton A. "Pletho's Calendar and Liturgy." *Doumbarton Oaks Papers* 4 (1948): 186-269.
Anderson, David. "Breaking the Silence: The Interview of Vanni Ronsisvalle and Pier Paolo Pasolini with Ezra Pound in 1968." *Paideuma* 10 (1981): 331-45.
Apuleius. *The Golden Ass*. Trans. S. Gaselee. Loeb Classical Library. Cambridge, MA: Harvard University Press, 1915.
Bachchan, Harbans Rai. *W.B. Yeats and Occultism: A Study of his Works in Relation to Indian Lore, the Cabbala, Swedenborg, Boehme, and Theosophy*. Delhi: Motilal Barnarsidass, 1965.
Bacigalupo, Massimo. *The Forméd Trace: The Later Poetry of Ezra Pound*. New York: Columbia University Press, 1980.
Banta, Martha. *Henry James and the Occult*. Bloomington: Indiana University Press, 1972.
Baumann, Walter. "Ezra Pound and Magic: Old World Tricks in a New World Poem." *Paideuma* 10 (1981): 209-24.
―――. "Ezra Pound's Metamorphosis during his London Years: From Late-Romanticism to Modernism." *Paideuma* 13 (1984): 357-73.
―――. "Secretary of Nature, J. Heydon." In *New Approaches to Ezra Pound*, edited by Eva Hesse, 303-18. Berkeley: University of California Press, 1969.
―――. *The Rose in the Steel Dust: An Examination of the Cantos of Ezra Pound*. 1967. Coral Gables, FL: University of Miami Press, 1970.
Bays, Gwendolyn. *The Orphic Vision: Seer Poets from Novalis to Rimbaud*. Lincoln: University of Nebraska Press, 1964.
Beer, John. *Coleridge the Visionary*. London: Chatto, 1959.

Beilby, Rev. Arthur E. "Two Other-World Explorers: Dante and Swedenborg." *Quest* 4 (1912-13): 229-48.
Bell, Ian F. A. *Critic as Scientist: The Modernist Poetics of Ezra Pound*. London and New York: Methuen, 1981.
Bernstein, Michael. *The Tale of the Tribe: Ezra Pound and the Modern Verse Epic*. Princeton, NJ: Princeton University Press, 1980.
Blackstone, Bernard. *The Consecrated Urn: An Interpretation of Keats in Terms of Growth of Form*. London: Longmans, 1959.
Blavatsky, Helena P. *The Key to Theosophy*. 1889. Pasadena, CA: Theosophical University Press, 1946.
Bloom, Harold. *Kabbalah and Criticism*. New York: Seabury, 1975.
———. "Myth, Vision, Allegory." *Yale Review* 54 (1964): 143-49.
Bowers, Faubion. "Memoir Within Memoirs." *Paideuma* 2 (1973): 53-68.
Brooker, Peter. *A Student's Guide to the Selected Poems of Ezra Pound*. London: Faber, 1979.
Brooke-Rose, Christine. *A ZBC of Ezra Pound*. London: Faber, 1971.
Brooks-Davis, Douglas. *The Mercurian Monarch: Magical Politics from Spenser to Pope*. Manchester: Manchester University Press, 1983.
Bryson, Mary E. "Metaphors for Freedom: Theosophy and the Irish Literary Revival." *Canadian Journal of Irish Studies* 3, no. 1 (June 1977): 32-39.
Bush, Ronald. *The Genesis of Ezra Pound's Cantos*. Princeton, NJ: Princeton University Press, 1977.
Butler, E.M. *Ritual Magic*. 1949. Cambridge: Cambridge University Press, 1979.
Campbell, Bruce F. *Ancient Wisdom Revived: A History of the Theosophical Movement*. Berkeley: University of California Press, 1980.
Cantor, Paul A. *Creature and Creator: Myth-making and English Romanticism*. Cambridge, MA: Cambridge University Press, 1984.
Cantrell, Carol H. "Quotidian to Divine: Some Notes on Canto 81." *Paideuma* 12 (1983): 11-20.
Chace, William M. *The Political Identities of Ezra Pound and T.S. Eliot*. Stanford, CA: Stanford University Press, 1973.
Colquhoun, Ithell. *Sword of Wisdom: MacGregor Mathers and 'The Golden Dawn.'* New York: Putnam's, 1975.
Cookson, William. *A Guide to the Cantos of Ezra Pound*. New York: Persea Books, 1985.
Dante Alighieri. *Paradiso*. Princeton, NJ: Princeton University Press, 1982. Vol. 1 of *The Divine Comedy*. Trans. C.S. Singleton. Bollingen Series, vol. 80. 3 vols. 1982.
Davenport, Guy. *Cities on Hills: A Study of I-XXX of Ezra Pound's Cantos*. Ann Arbor, MI: UMI, 1983.
Davie, Donald. *Ezra Pound*. New York: Viking, 1975.
———. *Ezra Pound, Poet as Sculptor*. London: Routledge, 1965.
Davis, Kay. *Fugue and Fresco: Structures in Pound's "Cantos."* Orono, ME: National Poetry Foundation, 1984.
Dean, Barbara. "Shaw and Gnosticism." *The Shaw Review* 16, no. 3 (1973): 104-22.

WORKS CITED AND CONSULTED 195

Dekker, George. *Sailing after Knowledge: The Cantos of Ezra Pound.* London: Routledge, 1963.
Dennis, Helen M. "The Eleusinian Mysteries as an Organizing Principle in *The Pisan Cantos.*" *Paideuma* 10 (1981): 273-82.
D'Epiro, Peter. *A Touch of Rhetoric: Ezra Pound's Malatesta Cantos.* Ann Arbor, MI: UMI, 1983.
Dodds, E.R. *Pagan and Christian in an Age of Anxiety.* New York: Norton, 1970.
Doherty, Gerald. "Connie and the Charkas: Yogic Paterns in D.H. Lawrence's 'Lady Chatterley's Lover.'" *D.H Lawrence Review* 13 (1980): 79-93.
Doolittle, Hilda. [H.D.] *End to Torment: A Memoir of Ezra Pound by H.D.* Edited by Norman Holmes Pearson and Michael King. New York: New Directions, 1979.
―――. *HERmione.* New York: New Directions, 1981.
Eastham, Scott. *Paradise and Ezra Pound: The Poet as Shaman.* New York: University Press of America, 1983.
Edwards, John H., and W.V. Vasse. *Annotated Index to the Cantos of Ezra Pound: Cantos I-LXXXIV.* Berkeley: University of California Press, 1957.
Eliade, Mircea, ed. *Encyclopedia of Religion.* 16 vols. New York: Macmillan, 1987.
―――. *Images and Symbols: Studies in Religious Symbolism.* Trans. Philip Mairet. New York: Sheed and Ward, 1961.
―――. *The Myth of the Eternal Return: Cosmos and History.* Trans. Willard R. Trask. Princeton, NJ: Princeton University Press, 1954.
―――. *Occultism, Witchcraft, and Cultural Fashions: Essays in Comparative Religion.* Chicago and London: University of Chicago Press, 1976.
―――. *The Sacred and the Profane.* New York: Harper, 1961.
Elliott, Angela. "Light as Image in Ezra Pound's *Cantos.*" Diss., Drew University, 1978.
―――. "Pound's 'Isis Kuanon': An Ascension Motif in *The Cantos.*" *Paideuma* 13 (1984): 327-56.
―――. "Pound's Lucifer: A Study of the Imagery of Flight and Light." *Paideuma* 12 (1983): 237-66.
―――. "The Word Comprehensive: Gnostic Light in the *Cantos.*" *Paideuma* 18 (1989): 7-57.
Ellmann, Richard. *The Identity of Yeats.* 1954. New York: Oxford University Press, 1964.
Ellwood Jr., Robert S. *Religious and Spiritual Groups in Modern America.* Englewood Cliffs, NJ: Prentice-Hall, 1973.
Emery, Clark. *Ideas into Action: A Study of Pound's Cantos.* Coral Gables, FL: University of Miami Press, 1958.
Epstein, Perle S. *The Private Labyrinth of Malcolm Lowry: "Under the Volcano" and the Cabbala.* New York: Holt, 1969.
Farnell, Lewis Richard. *The Cults of the Greek States.* 5 vols. Oxford: Clarendon, 1906-1909.
Finlay, John L. *Social Credit: The English Origins.* Montreal: McGill-Queen's University Press, 1972.
Fitts, Dudley. "Music Fit for the Odes." In *Ezra Pound: The Critical Heritage,* edited by Eric Homberger, 246-55. London: Routledge, 1972.

Flannery, Mary C. *Yeats and Magic: The Earlier Works.* Gerrards Cross, Buckinghamshire: Smythe, 1977.
Flory, Wendy S. *Ezra Pound and the Cantos: A Record of Struggle.* New Haven: Yale University Press, 1980.
Frazer, Sir James George. *The New Golden Bough: A New Abridgment of the Classic Work.* Edited by Theodor H. Gaster. New York: Criterion, 1959.
French, William, and Timothy Materer. "Far Flung Vortices and Ezra's 'Hindoo' Yogi." *Paideuma* 11 (1982): 39-53.
Friedman, Susan Stanford. *Psyche Reborn: The Emergence of H.D.* Bloomington: Indiana University Press, 1981.
Furia, Philip. *Pound's Cantos Declassified.* University Park and London: Pennsylvania State University Press, 1984.
Galbreath, Robert. "Explaining Modern Occultism." In *The Occult in America: New Historical Perspectives,* edited by Howard Kerr and Charles L. Crow. Urbana: University of Illinois Press, 1981.
―――. "The History of Modern Occultism: A Bibliographical Survey." *Journal of Popular Culture* 5 (1971): 726-54.
―――. "Introduction: The Occult Today." *Journal of Popular Culture* 5 (1971): 629-34.
Gallup, Donald. *A Bibliography of Ezra Pound.* 1963. London: Hart-Davis, 1969.
Géfin, Laszlo K. *Ideogram: History of a Poetic Method.* Austin: University of Texas Press, 1982.
Gibbons, Tom. "*The Waste Land* Tarot Identified." *Journal of Modern Literature* 4 (1972): 560-65.
Gilbert, R.A. "'The One Deep Student': Yeats and A.E. Waite." *Yeats Annual* 3 (1985): 3-14.
Gilbert, Stuart. *James Joyce's 'Ulysses.'* 1930. London: Faber, 1952.
Giovannini, Giovanni. *Ezra Pound and Dante.* Nijmegen, Utrecht, Netherlands: Dekker and Van De Vegt, 1961.
Goldfarb, Russell M. "Madame Blavatsky." *Journal of Popular Culture* 5 (1971): 660-72.
Gourmont, Remy de. *The Natural Philosophy of Love.* Trans. Ezra Pound. 1922. New York: Collier, 1972.
Grieve, Thomas. "The Seraphin Courveur Sources of Rock-Drill." *Paideuma* 4 (1975): 361-508.
Gross, Kenneth. *Spenserian Poetics: Idolatry, Iconoclasm and Magic.* Ithaca, NY: Cornell University Press, 1985.
Grover, Philip, ed. *Ezra Pound: The London Years, 1908-1920.* New York: AMS, 1978.
Grundberg, Carl. "Ezra Pound and the 'Trobar Clus.'" *San Jose Studies* 12, no. 3 (1986): 119-24.
Guest, Barbara. *Herself Defined: The Poet H.D. and Her World.* Garden City, NY: Doubleday, 1984.
Hall, Donald. *Writers at Work: The Paris Review Interviews.* 2nd series. New York: Viking, 1963.
Harper, George Mills. *The Neoplatonism of William Blake.* Chapel Hill: University of North Carolina Press, 1961.

———, and John S. Kelly. "Preliminary Examination of the Script of E[lizabeth] R[adcliffe]." In *Yeats and the Occult*, edited by George Mills Harper, 130-71. London: Macmillan, 1975.
———. *W.B. Yeats and W.T. Horton: The Record of an Occult Friendship*. London: Macmillan, 1980.
———, ed. *Yeats and the Occult*. London: Macmillan, 1975.
———. *Yeats's Golden Dawn*. London: Macmillan, 1974.
Harrison, Jane. *Prolegomena to the Study of Greek Religion*. 1903. New York: Meridian Books, 1955.
Harwood, John. "Olivia Shakespear and W.B. Yeats." *Yeats Annual* 4 (1986): 75-98.
Hastings, James, ed. *Encyclopaedia of Religion and Ethics*. 1917. 13 vols. New York: Scribner's, 1955.
Henricksen, Bruce. "*Heart of Darkness* and the Gnostic Myth." *Mosaic* 11 (1978): 35-44.
Herr, Cheryl T. "Theosophy, Guilt, and 'That Word Known to All Men' in Joyce's *Ulysses*." *James Joyce Quarterly* 18 (1980): 45-54.
Hesiod. *Hesiod: The Homeric Hymns and Homerica*. Trans. Hugh G. Evelyn-White. Loeb Classical Library. 1914. Cambridge, MA: Harvard University Press, 1970.
Hoeller, Stephan A. *The Gnostic Jung and the Seven Sermons of the Dead*. Wheaton, IL: The Theosophical Publishing House, 1982.
Homberger, Eric, ed. *Ezra Pound: The Critical Heritage*. London: Routledge, 1972.
Homer. *Homer: The Odyssey*. Trans. A.T. Murray. Vols. 104 and 105. Loeb Classical Library. 1919. Cambridge, MA: Harvard University Press, 1966.
———. *The Odyssey of Homer*. Trans. Richmond Lattimore. New York: Harper, 1965.
Hough, Graham. *The Mystery Religion of W.B. Yeats*. New Jersey: Barnes and Noble, 1984.
Hutchins, Patricia. *Ezra Pound's Kensington Years: An Exploration, 1885-1913*. London: Faber, 1965.
Hynes, Samuel. *The Edwardian Turn of Mind*. Princeton, NJ: Princeton University Press, 1968.
Inge, William Ralph. *The Philosophy of Plotinus*. 2 vols. London: Longmans, 1948.
Jackson, Thomas H. *The Early Poetry of Ezra Pound*. Cambridge: Harvard University Press, 1969.
Jenkins, Ralph. "Theosophy in 'Scylla and Charybdis.'" *Modern Fiction Studies* 15 (1969): 35-48.
Johnson, Josephin. *Florence Farr: Bernard Shaw's 'New Woman.'* Gerrards Cross, Buckinghamshire: Colin Smythe, 1975.
Jonas, Hans. *The Gnostic Religion*. Boston: Beacon, 1967.
Jung, C.G. *VII Sermons ad Mortuos*. Trans. H.G. Baynes. London: Stuart and Watkins, 1967.
Kearns, George. *Ezra Pound: The Cantos*. Cambridge: Cambridge University Press, 1989.
Kenner, Hugh. *Gnomon: Essays in Contemporary Literature*. New York: McDowell, Obolensky, 1958.

———. *The Poetry of Ezra Pound*. New York: New Directions, 1951.
———. *The Pound Era*. Berkeley: University of California Press, 1971.
Kerényi, C. *The Religion of the Greeks and Romans*. Trans. Christopher Holme. London: Thames and Hudson, 1962.
———. *Eleusis: Archetypal Image of Mother and Daughter*. Trans. Ralph Manheim. Bollingen Series, vol. 65, no. 4. New York: Pantheon Books, 1967.
King, Francis. *Ritual Magic in England*. London: Neville Spearman, 1970.
Knight, Gareth. *A History of White Magic*. London: Mowbrays, 1978.
Kodama, Sanehide. "The Eight Scenes of Sho-Sho." *Paideuma* 6 (1977): 131-45.
Kristeller, Paul Oskar. *The Philosophy of Marsilio Ficino*. Trans. Virginia Conant. Gloucester, MA: P. Smith, 1964.
Knox, Bryant. "Allen Upward and Ezra Pound." *Paideuma* 3 (1974): 71-83.
Kuch, Peter. *Yeats and A.E.: 'The Antagonism that Unites Dear Friends.'* Gerrards Cross, Buckinghamshire: Colin Smythe, 1986.
Kuhn, Alvin Boyd. *Theosophy: A Modern Revival of Ancient Wisdom*. New York: Henry Holt, 1930.
Lacarrière, Jacques. *The Gnostics*. Trans. Nina Rootes. Foreword by Lawrence Durrell. London: Owen, 1977.
Laughlin, James. "Ez As Wuz." *San José Studies* 12, no. 3 (1986): 6-28.
———. *Pound as Wuz: Essays and Lectures on Ezra Pound*. Saint Paul: Graywolf Press, 1987.
Lamplugh, Rev. F. *The Gnosis of Light*. London: John M. Watkins, 1918.
Laurie, Peter. "Peacocks in Koré's House: A Note on Pound's Alchemy." *Paideuma* 9 (1980): 333-37.
———. "The Poet and the Mysteries: Pound's Eleusis." Diss., Brown University, 1975.
Leary, Lewis, ed. *Motive and Method in the Cantos of Ezra Pound*. New York: Columbia University Press, 1954.
Legman, Gershon, et al. *The Guilt of the Templars*. New York: Basic Books, 1966.
Levenson, Michael H. *A Genealogy of Modernism: A Study of English Literary Doctrine 1908-1922*. Cambridge: Cambridge University Press, 1984.
Libera, Sharon Mayer. "Casting His Gods Back into the NOUS: Two Neoplatonists and *The Cantos* of Ezra Pound." *Paideuma* 2 (1973): 355-77.
———. "Ezra Pound's Paradise: A Study of Neoplatonism in the *Cantos*." Diss., Harvard University, 1971.
Liddel, Henry George, and Robert Scott, eds. *A Greek-English Lexicon*. 8th ed. New York: American Books, 1897.
Litz, A. Walton. "Pound and Yeats: The Road to Stone Cottage." In *Ezra Pound Among the Poets*, edited by George Bornstein, 128-48. Chicago: Chicago University Press, 1985.
Longenbach, James. "The Order of the Brothers Minor: Pound and Yeats at Stone Cottage 1913-16." *Paideuma* 14 (1985): 395-403.
———. "The Secret Society of Modernism: Pound, Yeats, Olivia Shakespear, and the Abbé de Montfaucon de Villars." *Yeats Annual* 4 (1986): 103-20. Edited by Warwick Gould.
———. *Stone Cottage: Pound, Yeats, and Modernism*. New York: Oxford University Press, 1988.

MacKenna, Stephen. *Plotinus.* 2 vols. 1916. London: Faber, 1969.
Mairet, Philip. *A.R. Orage: A Memoir.* New York: University Books, 1966.
―――. *Autobiographical and Other Papers.* Edited by C.H. Sisson. Manchester: Carcanet, 1981.
―――. "Allen Upward and His Order of Genius." *New Age* 40 (1927): 162.
Makin, Peter. *Pound's Cantos.* London: Allen, 1985.
―――. *Provençe and Pound.* Berkeley: University of California Press, 1978.
MacDowell, Colin. "'As Towards a Bridge Over Worlds': The Way of the Soul in *The Cantos.*" *Paideuma* 13 (1984): 171-200.
―――, and Timothy Materer. "Gyre and Vortex: W.B. Yeats and Ezra Pound." *Twentieth Century Literature* 31 (1985): 343-67.
―――. "'The Toys... at Auxerre': Canto 77." *Paideuma* 12 (1983): 21-30.
Martin, Heather C. *W.B. Yeats: Metaphysician as Dramatist.* Waterloo, ON: Wilfrid Laurier University Press, 1986.
Martin, Wallace. *The New Age Under Orage.* New York: Barnes, 1967.
Materer, Timothy. "Ezra Pound and the Alchemy of the Word." *Journal of Modern Literature* 11 (1984): 109-24.
―――. *Vortex: Pound, Eliot, and Lewis.* Ithaca and London: Cornell University Press, 1979.
McDougal, Stuart Y. *Ezra Pound and the Troubadour Tradition.* Princeton, NJ: Princeton University Press, 1972.
McIntosh, Christopher. *Eliphas Lévi and the French Occult Revival.* New York: Weiser, 1974.
McLuhan, Marshall. *The Letters of Marshall McLuhan.* Edited by Matie Molinaro, Corinne McLuhan, and William Toye. New York: Oxford University Press, 1987.
Mathers, S.L. MacGregor, trans. *The Kabbalah Unveiled.* Introd. M[oina] MacGregor Mathers. London: G. Redway, 1887.
Mead, G.R.S. *Apollonius of Tyana.* London: Watkins, 1901.
―――. *Did Jesus Live 100 B.C.?.* London: Theosophical Publishing Society, 1903.
―――. *Echoes from the Gnosis.* 11 vols. London: Theosophical Publishing Society, 1907-1908.
―――. *Fragments of a Faith Forgotten.* 1900. London: Theosophical Publishing Society, 1906.
―――. "Notes on the Eleusinian Mysteries." *The Theosophical Review* 22 (1898): 145-57, 232-42, 312-23.
―――. "Occultism." In Vol. 9 of *The Encyclopaedia of Religion and Ethics*, edited by James Hastings, 444-48. 13 vols. New York: Scribner's, 1955.
―――. "On a Speculation in Fourth-Dimensionalism." *Quest* 13 (1921-22): 48-49.
―――. *Orpheus.* 1896. London: Watkins, 1965.
―――. *Pistis Sophia: A Gnostic Gospel.* 1896. New Jersey: University Books, 1974.
―――. *Simon Magus: An Essay.* London: Theosophical Publishing Society, 1892.
―――, ed. *Quest.* London: Watkins, 1910-30.

———. "Some Remarks on Fourth Dimensionalism and the Time-Enigma." *Quest* 12 (1920-21): 993-505.
———. "The Augoeides or Radiant Body." *Quest* 1 (1909-10): 705-24.
———. *The Gospel and the Gospels*. London: Theosophical Publishing Society, 1902.
———. *The Doctrine of the Subtle Body in Western Tradition*. London: Watkins, 1919.
———. "'The Quest'—Old and New: Retrospect and Prospect." *Quest* 17 (1925-26): 289-307.
———. "The Resurrection of the Body." *Quest* 1 (1909-10): 271-87.
———. "The Rising Psychic Tide." *Quest* 3 (1911-12): 401-21.
———. "The Spirit-Body: An Excursion into Alexandrian Psycho-Physiology." *Quest* 1 (1909-10): 472-88.
———. *The World Mystery: Four Comparative Studies in General Theosophy*. 1895. London: Theosophical Publishing Society, 1907.
———. *Thrice-Greatest Hermes*. 3 vols. 1906. London: Watkins, 1964.
Michaels, Walter B. "Pound and Erigena." *Paideuma* 1 (1972): 37-54.
Miyake, Akiko. "The Greek-Egyptian Mysteries in Pound's '*The Little Review* Calendar' and in Cantos 1-7." *Paideuma* 7 (1978): 73-112.
Morford, Mark P.O., and Robert J. Lenardon. *Classical Mythology*. 1971. New York: Longman, 1977.
Moody, A.D. "Pound's Allen Upward." *Paideuma* 4 (1975): 55-70.
Moore, Virginia. *The Unicorn: William Butler Yeats' Search for Reality*. New York: Macmillan, 1954.
Moore, Robert Lawrence. *In Search of White Cows*. New York: Oxford University Press, 1977.
Murphy, William M. "Psychic Daughter, Mystic Son, Sceptic Father." In *Yeats and the Occult*, edited by George Mills Harper, 11-26. London: Macmillan, 1975.
Mylonas, George E. *Eleusis and the Eleusinian Mysteries*. Princeton, NJ: Princeton University Press, 1967.
Nänny, Max. *Ezra Pound: Poetics for an Electric Age*. Bern: Franke, 1973.
Nassar, Eugene Paul. *The Cantos of Ezra Pound: The Lyric Mode*. Baltimore: Johns Hopkins University Press, 1975.
Neault, James. "Apollonius of Tyana: The Odyssean Hero of Rock Drill as a Doer of Holiness." *Paideuma* 4 (1975): 3-36.
Nethercot, Arthur H. *The First Five Lives of Annie Besant*. London: Rupert Hart-Davis, 1961.
Norman, Charles. *Ezra Pound: A Biography*. 1960. London: Macdonald, 1969.
O'Brien, Elmer. *The Essential Plotinus*. New York: Mentor Books, 1964.
Oderman, Kevin. *Ezra Pound and the Erotic Medium*. Durham: Duke University Press, 1986.
O'Donnell, William H. "Yeats as Adept and Artist: *The Speckled Bird*, *The Secret Rose*, and *The Wind Among the Reeds*." In *Yeats and the Occult*, edited by George Mills Harper, 55-79. London: Macmillan, 1975.
Oppenheim, Janet. *The Other World: Spiritualism and Psychical Research in England, 1850-1915*. Cambridge, MA: Cambridge University Press, 1985.

Ouspensky, P.D. *Tertium Organum.* 1912. Trans. Nicholas Bessaraboffard and Claude Bragdon. London: Routledge, 1957.
Pagels, Elaine. *The Gnostic Gospels.* New York: Random House, 1979.
Page, Denys. *The Homeric "Odyssey".* Oxford: Clarendon Press, 1966.
Palandri, Angela Jung. "The 'Seven Lakes Canto' Revisited." *Paideuma* 3 (1974): 51-54.
Pearlman, Daniel S. *The Barb of Time: On the Unity of Ezra Pound's Cantos.* New York and London: Oxford University Press, 1969.
Peck, John. "Arras and Painted Arras." *Paideuma* 3 (1974): 61-66.
Perret, N.M. "'God's Eye Art 'Ou': Eleusis as a Paradigm for Enlightenment in Canto CVI." *Paideuma* 13 (1984): 419-32.
Philostratus. *Philostratus: The Life of Apollonius of Tyana.* Trans. F.C. Conybeare. Loeb Classical Library. 2 vols. 1912. Cambridge, MA: Harvard University Press, 1960.
Plotinus. *Select Works of Plotinus.* Trans. Thomas Taylor. Edited and with an Introduction by G.R.S. Mead. London: Bell, 1914.
Porphyry. *Porphyry: "On the Cave of the Nymphs."* Trans. Robert Lamberton. Barrytown, NY: Station Hill, 1983.
Powell, Barry B. *Composition by Theme in "The Odyssey."* Herstellung, Germany: Verlag Anton, 1977.
Pound, Ezra. *ABC of Reading.* 1934. New York: New Directions, 1960.
———. *The Cantos of Ezra Pound.* New York: New Directions, 1972.
———. *Collected Early Poems of Ezra Pound.* Edited by Michael King. New York: New Directions, 1976.
———. *Confucius: The Unwobbling Pivot and The Great Digest.* 1947. London: Peter Owen, 1968.
———. *Ezra Pound and Margaret Cravens: A Tragic Friendship, 1910-1912.* Edited by Omar Pound and Robert Spoo. Durham and London: Duke University Press, 1988.
———. *Ezra Pound/Dorothy Shakespear, Their Letters: 1909-1914.* Edited by Omar Pound and A. Walton Litz. New York: New Directions, 1986.
———. *Ezra Pound/John Theobald Letters.* Eds. Donald Pearce and Herbert Schneidau. Black Swan Books, 1984.
———. *Ezra Pound: Selected Poems.* Introd. T.S. Eliot. 1928. London: Faber, 1968.
———. *Ezra Pound: Translations.* Introd. Hugh Kenner. New York: New Directions, 1963.
———. *Gaudier-Brzeska: A Memoir.* 1916. New York: New Directions, 1970.
———. *Guide to Kulchur.* 1938. New York: New Directions, 1970.
———. *Impact: Essays on Ignorance and the Decline of American Civilization.* Edited by Noel Stock. Chicago: Henry Regnery, 1960.
———. *Jefferson and/or Mussolini.* 1935. New York: Liveright, 1970.
———. *Literary Essays of Ezra Pound.* 1954. Edited by T.S. Eliot. New York: New Directions, 1972.
———. *The Little Review: The Letters of Ezra Pound to Margaret Anderson.* Edited by Thomas L. Scott and Melvin J. Friedman. New York: New Directions, 1988.

———. *Pavannes and Divisions*. 1918. New York: New Directions, 1958.
———. *Personae: The Collected Shorter Poems of Ezra Pound*. 1926. New York: New Directions, 1971.
———. *Polite Essays*. London: Faber, 1937.
———. *Pound/Joyce: The Letters of Ezra Pound to James Joyce, with Pound's Critical Essays and Articles about Joyce*. Edited by Forrest Read. New York: New Directions, 1967.
———. *Pound/Lewis: The Letters of Ezra Pound and Wyndham Lewis*. Edited by Timothy Materer. New York: New Directions, 1985.
———. *Pound/The Little Review: The Letters of Ezra Pound to Margaret Anderson: "The Little Review" Correspondence*. Edited by Thomas L. Scott and Melvin J. Friedman, with the Assistance of Jackson R. Bryer. New York: New Directions, 1988.
———. *Selected Letters of Ezra Pound, 1907-1941*. 1950. Edited by D.D. Paige. New York: New Directions, 1971.
———. *Selected Prose of Ezra Pound, 1909-1965*. Edited by William Cookson. New York: New Directions, 1973.
———. *The Spirit of Romance*. 1910. New York: New Directions, 1968.
Quinn, Sister Mary Bernetta. *Ezra Pound*. New York: Columbia University Press, 1972.
Raine, Kathleen. *William Blake*. London: Thames and Hudson, 1971.
———. *Yeats, the Tarot and the Golden Dawn*. Dublin: Dolmen Press, 1975.
Ramacharaka, Yogi. *Fourteen Lessons in Yogic Philosophy and Oriental Occultism*. Chicago: The Yoga Publishing Society, 1903.
Rachewiltz, Boris de. "Pagan and Magic Elements in Ezra Pound's Works." In *New Approaches to Ezra Pound*, edited by Eva Hesse, 174-97. London: Faber, 1969.
Read, Forrest. *'76: One World and the Cantos of Ezra Pound*. Chapel Hill: University of North Carolina Press, 1980.
Reck, Michael. *Ezra Pound: A Close-Up*. New York: McGraw, 1967.
Reid, Robert W. *Marie Curie*. London: Collins, 1974.
Reitzenstein, Richard. *Hellenistic Mystery-Religions: Their Basic Ideas and Significance*. Trans. John E. Steely. Pittsburgh, PA: Pickwick, 1978.
Rieger, James. *The Mutiny Within: The Heresies of Percy Bysshe Shelley*. New York: Braziller, 1967.
Roberts, Marie. *British Poets and Secret Societies*. London: Groom Helm, 1986.
Rogers, Neville. *Shelley at Work: A Critical Inquiry*. 1956. Oxford: Clarendon, 1967.
Rossetti, Dante Gabriel. *The Early Italian Poets*. London: Anvil Press, 1981.
Rudolph, Kurt. *Gnosis: The Nature and History of Gnosticism*. Trans. and ed. Robert McLachlan Wilson. San Francisco: Harper & Row, 1977.
Rosenthal, M.L. "Pound at his Best: Canto 47 as a Model of Poetic Thought." *Paideuma* 6 (1977): 300-21.
Saurat, Denis. *Literature and Occult Tradition*. Trans. Dorothy Bolton. London: Bell, 1930.
Schneidau, Herbert N. *Ezra Pound: The Image and the Real*. Baton Rouge: Louisiana State University Press, 1969.

———. "Pound and Yeats: The Question of Symbolism." *ELH* 32 (1965): 220-37.
Schweighaeuser, Iohannes, ed. *Athenaei Naucratitae Deipnosophistarum*. 5 vols. Argentorati: Ex Typographia Societatis Bipontinae, 1802.
Schmitt, Charles B. "Reappraisals in Renaissance Science." *Historical Science* 16 (1978): 200-14.
Scholem, Gershom G. *Major Trends in Jewish Mysticism*. London: Thames and Hudson, 1955.
Schultz, Robert. "A Detailed Chronology of Ezra Pound's London Years, 1908-20, Part One: 1908-1914." *Paideuma* 11 (1982): 456-72.
———. "A Detailed Chronology of Ezra Pound's London Years, 1908-1920, Part Two: 1915-1920." *Paideuma* 12 (1983): 356-73.
Schuré, Edouard. *The Great Initiates: A Study of the Secret History of Religions*. Trans. Gloria Rasberry. Introd. Paul M. Allen. New York: St. George Books, 1966.
Scott, Bonnie Kime. "Joyce and the Dublin Theosophists: 'Vegetable Verse' and Story." *Eire-Ireland*, 13 (1978): 54-70.
Scott, W., ed. *Hermetica*. 4 vols. 1924-36. Boston: Shambhala, 1985.
Segal, Robert A. *The Poimandres as Myth: Scholarly Theory and Gnostic Meaning*. Berlin, New York, and Amsterdam: Mouton de Gruyer, 1986.
Senior, John. *The Way Down and Out: The Occult in Symbolist Literature*. 1959. Westport, CT: Greenwood, 1968.
Shepard, Leslie A. *Encyclopedia of Occultism and Parapsychology*. 3 vols. Detroit: Gale Research, 1972.
Sicari, Stephen. "The Secret of Eleusis, or How Pound Grounds His 'Epic of Judgement.'" *Paideuma* 14 (1985): 303-21.
Sieburth, Richard. *Instigations: Ezra Pound and Remy de Gourmont*. Cambridge, MA: Harvard University Press, 1978.
Sinistrari, Lodovico Maria. *Demoniality*. Trans. Montague Summers. New York: B. Blom, 1972.
Smith, Warren Sylvester. *The London Heretics: 1870-1914*. London: Constable, 1967.
Sophocles. *Women of Trachis*. Trans. Ezra Pound. 1956. New York: New Directions, 1956.
Spence, Lewis. *An Encyclopedia of Occultism*. 1920. New York: University Books, 1960.
Stock, Noel. *Ezra Pound's Pennsylvania*. Toledo, OH: University of Toledo Libraries, 1976.
———. *Poet in Exile: Ezra Pound*. Manchester: Manchester University Press, 1964.
———. *Reading the Cantos: A Study of Meaning in Ezra Pound*. London: Routledge, 1966.
———. *The Life of Ezra Pound*. New York: Random, 1970.
Stockenström, Göran. "The Symbiosis of 'Spirits' in *Inferno*: Strindberg and Swedenborg." In *Structures of Influence: A Comparative Approach to August Strindberg*, edited by Marilyn Johns Blackwell, 3-37. Chapel Hill: University of North Carolina Press, 1981.

Surette, Leon. *A Light from Eleusis.* Oxford: Clarendon, 1979.
———. "Economics and Eleusis." *San José Studies* 12 (1986): 58-67.
———. "Helen of Tyre." *Paideuma* 2 (1973): 419-22.
———. "The Birth of Modernism" (work-in-progress).
———. "*The Waste Land* and Jessie Weston: A Reassessment." *Twentieth Century Literature* 34 (1988): 223-44.
Tay, William. "Between King and Eleusis." *Paideuma* 4 (1975): 37-254.
Taylor, Anya. *Magic and English Theatre.* Athens: University of Georgia Press, 1979.
———. "The Occult in Romanticism." *The Wordsworth Circle* 8 (1977): 97-102.
Taylor, Thomas. *Thomas Taylor the Platonist: Selected Writings,* edited by Kathleen Raine and George Mills Harper. Princeton, NJ: Princeton University Press, 1969.
Terrell, Carroll F. *A Companion to the Cantos of Ezra Pound.* 2 vols. Berkeley: University of California Press, 1980-84.
———. "Mang-Tsze, Thomas Taylor, and Madam "Υλη." *Paideuma* 7 (1978): 141-54.
———. "Pound and KRH: An Introduction to Bowers' Memoir." *Paideuma* 2 (1973): 49-52.
Thatcher, David S. *Nietzsche in England: 1890-1914.* Toronto: University of Toronto Press, 1970.
Tindall, W.Y. *D.H. Lawrence and Susan His Cow.* New York: Columbia University Press, 1939.
———. *Forces of Modern British Literature: 1885-1956.* 1947. New York: Vintage, 1956.
———. "James Joyce and the Hermetic Tradition." *Journal of the History of Ideas* 15 (1954): 23-39.
———. *The Literary Symbol.* Bloomington: Indiana University Press, 1955.
Tryphonopoulos, Demetres P. "The *Cantos* as Palingenesis." *Paideuma* 18 (1989): 7-33.
———. "'The Fourth; The Dimension of Stillness': D.P. Ouspensky and Fourth Dimentionalism in Canto 49." *Paideuma* 19 (1990): 117-22.
———. "Ezra Pound's Occult Education." *Journal of Modern Literature* (forthcoming).
Tuveson, Ernest Lee. *The Avatars of Thrice Great Hermes: An Approach to Romanticism.* London: Associated University Press, 1982.
Twitchell, Jeffrey. "Art and the Spirit of Capitalism: Iconography and History in The Usura Cantos." *Paideuma* 19 (1990): 7-31.
Tytell, John. *Ezra Pound: The Solitary Volcano.* New York: Doubleday, 1987.
Upward, Allen. *Divine Mystery.* Santa Barbara, CA: Ross-Erikson, 1976.
———. *New Word.* New York: M. Kennerley, 1910.
Waite, Edward Arthur. *A New Encyclopaedia of Freemasonry.* 2 vols. New York: Weathervane Books, 1970.
Walbank, F.W. *The Hellenistic World.* Cambridge, MA: Harvard University Press, 1982.
Walker, Benjamin. *Gnosticism: Its History and Influence.* Wellingborough, Northamptonshire: Aquarian Press, 1983.

Wasson, R. Gordon, Albert Hofmann, and Carl A.P. Ruck. *The Road to Eleusis: Unveiling the Secret of the Mysteries.* New York and London: Harcourt Brace Jovanovich, 1978.
Watkins, Geoffrey N. "Yeats and Mr. Watkins' Bookshop." In *Yeats and the Occult*, edited by George Mills Harper, 307-10. London: Macmillan, 1975.
Webb, James. *The Harmonious Circle.* New York: G.P. Putnam's Sons, 1980.
———. *The Occult Establishment.* La Salle, IL: Open Court, 1976.
———. *The Occult Underground.* La Salle, IL: Open Court, 1974.
———, ed. *A Quest Anthology.* New York: Arno Press, 1976.
Welburn, Andrew J. *Power and Self-Consciousness in the Poetry of Shelley.* London: Macmillan, 1986
Weston, Jessie L. *From Ritual to Romance.* Cambridge, MA: Cambridge University Press, 1920.
Wilhelm, James J. "Addenda and Corrigenda for *The American Roots of Ezra Pound.*" *Paideuma* 17 (1989): 238-44.
———. *Dante and Pound: The Epic of Judgement.* Orono: University of Maine Press, 1965.
———. *The American Roots of Ezra Pound.* New York: Garland, 1985.
———. *The Later Cantos of Ezra Pound.* New York: Walker, 1977.
Wilson, Edmund. *Axel's Castle.* New York: Scribner's, 1931.
Wilson, F.A.C. *W.B. Yeats and Tradition.* London: Gollancz, 1958.
———. *Yeats's Iconography.* London: Gollancz, 1960.
Wind, Edgar. *Pagan Mysteries in the Renaissance.* New Haven: Yale University Press, 1958.
Yates, Frances A. *Giordano Bruno and the Hermetic Tradition.* London: Routledge, 1964.
———. *Theatre of the World.* London: Routledge, 1969.
———. "The Hermetic Tradition in Renaissance Science." In *Art, Science, and History in the Renaissance*, edited by Charles S. Singleton, 255-74. Baltimore: Johns Hopkins University Press, 1967.
———. *The Occult Philosophy in the Elizabethan Age.* London: Routledge, 1979.
———. *The Rosicrucian Enlightenment.* London: Routledge, 1972.
Yeats, W.B. *A Packet for Ezra Pound.* 1929. Shannon: Irish University Press, 1970.
———. *Letters of W.B. Yeats.* Ed. Allan Wade. London: Hart-Davis, 1954.

INDEX

References to individual Cantos are printed in **boldface** type.

ABC of Reading (Pound), 11
Adams, Stephen J., 63, 93 n. 4
Adonis, 136-37, 151-52, 180
Aegisthus, 168
Aeneas, 136-37
Aeneid. See Virgil
Agresti, Olivia Rossetti, xii, 18 n. 2, 47, 65-66
Albigensianism, 37-39, 127, 134-36, 166; and the Catholic Church, 38, 134-36
Alchemy, 170-71
A Lume Spento (Pound), 63
Amphion, 164
Anastos, Milton A., 140
Anchises, 136-37, 180
Anderson, David, 54 n. 1
Anderson, Margaret, 82, 97 n. 41
Andreae, Johann Valentin, 43
Aphrodite, 109, 137-38, 142, 147, 148, 167, 175, 176, 183
Apollonius of Tyana, 13, 57 n. 24, 174-76, 182
"Apparuit" (Pound), 63
Apuleius, 4
Artemis, 117, 180
Athena, 114, 121-22, 125
Atkinson, W.W. [pseud. Ramacharaka, Yogi], 66-67, 94 n. 10
Augoeides, 170-72, 177, 183

Bacchus. *See* Dionysus
Bacigalupo, Massimo, 181
Bacon, Francis, 45
Balzac, Honoré, 13, 65
Barry, Iris, 63
Beinecke Rare Book Library, xii, 18 n. 2, 23, 65-66, 82-83, 97 n. 41, 109, 185 n. 10, 185 n. 13
Bell, Ian F.A., xiii, 21 n. 24, 131
Bergson, Moina, 132
Bernouard, Franois, 161
Bernstein, Michael, 101-102
Binyon, Laurence, 165
Bion, 148
Bird, William, 47
Blavatsky, Helena Petrovna, 13, 23-24, 49-53, 57 n. 26, 85, 99 n. 57. *See also* Theosophical Society; Theosophy
Bloom, Harold, 39
Boat, 113, 119, 123, 153 n. 11
Bowers, Faubion, 62-63
Brancusi, Constantin, 13
British Museum, xii
Brook-Rose, Christine, 134
Bruno, Giordano, 42

Cabala, xii, 39-40
Cadmus, 175
Cantos, The (Pound), 101-88 passim; cryptological reading of, 6;

Eleusinian mysteries in, xi, 105-106, 135-38, 143-46 passim; enlightened souls in, 106; exoteric/esoteric nature of, 7-8, 101, 150-51, 160; genesis of, 61; Hellenistic religious thought in, 101; *hieros gamos* in, 107, 120, 142, 144, 147-48, 152, 175; main scheme of, xi, 10; Neoplatonism in, 138-42; *mythos* of, xi, 102; as palingenesis, 6-9, 62, 91, 101-108, 114, 120, 130, 152, 160, 161-62, 177-78; *individual cantos*: **1**: 106, 108, 109, 146, 168; **2**: 152; **3**: 133; **4**: 117, 133, 179; **5**: 134, 138; **8**: 133, 139-41 passim; **14**: 109; **15**: 91-92, 109, 124-25, 126; **16**: 109; **17**: 104, 108-127, 150; **20**: 133, 146; **23**: 104, 127-142, 180; **24**: 133; **26**: 133, 139, 141; **36**: 107, 125, 143, 151; **39**: 109, 125, 142, 143, 146, 150; **41**: 143; **42**: 142, 144, 146; **43**: 142, 143, 144, 146; **44**: 142, 144; **45**: 142, 143, 144-46; **46**: 142, 144, 146; **47**: 104, 107, 109, 125, 137, 142, 143, 146-52; **49**: 3, 142, 143, 152; **50**: 143; **51**: 3, 142; **72**: 184 n. 9; **73**: 184 n. 9; **74**: 103, 119, 178; **76**: 165, 166; **77**: 65; **79**: 84; **81**: 7, 107; **82**: 159; **83**: 140; **84**: 159; **85**: 163, 165; **87**: 46, 165, 166; **88**: 3; **89**: 65; **90**: 88, 104, 143, 159, 160, 162-69, 173, 177; **91**: 45, 67, 88, 104, 110, 143, 152, 159, 160 162, 169-84; **93**: 65, 126, 152; **94**: 119, 120, 176; **96**: 98 n. 48, 119; **98**: 114, 119; **99**: 161; **100**: 120; **101**: 110; **106**: 125, 161; **110**: 1; **116**: 162; **117**: 7, 160-61
Cantrell, Carol H., 137
Carmagnola, 126
Castalia, 167
Catholic Church, 2, 18 n. 2
"Cavalcanti" (Pound), 7, 179
Caves, 112-13
Ceres. *See* Demeter

Circe, 109, 125, 147, 149-50, 161, 176
Cocteau, 13
Collected Early Poems of Ezra Pound (Pound), 93 n. 6
Confucius, 13
Corpus Hermeticum, 13, 41-43, 126
Curie, Marie, 131-33
Curie, Pierre, 131-32

Dante, 7, 13, 47, 108, 130 178
Davenport, Guy, 121, 125, 130
Davis, Andrew Jackson, 48
Davis, Kay, 105, 107, 153 n. 5
Deipnosophistae. *See* Stesichorus
Dekker, George, 104
Delphi, 164, 166
Demeter, 3, 29
D'Epiro, Peter, 155 n. 34
Descent. *See* Katabasis.
Diana. *See* Artemis
Dionysus, 30, 115, 116, 121, 168. *See also* Iacchos and Zagreus
Divine Mystery, The (Upward), 77
Doctrine of the Subtle Body, The (Mead), 67, 90-91, 130-31, 169-74, 178, 184
Dodona, 166
Doolittle, Hilda. *See* H.D.
Douglas, Major C.H., 80
Draft of XXX Cantos, A (Pound), 102, 161
Drake, Sir Francis, 178-79
Dromena. *See* Palingenesis

Echoes from the Gnosis (Mead), 89-90, 110-11
Eder, David, 81
Egypt, 126
Eidos, 7, 10, 107, 137, 177
Electra, 168
Eleusinian Mysteries, xii, 4-5, 29-31, 105, 125, 152 n. 4. *See also* Eleusinian Mysteries in *Cantos, The*
Eleven New Cantos (Pound), 102, 142-43
Eliade, Mircea, 26, 107

Eliot, T.S., 3, 27
Elizabeth I, Queen of England, 175, 178-79
Elliott, Angela, xiv, xviii n. 1, 56 n. 22, 92 n. 1, 96 n. 31, 97 n. 33, 99 n. 49, 131, 154 n. 24, 156 n. 39, 186 n. 25
Ellmann, Richard, xiii, 24
Ellwood, Jr., Robert S., 50-51
Emery, Clark, xiii, xviii n. 1, 20 n. 14, 21 n. 27, 92 n.1, 142, 143, 147, 152, 156 n. 39, 158 n. 48, 159, 186 n. 25
End to Torment (H.D.), 64-65, 68
Epopteia. See *Palingenesis*
Erebus, 167, 168
Erigena, Johannes Scotus, 13, 46, 166
Este, Borso d', 126
Este, Niccolo d', 133, 155 n. 31
Ezra Pound and Eleusis. See Eleusinian Mysteries
Ezra Pound and Margaret Cravens (Pound), xii, 82
Ezra Pound and Dorothy Shakespear (Pound), 68, 69, 72-75 passim, 82-84
Ezra Pound and John Theobald (Pound), xii, 78, 82, 84, 89, 99 n. 57

Fa-Han, 133
Farr, Florence, 71
Ferrara-Florence, Council of, 41, 127, 141
Festugière, A.J., 5
Ficino, Marcilio, 5, 13, 41-42, 88, 139
Fifth Decad of Cantos, The (Pound), 102, 143
Finley, John, L., 95 n. 19
Flint, F.S., 79
Flory, Wendy S., xiii
Fludd, Robert, 44
Ford, Ford Madox, 11, 16
Fox Sisters, 48
Fragments of a Faith Forgotten (Mead), 25, 27, 83, 87, 147-48
Frazer, Sir James, 5, 75, 165
Freemasons, 13, 45-46, 47

French, William, xiv, 20 n. 15, 59, 66
Friedman, Susan Stanford, 93 n. 7
Frobenius, Leo, 5
Furia, Philip, 157 n. 41

Galbreath, Robert, 26
Gates, 110, 113, 120
Gaudier-Brzeska: A Memoir (Pound), 73, 89-90, 141
Géfin, Lazlo, 9
Geryon, 3, 146
Giovannini, Giovanni, 97 n. 41
Gnosis, xii, 8-9, 20 n. 13, 34, 104-105, 182
Gnosticism, xii, 33-36, 55 nn. 16-17, 121
Green, H.C., 65
Gregory, Lady Augusta, 68
Grieve, Thomas, 165
Grosseteste, Robert, 13
Guest, Barbara, 64
Guide to Kulchur (Pound), 3, 7-16 passim, 65, 67, 87, 91, 106, 127, 138, 140, 143, 144, 161
Gurdjieff, G.I., 13, 82

Hades, 29
Hall, Donald, 61, 74
Harper, George Mills, xii, xiii, 70-71, 74
Harrison, Jane Ellen, 115
Hastings, Beatrice, 80
H.D., 13, 60, 64-68, 94 n. 12; and spiritualism, 65; and "Yogi books," 65-66, 68; *works: End to Torment*, 64-65, 68; *HERmione*, 62
Helen of Tyre, 36, 87, 147, 175, 186 n. 23
Helios, 126, 129, 154 n. 20, 180
"Hell Cantos" (Pound), 130
Hellenistic syncretism, 28, 31-33, 41, 77
Herakles, 129-32, 166
Hermes, 109, 121-22, 149
Hermes Trismegistus, 41, 88, 126
Hermeticism, xii, 41-43
HERmione (H.D.), 62
Hesiod, 137

Heydon, John, 13, 45, 57 n. 24, 163, 165-66, 182
Heyman, Katherine Ruth, 60-64, 65, 93 n. 4
Hierophant, 30, 136
Hieros gamos, 14, 18, 55 n. 11, 90, 105, 107, 120, 127, 136, 142-48 passim, 152, 175
Hodgson, Richard, 52-53
Homer, 105, 109, 111, 112, 114, 117, 125, 161, 165, 175
Homeric Hymn to Aphrodite, 137
Homeric Hymn to Demeter, 29
Horton, W.T., 70-71
Hough, Graham, 23-24
Hutchins, Patricia, xii, 63, 82, 84, 93 n. 5, 95 n. 22
Hynes, Samuel, 26, 54 n. 6, 155 n. 28

iacchos, 30; *See also* Dionysus
Iamblichus, 13
"I Gather the Limbs of Osiris" (Pound), 10
Iliad. *See* Homer
Inge, Dean, 33
Initiation. *See Palingenesis*
Ino, 175
Isis, 167
Ithaca, 125, 126
Izzo, Carlo, 145

Jackson, Holbrook, 78-79
Jefferson and/or Mussolini (Pound), 102
Joan of Arc, 183
Jonas, Hans, 28, 32, 33-34, 35, 147
Jove. *See* Zeus
Joyce, James, 27

Katabasis, 30, 103-105, 107, 109, 115, 117-19, 123, 127, 128, 130, 136-38 passim, 142, 146, 148, 168, 180. *See also Palingenesis*
Kenner, Hugh, xiii, 99 n. 49, 131, 166
Kerényi, C., 152 n. 4, 153 n. 7
Kingsland, William, 51
knights Templar, 46, 164, 166
Knox, Bryant, 74, 75
Koré, 29, 125, 148

Kristeller, Paul Oskar, 41
Kuch, Peter, 51-52
Kuhn, Alvin Boyd, 49

Lacarrière, Jacques, 33
Lamberton, Robert, 111, 112
Laughlin, James, 21 n. 25, 31, 152 n. 4, 157 n. 45
Laurie, Peter Hamilton, 97 n. 39, 153 n. 5
Layamon, 181
Leadbeater, Charles Webster, 85, 98 n. 45
Leopoldo, Pietro, 144
Leucochoe, 175
Leucothea, 114, 175, 181-82
Levenson, Michael H., 73, 98 n. 42
Lexicon, Greek-English, 129-30
Libera, Sharon Mayer, xiii, 13, 91-92, 104, 108, 118, 123, 138-39, 141, 153 n. 9, 153 n. 10, 156 n. 37
Lilly Library, xii, 47
Literary Essays (Pound), 10, 11, 17, 161
Little Review: The Letters of Ezra Pound to Margaret Anderson, the (Pound), 82, 97 n. 41
Litz, A. Walton, xiii
Logos, 32, 126
Longenbach, James, xii, xiii, 92 n. 1, 94 n. 13, 94 n. 15, 95 n. 16, 153 n. 6

Macleod, Fiona, 86
McLuhan, Marshall, 54 n. 7
McPherson, Douglas, 8
Maensac, Austors de, 134
Maensac, Peire de, 133-34
Magic, 37. *See also* Occultism
Magnus, Albertus, 13
Magus, Simon. *See* Simon Magus
Maier, Michael, 44
Mairet, Philip, 78, 81, 95 n. 21
Makin, Peter, 19 n. 12
"Malatesta Cantos" (Pound), 139-40
Malatesta, Novvy, 141
Malatesta, Sigismundo, 41, 126, 140-41, 143

Manes, 13, 102-103
Manicheanism, 37
Masons. *See* Freemasons
Materer, Timothy, xiv, 57 n. 24, 66
McDowell, Colin, xiv, 67, 98 n. 47, 160, 184, 184 n. 2
Mead, G.R.S., xii, 5, 13, 82-92, 99 n. 53, 99 n. 57, 106, 152 n. 4, 159; in Taylor, Thomas, 107-108; works: *The Doctrine of the Subtle Body*, 67, 90-91, 130-31, 169-74, 178, 184; *Echoes from the Gnosis*, 89-90, 110-11; *Fragments of a Faith Forgotten*, 25, 27, 83, 87, 147-48; "Foreword," *Selected Works of Plotinus*, 91; "Occultism," 25; *Orpheus*, 87-88, 106, 116-17; *The Quest*, 68, 85-86; "The Rising Psychic Tide," 26-27; *Simon Magus*, 87, 148; *Thrice-Greatest History*, 88-89, 126; *The World Mystery*, 83
Medici, Cosimo de', 41, 88, 141
Memnon, 122
Mencius, 165
Mesmer, Franz Anton, 46
Mesmerism, 46
Metamorphoses. *See* Ovid
Metamorphosis, 3-4, 108-109, 115-16, 164, 172
Mirandola, Pico della, 5, 13
Mithraic mysteries, 110, 166
Mitrinovic, Dmitri, 81
Miyake, Akiko, xiv, xviii n. 1, 125, 153 n. 13, 154 n. 25
"Moeurs Contemporaines" (Pound), 66
Molay, Jacques de, 46, 165
Montségur, 38, 135, 136, 166
Moore, Robert Lawrence, 48
Moore, Virginia, 97 n. 32, 99 n. 50
Morris, William, 64
Mozart, Wolfgang Amadeus, 13
Mussolini, Benito, 143
Myesis, xii, 30
Mylonas, George E., 29-30, 152 n. 4
Mystes, 4, 30, 117, 119, 126, 147, 162, 169, 177

Nänny, Max, 20 n. 16
Nekuia, 102, 146, 147
Neoplatonic tradition of reading the epic, 111-12
Neoplatonism, xii, 36-37, 56 nn. 19-20, 105, 127, 138-39
Nerea, Cave of, 110, 117-18, 119, 120, 123
Nereus, 110
Nethercot, Arthur H., 85
New Age, The. *See* Orage, A.R.
New Word, The (Upward), 75-77
Norman, Charles, 62, 63
"Note Precedent to 'La Fraisne' " (Pound), 67, 94 n. 11
Nous, 3, 138, 142

O'Brien, Elmer, 36-37
Ocellus, 13, 175
Occultism, definition of, xii, 24-27, 53; during Hellenistic age, 28-29; and science, 25-26, 51, 73, 131-33, 186 n. 19
Oderman, Kevin, xiv, 19 n. 10, 99 n. 49, 143, 185 n. 18
Odysseus, 105-109 passim, 114, 115, 125, 127, 129-30, 143, 149-50, 161, 168, 174, 175, 181-82
Odyssey. *See* Homer
Olcott, Colonel Henry, 49, 52, 85
Oppenheim, Janet, 53
Orage, A.R., xii, 13, 75, 78-82; Leeds Art Club, 79; Nietzsche, on Friedrich, 79; psychoanalysis, 81-82; The Theosophical Society, 77-79
Orpheus (Mead), 87-88, 106, 116-17
Orphism, 31-32, 87, 116
Ouspensky, P.D., 82
Ovid, 3-4, 105, 136

Palingenesis, 2-4, 28, 87, 89, 101-88 passim
Pearlman, Daniel, xi, 104, 131
Peck, John, 133
Pecten cteis, 120, 150-51, 154 n. 17
Péladan, Joséphin, xi, 13, 38-39, 135
Penty, A.J., 78-79

Persephone. *See* Koré
Personae (Pound), 68, 163
Philostratus, 98 n. 48, 174, 175
Pisan Cantos (Pound), 64, 102-103, 140, 159
Pistoria, Leonardo da, 41
Plato, 5, 13, 36
Plethon, Georgius Gemistus, 13, 41, 88, 127, 138-42
Plotinus, 13, 36-37, 91, 108, 138
"Plotinus" (Pound), 66
Pluto, 3
Poitier, Guillaume de, 173
Porphyry, 13, 138, 149, 178, 183; commentary on *Odyssey*, 109-14
Poseidon, 140, 182
Pound, Dorothy. *See* Shakespear, Dorothy
Pound, Ezra: Albigensians, 38-39, 46; American paideuma, 143; at the British Museum in 1906, 60; Catholic Church, 2; "Celestial Tradition," 11-15, 38-39, 87-88, 140-41, 166-67; Eleusis, xiv, 2, 13, 30-31, 135, 137, 173; Fontainebleau, visit to, 82, 96 n. 29; Gnosticism, 36; Hellenistic rituals, 106; Heydon, John, 45; hierophant of art, as, 123; H.D., introduces to occult, 64-65, 93 n. 7; *hieros gamos* in, 18, 30-31, 90, 104; Horton's letters to Yeats, in, 70-71; imagistic poetics and science, 11; letters to parents, xii, 68, 82-83, 97 nn. 34-36; London years, xii, 9, 23, 26-27, 59, 68-69; Mead, G.R.S., 82-84, 87, 90, 92; Mead's Quest Society lectures, attendance at, 68, 83; Mead, debt to, 87-88, 90; metamorphosis, 2-3; myth, 15-16; Neoplatonism, 37, 56 n. 19; Nietzsche, Friedrich, 80; occult, xi, 47-48, 53, 65-66, 82, 84; Orage's mysticism, disapproval of, 47; paganism, 16-18; *The Quest*, in, 68, 82, 84, 86; religious beliefs of, 1-2, 11, 21 n. 25; reading of *Odyssey*, 114; scholarship on Pound and the occult, xiii-xiv; Shakespear, Olivia, 71-72; Swedenborg, 47; symbolism, 72-74, 89-90; Taylor, Thomas, 43; Upward's work, on, 75-76, 80; Venice, in, 123; Yeats's psychic research, disapproval of, xiv, 47, 69-70; Yeats, at Stone Cottage with, 47, 69
Provence, 38-39, 135-36, 173
Psellus, 13, 88, 138
"Psychology and Troubadours" (Pound), 10, 11, 15-16, 36, 68, 73, 87, 92, 177
Pythagoras, 13, 166
Pythagoreanism, 31-32, 87

Quest Society, The, 74, 83-84, 86
Quest, The, 68, 85-86

Ramacharaka, Yogi. *See* Atkinson, W.W.
Rachewiltz, Boris de, 56 n. 22, 152 n. 4, 164, 165, 177, 179, 180, 187 n. 30
Rachewiltz, Mary de, 18 n. 2
Raine, Kathleen, xiii
Ra-Set, Princess, 176-78 passim, 180
Read, Forrest, 19 n. 8
Reid, Robert, 132-33
Reina, 173-74
Reitzenstein, Richard, 4, 6-7
"Religio" (Pound), 17-18, 87, 90
Rock Drill (Pound), 103
Rosenkruz, Christian, 43
Rosicrucianism, 43-45
Rossetti, Gabriele, 47, 65-66
Rudolph, Kurt, 33, 34

San Ku, 165, 166
Santayana, George, 166
Saurat, Denis, 90
Schmitt, Charles B., 42
Schneidau, Herbert N., xiv, 9-11 passim, 185 n. 17
Scholem, Gershom G., 40
Schultz, Robert, 95 n. 24

Schwob, Marcel, 64-65
Scriabin, Alexander, 63
"Scriptor Ignotus" (Pound), 60-61
Segal, Robert, 55 n. 16
Selected Letters of Ezra Pound (Pound), 8, 10, 62, 63, 69, 75, 80, 104-105, 119, 133, 145-46
Selected Prose of Ezra Pound (Pound), 2, 11, 76-78 passim, 80, 56 n. 20, 96 n. 25, 120, 131-32, 143
Selected Works of Plotinus (Mead), 91
Selloi, 165-66
Shakespear, Dorothy, xii, 72, 82-84. See also Ezra Pound/Dorothy Shakespear
Shakespear, Olivia, xii, 71-72, 94 n. 15; introduces Pound to Yeats, 23
Sibylla, 167
Sieburth, Richard, 161
Sigismond. See Malatesta, Sigismundo
Simon Magus, 36, 87, 147-48, 151, 171, 186 n. 23
Simon Magus (Mead), 87, 148
Sinistrari, Lodovico Maria, 67, 94 n. 11
Smith, Warren Sylvester, 24, 48
Smith, William Brook, 62
Society for Psychical Research, 52-53, 79
Sophia, 147
Spenser, Edmund, 44-45
Spirit of Romance, The (Pound), 108
Spiritualism, 48-49
Stesichorus, 128-31, 133
Stock, Noel, xiv, xviii n. 1, 2, 5, 19 n. 5, 164, 186 n. 25
Summers, Montague, 94 n. 11, 94 n. 12
Sun. See Helios
Surette, Leon, xiv, 80, 95 n. 20, 104, 173; *Light*, xi-xii, xiv, 3-4, 30, 38-39, 61, 135, 147, 153 n. 13, 158 n. 49, 160, 168-69, 182, 186 n. 24, 188 n. 31; "The Birth of Modernism," 20 n. 13, 94 n. 9, 152 n. 1

Swabey, Henry, 8
Swedenborg, Emanuel, 7, 13, 46-48
Swedenborgianism, 46
Symbolism, 72-74
Symons, Arthur, 73
Synesius, 130-31

Tamuz, 148
Taylor, Thomas, 37, 43, 57 n. 23, 105-106, 111, 112, 116, 149-50
Tempio Malatestiano, 41, 142
Terracina, 175
"Terra Italica" (Pound), 16-17, 38, 88, 89, 135-36, 175
Terrell, Carroll F., xiv, 62, 104, 122, 166, 169-70, 173, 175, 176, 185 n. 11
Thatcher, David S., 95 n. 23
Theobald, John. See *Ezra Pound/John Theobald*
Theodora, Empress, 175
Theophany, 127, 137-38
Theosophical Society, The, 23-24, 49-50, 52, 77-79, 85-86. See also Blavatsky, Helena Petrovna
Theosophy, xii, 48-53. See also Blavatsky, Helena Petrovna
Theurgy, xii, 24, 47, 69. See also Occultism
Thrice-Greatest History (Mead), 88-89, 126
Thrones (Pound), 103
Titans, 116-17
Translations (Pound), 69-70
"Tree, The" (Pound), 68, 163
Troubadours, 127
"Troubadours—Their Sorts and Conditions" (Pound), 134
Twitchell, Jeffrey, 157 n. 44
Tytell, John, 61, 66

Undine, 174-75
Upward, Allen, xii, 13, 74-78; works: *The New Word*, 75-77; *The Divine Mystery*, 77
"Ur-Cantos" (Pound), 45, 57 n. 24, 182
Usura, 3, 144-45, 146

Valli, Luigi, 7, 19 n. 12
Venice, 117, 122-23
Ventadorn, Bernart de, 161, 173
Venus. *See* Aphrodite
Virgil, 102, 105, 109
Vorticism, 9, 10, 90

Waite, A.E., 86
Webb, James, 79, 81, 95 n. 20
Weston, Jessie L., 185 n. 11
Wilhelm, James J., xiii, 37, 65-66, 92 n. 3, 161
Wilson, F.A.C., 70
Wind, Edgar, 4-6
World Mystery, The (Mead), 83

Yates, Francis, 13, 39, 41-45 passim
Yeats, William Butler, xii, 13, 59, 68, 69-71, 183; critics on Yeats and the occult, xiii, 54 n. 3; Horton, W.T., 70-71; theosophical phase, 23-24, 53; introduces Pound to occult circles, 24, 67; Mead, G.R.S., 97 n. 32; symbolism, 73-74
Ygdrasail, 163

Zagreus, 115, 116-17, 121
Zeus, 29, 165-66, 168
Zothar, 125

www.ingramcontent.com/pod-product-compliance
Lightning Source LLC
Chambersburg PA
CBHW052022070526
44584CB00016B/1864